POLITEXT 185

The ISPS Code - 2
Development of port ordinances

POLITEXT

Ricard Marí Sagarra
Ramiro Santalices Fernández

The ISPS Code - 2
Development of port ordinances

EDICIONS UPC

Publication sponsored by the Ministry of Public Works (2009)

First edition: September 2009
Reprint: November 2009

©   los autores, 2009

©   Edicions UPC, 2009
     Edicions de la Universitat Politècnica de Catalunya, SL
     Jordi Girona Salgado 1-3, 08034 Barcelona
     Tel.: 934 137 540   Fax: 934 137 541
     Edicions Virtuals: www.edicionsupc.es
     E-mail: edicions-upc@upc.edu

Production: LIGHTNING SOURCE

Legal deposit: B-36521-2009
ISBN: 978-84-9880-370-9

This work may only be reproduced, distributed, publicly disclosed or transformed with permission from its copyright holders, with the exception provided by the law. If you need to photocopy or scan a part of this work, please contact CEDRO (Spanish Centre for Reprographic Rights) at www.cedro.org.

Index

Introduction 11

    Introduction 11
    Objectives 11
    Methodology 11
    Work schedule 12

1. Security in general 13

1.1   The concept of security 13
1.2   Preventive security 15
1.3   Security on an International scale 15
1.4   The International Ship and Port Facility Security Code (ISPS) 16

2. Terrorism 19

2.1   National terrorism 19
2.2   International terrorism 20
2.3   International and national regulation 23
2.4   Threats to means of transport and port facilities 25
2.5   Global answers 27
2.6   The International Ship and Port Facility Security Code: Objectives 28
2.7   The Spanish port organisation 30
        2.7.1 Ports of general Interest 33
        2.7.2 Port space under the competence of regional governments 34
        2.7.3 Service areas in ports managed under concession 34
        2.7.4 Other ports and facilities depending on State Administration 35
2.8   Public Service in the Ports of General Interest 35
2.9   Competences and Powers of the Port Authorities 38
2.10 Relationships between the General Directorate of the Merchant Navy and the Public Entity Ports of the State 40

3. The International Ship and Port Facility Security Code and the port regulations 43

3.1	Introduction: the context in Europe	43
3.2	Role of maritime transport in EU trade	44
3.3	Flag-bearing fleets and fleets controlled by the EU	44
3.4	The ports of the Community	45
3.5	Spain	46
3.6	European Regulation	50

**4. Policing regime in the ports of general interest.
Regulation of Exploitation and Policing** 53

4.1	The old Port Regulation on Services, Police and Regime	58
4.2	The legal grounds for the Regulation of Exploitation and Policing	60
4.3	The regulation of exploitation and policing and public security	62
4.4	Harbour guards. Historical evolution. Public function. Security guards	65
	4.4.1 Harbour guards in Law 27/92, modified by Law 62/97	67
	4.4.2 The position of Harbour guards with respect to LO 2/86, of 13th March, on Security Forces and Bodies, LO 1/92, of 21st February, on the Protection of Public Safety and Law 23/92, of 30th July, on Private Security	68
4.5	Agents of Authority. Doctrine	77
4.6	Jurisprudence	78
4.7	Security forces in the port. Functions	79
4.8	Maritime Service of the Civil Guard	82
4.9	Public security. Public Order	83
	4.9.1 Private security and the Ports of General Interest	84
4.10	Training and drills in matters of port security in the PBIP	86

5. The Law of the Ports and the Regulation of Exploitation and Policing. The future 89

5.1	Law 48/03 of economic regime and the rendering of services in the Ports of General Interest and the Regulation of Exploitation and Policing	89
5.2	Law 27/92 and Port Regulation	94

6. The International Ship and Port Facility Security Code (ISPS Code) and obligations derived from it for the contracting governments 99

6.1	The obligations of the contracting Governments	102
6.2	Responsibilities of the contracting Governments	103
6.3	Declaration of maritime protection	104
6.4	Ship Security	104
6.5	The port facility	105
6.6	International certificate of protection	105
	6.6.1 Responsibilities of the contracting Governments	105
	6.6.2 Determination of the level of protection	106
	6.6.3 The port facility	106
	6.6.4 Information and communication	107

6.7	Responsibilities of the contracting Governments	107
	6.7.1 Protection of the evaluations and responsible authority	107
	6.7.2 Recognised protection organisations	107
	6.7.3 Points of contact and information on the protection plans of the Port Facilities	109
	6.7.4 Documents of identity	110
	6.7.5 Ships that do not have to comply with part A of this Code	110
	6.7.6 Threats to ships and other events at sea	111
	6.7.7 Equivalent measures for port facilities	111
	6.7.8 Approval of the PFSP	112
	6.7.9 Declaration of compliance of a port facility	112
6.8	Communication protocol for the different levels of protection in Spain.	112
	6.8.1 Determination of the level of protection	112
	6.8.2 Procedure to determine the level of protection	113
	6.8.3 Communication of the levels of protection	114
	6.8.4 Response to a specific and determined threat	115
	6.8.5 Communication procedure for threats and levels of protection	115
6.9	The Ministries and Organisms involved in its implementation	115
6.10	Towards a new port police	117
	6.10.1 Legal labour statute that seeks recognition of the function of the police	117
	6.10.2 The position of the unions	120
6.11	Private security	121
	6.11.1 Security guards	121
	6.11.2 Chiefs of Security	122
	6.11.3 Private security in foreign ships	122
	6.11.4 Private security in the ports	123

7. The Code and the Port Facilities Security Plan 125

7.1	Introduction	125
7.2	Port organisation. Autonomy and management efficiency	129
	7.2.1 Ports of General Interest	130
	7.2.2 Autonomic Ports	130
	7.2.3 Private Terminals	131
7.3	Purpose of PFSP	131
7.4	Situations that could cause panic	135
7.5	Control of the concentration	135
7.6	Practices	137
7.7	Contents of the PFSP	138
7.8	Confidentiality	139

8. Port Facilities Security Plan (PFSP) 143

8.1	Elaboration of the PFSP	145
8.2	Access to the port facility	155

		8.2.1 Detector gates	158
		8.2.2 Portable equipment	158
		8.2.3 X ray equipment	158
8.3		Operational limitations of the equipment and of the protection systems	159
8.4		Restricted areas inside the port facility	166
8.5		Handling cargo	169
8.6		Delivery of the ship's provisions	172
8.7		Unaccompanied baggage	173
8.8		Monitoring the protection of the port facility	174
8.9		Different levels of protection	175
8.10		Activities not regulated by the Code	175
8.11		Approval of the port facilities protection plan	175
8.12		Implementation of the port facilities protection plan	176
8.13		Maintenance and modification of the port facility protection plan	177
8.14		Control of arms and explosives in the port facility	177
		8.14.1 Types	178
		8.14.2 Transport of arms	181
8.15		Explosives	181

9. Roles of the port 185

9.1	The port as a frontier	186
9.2	The port as customs	187
9.3	Customs and frontier	189
9.4	International standards	190
	9.4.1 Agreement for the representation of illicit acts against the security of maritime navigation	190

10. General service and policing regulation project in Ports of general interest, now known as "Regulation of exploitation and policing" 195

10.1	Power to sanction	195
10.2	The scope of the Regulation of Exploitation and Policing	198
10.3	ISPS Code. EU Regulation and Project for the Directive	201
10.4	The Proposal of the Community Directive	206
	10.4.1 The hypothetical Regulation of Exploitation and Policing	213
10.5	Security Contents of the Regulation and Ordinances	214

11. Conclusions 223

Bibliography 227

Introduction

A new regime for safety in international maritime transport came into force on 1st July 2004. It was developed by the International Maritime Organisation (IMO) which established a series of measures aimed at strengthening the maritime protection of the ship and the port facilities, and to prevent and suppress, among others, acts of terrorism against the activity of maritime transport.

In this sense, the main aspects to be analysed are those related to the port security authorities at a national level, the port police, the recognised protection organisations, the monitoring of the protection of the port facility, the different figures created by the ISPS Code, port ordinances and their inclusion and coherence with the Spanish port system.

Objectives

This study aims to achieve the following objectives:

- To mark the relationships and dependences of the ISPS and the port ordinances with other safety plans in order to harmonise the Spanish regulatory system.
- To define the role of concessionary companies in a port facility.
- Designation and intervention of the port and the Port Authority as a recognized protection organisation.
- Identify the legal aspects of the ship-port facility interface.
- To formally collate and unify protection in the Spanish port system, by guaranteeing the coordination and homogeneity among the different security plans and other legislation of obligatory application.
- To extract the parts directly related to the emergency plans from the above mentioned legal instruments, by identifying the weak points of the relationship between them.

Methodology

To relate the legislative provisions that make it possible to implement the provisions contained in the ISPS Code, with a special focus on article 132 of the Law of Economic Regime and Rendering of Services in the Ports of General Interest (LREPS).

To analyse the legal grounds, regulations and tendencies in order to be able to define the interrelationship between the ISPS Code, the Port Ordinances and the other legal bodies required to achieve their implementation and coherence in the Spanish legal system.

Work schedule

The texts and provisions of the ISPS will be obtained for examination regarding the duties and obligations of the contracting governments. The knowledge obtained will make it clear that the initiation and maintenance of the processes and procedures required for the implementation of the applicable elements of the ISPS are a question for the national governments that are members of the International Maritime Organisation and are signatories of the Code and of the corresponding conventions.

A study will be made of the application mechanisms at a national level, and of what the Ministerial Orders are. These must be of an authorising nature determining the future development of the Port Ordinances. The LREPS establish an ample and thorough control by the Port Authority in the area of the port relating to the certain areas (dangerous goods, occupational hazards, etc.) notwithstanding the competences that correspond to other organs of the Public Administrations and of the responsibilities that correspond in this matter to the users and dealers in the port.

All of these measures will be necessary to guarantee the homogeneity and collation among all the port facilities on Spanish soil and to achieve their coordination at a national level.

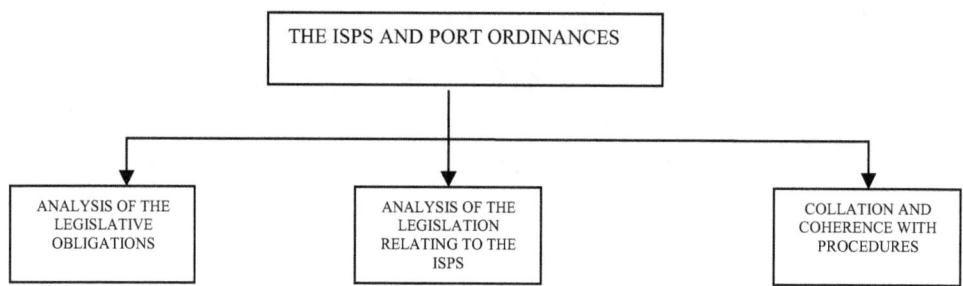

1 Security in general

1.1 The concept of security

Security, without adjectives, is a concept that has several meanings. The one that we are interested in is that which is applied to a branch of the public administration and whose aim is to cater for public safety.

In short, public safety as a state of affairs in which life evolves pacifically and people coexist without unwelcome surprises because the State guarantees reasonable conditions for the progress of daily life.

Security is better understood in the negative sense, as the absence of situations that cause alarm or unease in citizens.

Public safety is a matter for everyone and the State is the guarantor of this situation so that the citizens can enjoy their rights without outside disturbances spoiling that enjoyment. Public safety is guaranteed by the State who exercises it through the Ministry of the Interior in so far as it organizes and directs the State's Security Forces and Corps (FCSE). There is also a place for other security forces such as the regional police forces which play integral roles in matters of security with the exception of some competences that remain in the hands of the State. Local police contribute to this public safety within the scope of their competences.

Within the framework of article 4 of Organic Law 1/92 on the protection of public safety, an administrative police framework known as *special police* is contemplated. In areas of activity not specifically attributed to entities depending on the Ministry of the Interior it may intervene in so far as is necessary to guarantee that the objectives laid down in paragraph 2 of article 1 are achieved.

Through their agents, these entities shall offer the necessary executive aid to any other public authorities who require it to guarantee compliance with the laws.

Paragraph 2 of article 1 of OL 1/92 limits the scope of action of these special police to the exercise of the administrative powers established in the Law, in order to:

- guarantee coexistence,
- eradicate violence,
- attain a pacific use of the public roads and spaces
- prevent crimes and offences from being committed.

The competence of the special administrative police forces, including harbour guards, is not a trivial matter as it implies, as can be seen, an array of possibilities for actions which are hardly insignificant in general terms and more specifically in the area of port services.

As already mentioned, they also have an executive duty of an auxiliary nature with the public authorities to guarantee compliance with the laws.

In the first 4 articles of OL 2/86 on Security Forces and Corps, it is stated that public safety is the exclusive competence of the State and its maintenance corresponds to the Government of the Nation.

The Autonomous Communities shall participate in maintaining public safety in the terms that are established in the corresponding Statutes and in the framework of this Law.

Local corporations shall participate in maintaining public safety in the terms established in the regulatory Law on the Bases of Local Regime and in the framework of the Law that we are considering.

Maintaining public safety shall be the exercise of the different Public Administrations through the Security Forces and Corps.

Article 2 defines the Security Forces and Corps as including:

- The security forces and corps that report to the Government of the Nation.
- Police forces reporting to the Autonomous Communities
- Police forces reporting to local corporations.

Article 3 states that the members of the Security Forces and Corps shall adapt their actions to the principle of reciprocal cooperation and they shall be coordinated through the organs established to that effect by the Law.

Once again Article 4 makes reference to the special police forces after stating that they all have the duty of lending the necessary support to the Security Forces and Corps in the investigation and persecution of crimes in the legally established terms.

However, this general obligation becomes a special demand for people and entities that exercise functions of surveillance, security or custody referring to personnel and goods or public or private services as they have a special obligation to help or collaborate with the Security Forces and Corps at all times.

Harbour guards perform functions of surveillance, security or custody referring to personnel and goods or public services, such as ports of general interest.

On this legal ground, the Regulation of Exploitation and Policing and the development of article 106 of the Law of Ports can build a whole framework of obligations and responsibilities so that the functions of the port police can be exercised to the full, though we must not forget that in this latest

Organic Law the Civil Guard is responsible for the custody of the ports, just as they are in airports and that that they also carry out tasks in Tax affairs as State Security.

It also refers to those who exercise private functions in a clear relation to Law 23/92 on Private Security. This matter will be studied in detail in another chapter of this text.

1.2 Preventive security

Preventive security is the consequence of a general organisational system which, through the use of material and human means, aims at avoiding antisocial behaviour. The exteriorisation of these means gives the citizens the sensation that their activities, life and possessions are guaranteed against external threats.

It is a matter for everyone. The citizens, by adopting a series of elementary measures in their daily activities to avoid putting their lives and assets at risk or in some cases by contracting private security services. The different police that we saw, by controlling different sectors of activity within their areas of competence. And the Security Forces, by offering a general service.

The former is achieved by fencing areas, controlling accesses with electronic surveillance, checking passengers, controlling cargos, monitoring the docks with rounds or cameras, etc., so that this arrangement is capable of dissuading intruders or anyone who aims at threatening security, the possessions or the lives of people in their family or professional surroundings.

The truth is that if all these physical and apparent means are not too aggressive or disproportionate and provided that they respect the dignity of people and their rights, the citizens have a reasonably positive feeling that they are safe and protected.

The Regulation of Exploitation and Port Policing shall take into account that the deployment of harbour guards and passive security measures and the possibility that they implement a system that is capable of sanctioning those non-compliances with the most elementary rules established in it will constitute a modern and efficient organisation that will lead to the security of the port area with the implementation of the International Ship and Port Facility Security Code (ISPS), in the affected maritime terminal.

1.3 Security on an international scale

In the introduction it was stated that the ship is, in itself, considered an international element because its voyages are subject to the changing legislation of the ports in which it loads and unloads passengers or goods, or docks.

The nationality of the different crew members and passengers can be very varied and the origin and destination of the merchandise very diverse.

Therefore, since the beginnings of commercial navigation, agreements and pacts have been sought which were more or less ample and more or less stable, in an attempt to provide a certain legal security in the navigation, to the ships, to the passengers and to the cargos.

In another section we mentioned that security was many sided as it could refer to security in navigation, port security, the security of the passengers, of the cargos, to commercial security, to legal security, which means that the reference depends on the adjective we use.

Here we are talking about public safety and specifically to that referring to preventing attacks on ships, passengers, crew members and cargos and the security of the port facilities and of the people and assets within.

Various agreements provided by international organisms have tried to answer these demands. The ISPS Code represents a milestone in international public safety as it establishes a homogenous international system, rules and people responsible who will try to make the provisions understood so that the security procedures thus standardised will give minimum guarantees of preventing aggressions against port facilities and ships.

1.4 The International Ship and Port Facility Security Code (ISPS)

The ISPS Code is an important international instrument whose objective, within the affected ports, is to see that certain areas, known as *port facilities*, are a security capsule whenever the ship interrelates with the terminal. This is known as *ship-port interface*. For this very special area and for the moment in which the interface occurs the Code has special preventive security measures.

It is aimed, therefore, at certain ships dedicated to international travel:

- passenger ships, including high speed passenger ships;
- cargo ships, including high speed ships, with a gross tonnage equal to or above 500;
- high sea mobile drilling units; and
- the port facilities that render services to these ships dedicated to international travel.

For this purpose it has established up to three levels of security that will be activated according to the threats and designates responsibilities for security on the ships, in the maritime companies that build ships and in the port facilities.

In applying different security plans these people will know at all times which measures to adopt according to the circumstances.

Among those responsible for security we wish to pay special attention to the Port Facility Security Officer (PFSO)

The PFSO is the person designated to respond for the elaboration, implementation, revision and updating of the Port Facility Security Plan (PFSP) and for coordination with the ship security officers (SSO) and with the company security officers (CSO).

A PFSO shall be designated for each port facility. The same person may be designated as security officer for more than one port facility.

The *tasks* and *responsibilities* of the PFSO will include but are not limited to the following:

1. Perform an initial evaluation of the port facility, taking into consideration the security of the port facility.
2. Guarantee the elaboration and maintenance of the PFSP.
3. Implement the PFSP and make practices with it.
4. Make periodical inspections at the port facility by guaranteeing that the protective measures are adequate. This is where the PFSO shall organise the work of the harbour guards as these demands are within their competences.
5. Recommend and include, as appropriate, modifications in the PFSP in order to correct deficiencies and update the plan.
6. Encourage the awareness of protection and monitoring among port facility personnel.
7. Make sure that the adequate training has been given to the personnel responsible for the protection of the port facility.
8. Report to the authorities on the events that imply a threat to the port facility and keep a record of them.
9. Coordinate the implementation of the PFSP with the SSO and the CSO
10. Coordinate with the necessary protection services.
11. Make sure that the regulations relating to the personnel responsible for the protection of the port facility are met.
12. Guarantee the operation, testing, calibration and adequate maintenance of the protective equipment, if applicable.
13. Help the SSO to confirm the identity of the people who wish to go on board, when so requested.

The PFSP is a plan that has been elaborated to guarantee the protection of the port facility and the ships, people, cargos, the units of transport and the provisions of the ships in the port facility, from the risks that affect maritime security.

Public ports, in Spain, are moving slowly towards being privately managed, although the ports of general interest continue in the hands of the State, regardless of the fact that in recent times the Autonomous Communities have acquired greater competence over them and in some cases they have even requested the competence be transferred to them.

From the perspective of the ISPS Code, we must point out that, in an open manner and from the beginning we shall not talk about ports, as the Code always refers to port facilities. This is how it is and therefore inside a port there can be several port facilities (docks for cruise ships, coal ships, containers, oil tankers....) and each one with their corresponding plans and PFSO, when there is only one per facility.

This is vital if we wish to understand that the intention is that the port facilities become security capsules within a more extensive port area, but in which the measures of security are not strict.

The port of general interest, in Spain, would become a second security circle, around a first capsule that represents the specific port facility. Therefore, a typical Port of General Interest could have:

- one or several port facilities for cruise ships,
- a port facility for containers,
- a port facility for general cargo,
- a port facility for liquid bulk
- a ro-ro terminal
- etc.

We could say that within the Spanish ports (state, autonomous or private terminals) there are areas of service that have access control and a more general security and special security areas, with stricter controls, such as the port terminals and which have specific protection plans, port facility protection officers, security personnel and action, control and management protocols.

2 Terrorism

2.1 National terrorism

National terrorism, at the present moment, is limited to the terrorist actions that could be committed by the criminal band ETA, which has been operating in Spain since the end of the nineteen-fifties. Based on the postulations of a Marxist Leninist ideology, this criminal band seeks the independence of the Basque Country and the reunification of the "Basque nation" which would be made up of three French provinces, Navarre and the Spanish Basque country.

This is a terrorism that we could call *nationalist* as its objectives are based on building an independent Basque Country where socialism is implemented. The criminal band ETA is an organised group with a common ideal which, through acts of terrorism, seeks to impose the idea of a *nation* and fight to obtain this objective, after independence.

On many occasions it has used weapons and explosives and its level of organisation and infrastructure is high. This has enabled it to survive for over four decades albeit with its ups and downs. It is a criminal band with clearly defined objectives. As it seeks to gain social support it tries not to disturb its immediate environment with attacks, to get involved in social conflicts with terror campaigns and attacks against the State, as it is considered the oppressor.

With this approach it also seeks international support and is very selective with the attacks it commits outside of Spain.

For a long time now it has kept its governing bodies in France, with a logistical, international and operative infrastructure that allows it to keep committing its criminal actions and sabotages from the underground.

Along the way they have left almost a thousand victims and a constant blood bath in what is expressed in a term known as *low intensity terrorism*, probably because of the increasingly lower incidence of this criminal band on Spanish political life.

In France it trains criminal groups known as *commands* and keeps them on a permanent training period holding them on standby for actions against specific objectives in certain areas of Spain or against different state or economical targets.

As we said, it does not practice indiscriminate terrorism but rather in favour of its interests that seek one day to obtain a majority support for its thesis and power through political representation or similar groups to implant socialism.

The leaders of the criminal band have been accommodating their political objectives to such an extent that the party that was most involved with it has been declared illegal.

The incidence of ETA in port-maritime security has not been very relevant, although there were significant episodes between 1979 and 1982 when they trained a *command* of divers to threaten the underwater body of the ships belonging to the Navy and which represented certain economic interests or interests of another nature.

On 10th February 1981 it attacked the Navy destroyer "Marques de la Ensenada" in the port of Santander. On 24th June 1979 the French ship "Montlhery" was sunk while it was docked in the Puerto de Pasajes (Guipuzcoa). The terrorist act was carried out underwater where two holes were made on the starboard side about 2.2 metres under the keel. The ship was dedicated to transporting Ford cars built in Spain to England. They have committed other similar actions and tried several more. They have also used a remote controlled boat loaded with explosives.

Having said this, it can be said that to date ETA has not committed terrorist acts with the intention of causing thousands of deaths, maybe because one day it wishes to come to power or influence a large part of the territory and this could lead to it losing social support by generating a face-on rejection of the important social backing that it has, within what would be its final strategy of conquering political power,

We cannot discard the possibility that ETA perpetrates more attacks on the means of transport or against the interests of Spanish port-maritime security. It will all depend on the moment and the opportunity and capacity to commit a terrorist action of this nature. However, it can be said that to date it has kept its preferential objectives elsewhere, without discarding the possibility that a State ship or gas or petrol station could become part of its evil plans because of the state or economic interests that they represent and the repercussion it would have in the media.

Once the interests present in each case within the port area have been analysed, any port security plan should contemplate the eventuality of this threat to port security. The security forces deployed in the ports and the harbour guards and other security agents, including private ones, must be aware of this threat and be prepared for the possibility of a terrorist attack.

The Regulation of Exploitation and Policing must use communication and information systems and action protocols against this type of anti-social aggression on the understanding that the security forces shall be the main protagonist in the resolution of this type of crisis.

2.2 International terrorism

Radical Islamic terrorism has attacked the transport network, namely local trains in Madrid causing numerous deaths. If airplanes have been used as instruments of terrorism and trains have been targeted to cause the massacre in Madrid on 11th March 2004, any decently experienced analyst would realise that a ship offers a huge potential to be used as an instrument for a large scale criminal action or as the object of a criminal attack.

Now more than ever security is a matter for everyone and everyone should get involved in preventive security. The increase in maritime security has been required by the International Maritime Organisation (IMO) in relatively recent times[1].

On the other hand, the IMO had already made several recommendations of interest as a preamble for what would become the Code, although there were also other reasons. Among them, the following Resolutions are worthy of mention:

A. 872 (20) approved on 20/11/97, has given guidelines for preventing and suppressing smuggling drugs, psychotropic substances and chemical products on ships dedicated to international maritime transport as these are at the end of the day the ones that enter the ports of general interest.

A. 584 (14) aimed at establishing a programme of measures to prevent the occurrence of illicit acts of an antisocial nature that could endanger the security of the ships, the passengers and the crews.

Letter 443 which contemplates measures to prevent illicit acts, applicable to passenger ships that make international voyages equal to or greater than 24 hours as well as the port facilities associated with these voyages.

A. 924 (22) relating to procedures for preventing terrorism that endangers the security of passengers, crews and ships.

We understand terrorism as being any deliberate antisocial illicit act that, due to its nature or context, could prejudice the ships used in both national and international maritime transport, or their passengers or their cargo or the port facilities associated with them. It also refers to third parties when damage can be caused to the ship or to strategic and sensitive objectives from the ship.

Behind every terrorist act there is an organised criminal group with sufficient capacity to plan and execute criminal acts with a huge social impact due to the material or human damage caused. The repercussions of these acts in the media feed back to the group, giving it the sensation of power and they become platforms to capture new terrorists in favour of the ideas and their actions which then become the motivation for the criminal actions of the group.

The idea that unites the group is the motor that drives unconditional and transcendent loyalties to follow a leader who personifies this idea and establishes who is the enemy and the terrorist objectives. The strong ideology of the group (political, religious...) justifies any kind of action no matter how pitiless it may seem and transcends the reason to reach a fanaticism that excludes all that which is not in favour of the established objectives.

Special reference must be made to what is known today as the *global war*, the threats that it represents for society and especially that means of transport may be used as a lethal weapon aimed at causing a

---

[1] On 12th October 100 there was a terrorist attack in Aden, Yemen. The target was the American war ship "USS Cole". The "Cole" was in the port of Yemini to refuel when a small boat, loaded with explosives, was detonated on the other side of the ship and made a huge hole in its hull. 17 marines were killed and 39 were wounded in the attack. The two terrorists crashed a speed boat into the hull of the ship. Others involved were sentenced to death in 2004.

large number of victims and countless damage in an indiscriminate manner at the same time as using terror to alarm and dominate governments as well as the population. Therefore an analysis will be made of the preventive measures that could dissuade the use of a ship as a means or objective of terrorism to cause widespread damage to both people and properties.

With the ISPS Code as the driving force, proposals will be made and ideas and opinions will be expressed about security on ships and in ports and about the responsibilities of the different institutions and maritime and port operators, both public and private, in control, surveillance and in security in the ample meaning of the word. In short, a shared reflection that invites us to be aware of the risks that a terrorist threat against maritime transport entails.

At the same time, the competences and responsibilities of the Security Forces and Corps shall be analysed. Apart from the internal security plans of the ships and of the measures to be implemented by the ship-owners and the Port Authorities and by the Merchant Navy, the Security Forces and Corps have to play a vital role in the prevention and investigation of elements and terrorist groups, as well as their action methods and procedures. They must be capable of coordinating all those involved in security and fundamentally, in controlling a system for gathering information and maintaining communication with the different maritime operators and be capable of channelling useful data and indications towards an adequate prevention.

It seems clear, at least for the most documented analysts, that the concept of *global war* must be connected with a certain type of terrorism that no longer has defined objectives such as the conquest of power through subversion, that does not operate in a specific country or area, that is not selective and does not seek support among the population where it executes its actions and it does not fear the consequences.

The criminal act is aimed at causing terror in its pure essence, in alarming humanity and in causing the largest number of victims and most damage possible regardless of its social condition.

There are other types of terrorism, and in Spain, we have more than enough experience of its effects and although they are censurable, they are more local and more foreseeable. We are talking about terrorisms that seek the independence of a certain territory, others that seek the long term imposition of a certain ideology or which wish to transform a certain country or area. They are equally censurable, but what has really gone beyond any expectation and because everyone feels threatened by it, is the recent manifestation of Islamic terrorism, which embedded in an all encompassing fanaticism wishes to attack any centre of military, political or economical power that affects its interests.

It uses religious fanaticism to keep its elements loyal to the point in which suicide has become a normal means of committing their actions against groups of people and means of transport as we could see, muted and impotent, in New York or Madrid. It is not therefore a matter of carrying out a series of low intensity related actions, if we might use the expression, but rather, of preparing a great action over several years involving their own life, provided that they achieve their objectives.

In the ports, and just as stated above, everyone who has any type of responsibility and especially regarding security and all personnel of the Port Authority and port facility operators must be made aware that sea transport is among the preferential objectives of the most radical Islamic terrorists and that these attacks are possible in our ports and against the interests of maritime and port security.

Prevention is vital and requires the involvement of a good security plan that evaluates and analyses the risks. It must be able to offer the bases and the necessary training for security personnel, public or private, to be in a position to detect those anomalous conducts perpetrated by intruders who take notes and provide data from their hideouts to make an attack possible.

Confidentiality, which we shall talk about, suspicion, observation and surveillance, both personal and electronic, is vital in detecting indications that allow the Security Forces to check on potentially dangerous behaviours and attitudes.

2.3 International and national regulation

It is obvious that there are no crimes specific to terrorism. The terrorist is a delinquent who, with more or less organisation, commits premeditated crimes just like any other delinquent, except for the fact that he/she concentrates on certain crimes such as murder, havoc, damage, etc., because they are the most appropriate for his/her criminal strategies.

Sabotage is one of the ways of exteriorising terrorism of al kinds. According to the Dictionary of the Royal Spanish Academy, sabotage is understood as being any damage or deterioration to installations, products, etc., as a procedure for fighting against the owners, against the State or against the occupying forces in social or political conflicts. Figuratively, it is also the hidden opposition to or obstruction of projects, orders, decisions, ideas, etc.

Potentially, sabotage is one of the possible criminal actions against a ship or port facility. To be more precise in this context sabotage is limited to the situation in which a port facility, a ship docked in it, its cargo or passengers are victims of an illegitimate external or internal aggression that is aimed at causing damage leaving it inoperative, destroying its cargo or causing personal damage to its crew or passengers in the context of the intentional aggression perpetrated normally by terrorist groups or elements. It also refers to the taking over of the ship by the members of a terrorist group, to use it intentionally against a strategic facility or to attack another ship in order to cause considerable personal and material damage.

Sabotaging a ship can cause a large number of victims and material damage (the deaths caused by mass murder). Murder is another of the more commonly committed crimes by terrorists.

Terrorism is understood as the domination of terror. It is the succession of acts of violence committed to induce terror.

In reference to international regulation, Spain ratified the Agreement and Protocol of 10th March 1988[2]. The Agreement relates the repression of illicit acts against the security of maritime navigation and fixed platforms located on the continental platform. A United States initiative is now leading the way to update it.

Article 3 stands out in its content. It defines what is understood as aggression against security in navigation, a concept close to terrorism. Thus, a crime is committed by any person who

---

[2] By Instrument of 15th June 1989, which was published in BOE number 99, of 24th April 1992.

intentionally takes over a ship or controls it with violence, threatens violence or any other form of intimidation; or perpetrates any violent act against a person who is on board a ship if said act could put its navigation in danger; destroys a ship, causes damage to it or to its cargo, or places or gets another to place, by any means, an artefact or substance that could destroy it, cause damage to its cargo or put the navigation of the ship in danger; destroy or cause damage to the maritime navigation facilities and services or seriously impedes their operation; distributes information knowing that it is false, thus putting the safe navigation of the ship in danger, or injures or kills any person.

Internally, the penalty for most of these actions can be found and handed out within the Penal Code Organic Law 10/95 of 23rd November, as a crime of damage and havoc, considered similar to sabotage.

Article 346, in so much as it affects us, considers that havoc or damage is committed by those who by provoking explosions or by using any other similar means, cause the destruction of, among others, airports, ports, collective means of transport or the immersion or stranding of the ship.

Article 571 and following of the Penal Code deal with terrorism: it considers terrorists as those belonging to, acting in service or collaborating with armed bands, organisations or groups whose objective is to subvert constitutional order or seriously alter public peace, commit crimes of havoc or fires in certain circumstances.

It also considers the deposit of arms or ammunition or holding or depositing substances or artefacts which are explosive, inflammable, incendiary or asphyxiant or of their components, as well as manufacturing, trafficking, transporting or supplying them in any form and the mere collection or use of such substances or of the adequate means or artifices…. (art. 573).

Weapons and explosives, as more or less sophisticated instruments, will be the normal means of aggression to take a ship or to attack a port.

Their control is linked to the monitoring of cargos, provisions and personal effects of the people on board when the ship is not taken over by force and is used against the port facility as a gigantic weapon with the intention of causing huge personal or material damage.

In the same way the Penal Code considers as terrorists those who, with the intention of forwarding funds to the above mentioned terrorist groups, or with the intention of favouring their objectives, attack against possessions….(art. 575) and those who carry out, perpetrate or facilitate any act of collaboration with the activities or objectives of a terrorist band.

Acts of collaboration are considered as the information or monitoring of people, possessions or facilities, the construction, conditioning, leasing or use of lodgings or deposits; concealing or transferring people related to armed bands, organisations or terrorist groups; the organisation of training practices or attending them, and in general, any other equivalent form.

Before any attack a study is required of the situation, of the means of surveillance that the facility has, photographs to be taken, notes on means of passive security to be able to overcome them, etc. These are collaborations that are sanctioned and logically as they are at the beginning of any criminal action, must be detected.

Acts of terrorism are also considered as those perpetrated by people who, without belonging to a terrorist group and with the purpose of subverting constitutional order or seriously altering public peace, commit murders, cause certain injuries[3], illegal detention, kidnappings, threats or duress against people, or who perpetrate any crimes including fire, havoc or the possession, trafficking and depositing of weapons or ammunitions (art. 577).

In order to take over a ship by force in the port or at sea it is obvious that certain crimes against liberty must be committed: the Captain or the members of the crew are forced aside and held illegally. This conduct is typified and included in the Penal Code.

In crimes related with the activity of terrorist organisations, the sentence of a foreign judge or court will be similar to the sentences of the Spanish judges or courts for the effects of recurrence (art. 580).

Sabotage is the means or the end of terrorism as it may be and usually is its instrument.

The Security Forces and those police (from Autonomous Communities) that have taken on the competences in the matter in hand must investigate those elements or terrorist groups that are in a position to carry out any of the actions described, either because of the characteristics of their organisation or because of the violent methods and procedures they use in the persecution of their objectives. Any suspicion relating to the matter must be reported to them. Occasionally, detecting a person taking notes in a secret fashion in a port or about a specific ship could be the link that thwarts an attack if this fact is reported to the police. We could give more examples.

Within the missions given to them by the Law of Ports and which must be contemplated in the new port Police Regulation, harbour guards must be aware that preventive surveillance and the detection of intruders are important weapons in avoiding terrorist attacks.

2.4 Threats to the means of transport and the port facilities

An *event that effects maritime protection* is understood as any act or circumstance that raises suspicion and which constitutes a threat to the protection of a ship, including high sea mobile drilling units and the high speed ships from a port facility, ship-port interface or a ship to ship activity.

The Code understands *maritime security* as the combination of preventive measures that are aimed at protecting maritime transport and port facilities against the threat of deliberate illicit acts.

Merchant ships which are primarily the object of the most radical international terrorism seem to be, those known as *cruise* ships. Before the dreadful 11th September cruise ships were the sector that was growing the most within the travel industry. The Cruise Lines International Association (CLIA) of New York represents the most important lines in the world therefore we are talking about American interests. But no developed country is foreign to this business sector related to the leisure and tourist industry, a sector in which Spain is a world leader and the destination of much of this traffic, if not the departure and arrival point of these voyages, particularly in the Mediterranean, which is a potentially dangerous area due to its geo-strategic and political situation.

---

[3] Those typified in articles 149 or 150 of the Penal Code.

The port facility, considered on its own, will be a difficult strategic objective, with the exception of certain terminals whose strategic repercussion may acquire its own relevance and become an objective. These could be the case of oil, chemical or gas product terminals.

Let's analyse any criminal action, from outside the hull of the ship, docked in port with the intention of sinking it so as to cause the greatest possible number of victims and personal injury.

The preparation of the attack involves the need to transport an important amount of explosives to the ship or the vicinity of the ship with sufficient destructive power to overcome the barrier that the hull represents.

Taking experience into account, the most predictable methods would be one of the following:

- One or several terrorists, acting as divers, transport the load and attach it to sensitive areas of the hull under the float line on the underwater of the ship. All conventional and home made procedures such as stick bombs are possible[4]. The success of the action, if intense enough, usually depends on sinking the ship and claiming victims among the crew and passengers.

- Pilots (suicide or not) on board small boats loaded with explosives drive them against the side of the ship facing the sea at the point where they can cause greater material damage or provoke more personal victims as the case may be.

- Small remote controlled boats (even airplanes) to minimise risks, with the capacity to transport small loads of explosives to a previously selected spot where they are detonated. As they are small loads they are usually used against specific objective or ships with personalities on board and are activated by remote control.

- Loads are attached between the dock and the ship. As the most important port facilities are now perfectly limited by the traffic affected by the Code, the terrorist or terrorists will have a lot of time to prepare the attack, which means that they can opt for this criminal action instead of attacking the ship directly, which nevertheless, will suffer the consequences of any explosion.

- The ship in port and especially cruise ships are susceptible to being attacked with weapons in a move to take over the ship and hold the crew and passengers hostage. This criminal action should not be discarded as it offers the possibility of being prolonged in time. The control of accesses, both to the port and to the facilities and preventive security measures are vital in foreseeing and thwarting this type of action, which can also be perpetrated from water side when the stay in the port is prolonged.

The Policing Regulation and port Ordinances must foresee the certain possibility that harbour guards, or alternatively security guards, within the framework of the Private Security Law, are in a position to skipper small boats to offer security to certain ships.

---

[4] On 24th June 1979, the French ship "Montlhery" was sunk while it was docked in the Port of Pasajes (Guipuzcoa). The terrorist attack was perpetrated by divers who made two holes in the hull of the ship on the starboard side, about 2.2 metres below the keel. This ship was dedicated to the transportation to England of Ford cars built in Spain..

Acceptable control and other important security measures are observed, especially in cruise ships, for the passengers themselves and their personal effects on the side of the ship that faces the dock but there is little surveillance on the water side.

The Security Forces can carry out controls on that side in their boats although they will always be random and discontinuous inspections to provide extra security, but preventive security must be guaranteed in the Port Security Plan or in the Port Facilities Security Plan (PFSP) and must be more frequent to prevent suspicious boats that could represent danger from coming alongside.

In the light of these deficiencies, cruise ships in our ports are demanding the use of their own security personnel and performing this service with their own boats, which regardless of their efficiency, could lead to a legal conflict because really the security services correspond to the State and are their exclusive competence in the broadest sense and it would not be right for a foreign security service to act off the limits of the ship because this would be an affront to sovereignty and could be a source of conflict if, using their own criteria or those of the country of their flag, they were to impose restrictions on the boats that navigate near the ship, especially when these security services that are on board the cruise ships do not know the port environment and the specific problems of teach maritime territory.

This is not a trivial problem and must be addressed in the future Policing Regulation because the area of water included in the port services area must also be the responsibility of the port Authority.

2.5 Global answers

Global answers regarding awareness and preventive measures are needed from all those involved in all areas of action and specifically in the port maritime area.

In the international context, the IMO is seeking to get all the nations to agree on the basic measures that the contracting Governments need to adopt.

The implementation of the ISPS Code is a good example of this. But the important international agreements, which involve a large number of countries with such different and often opposing interests are normally such small agreements that many countries do not even implement them because they lack the minimum organisational, legal and economical instruments to do so.

Security nowadays has a high cost and the countries of the third world are not really in a position to offer safe ports for international maritime navigation. Therefore, the Code has tried to focus security on something specific; the ship-port interface as a limited and concrete space which must concentrate the most elementary security measures and has involved ships and facilities and certain people responsible for their safety in it.

On the other hand, the limitations are also of a different nature as certain countries are clearly more vulnerable than others and some are preferential targets, which means that each one applies the Code with more or less rigour.

In a much more limited and closer geographic context, with important common interests, in an economically developed area of the world, it is clearly much easier to make a large number of interests common. This has already been done in other activity areas and CE number 725/2004 of the European Parliament and of the Council of 31st March 2004 goes further in its demands.

The ISPS Code is aware of this limitation and when it addresses the responsibility of the contracting governments, it admits the possibility of reaching alternative agreements on security. Thus, paragraph 4.26 of part B of the Code, states: "When determining how to implement chapter XI-2 and part A of this Code, the contracting governments may sign one or more agreements with one or more contracting governments."

The area of application of an agreement shall be limited to short international voyages on fixed routes between port facilities located in the territory of the parties entering the agreement. After signing an agreement the contracting governments should consult other contracting governments and administrations that have an interest in the agreement.

The ships that carry the flag of a country that is not part of the agreement will only be allowed to navigate in the fixed routes covered by the agreement if their administration admits that the ship must comply with the provisions of the agreement and demands that it does so. In no case should these agreements compromise the level of security of other ships and port facilities that are not covered by the agreement in question and specifically, no ship covered by an agreement of this nature will be allowed to carry out ship to ship activities with a ship that is not covered by the agreement.

Any interface operation carried out by the ships to which this agreement applies must be covered by it. The performance of each agreement will be continuously supervised and shall be modified according to the circumstances and in any case, shall be revised every five years.

In short, we can say that the more countries that are part of an agreement the less the level of compromise and compliance. That is why international treaties with a large number of contracting states attain the general principles and there is a higher level of involvement and response among countries with common interests, in certain areas, with similar problems, etc.

In these circumstances each time a ship goes to dock in different ports in different countries and with different threats, the global answers make the procedures more homogenous which makes better security possible.

On the other hand, if everyone gets involved in preventive security and this is balanced with a certain awareness of this type of problem the risks will be decreased. These worries must be constant and be evidenced in the different regulation texts.

The Regulation of Exploitation and Policing is an ideal instrument in which to include all these international requirements in a short but concise synthesis of what port security must be and what the techniques and procedures for maintaining port security are to give a response to current needs in a modern country.

2.6 The International Ship and Port Facility Security Code. Objectives

As the Code itself states in its preamble, following the tragic and alarming events of 11th September 2001 that caused thousands of deaths in an unprecedented attack, the twenty-second Assembly of the IMO (the Organisation) agreed unanimously that new measures must be drawn up with relation to the protection of ships and of port facilities. These would be adopted in the Conference of December 2002 of the International Agreement Contracting Governments for the safety of human life at sea (SOLAS, 1974), known as a diplomatic Conference on maritime protection.

The preparations for the diplomatic Conference were commissioned to the Maritime Security Committee of the Organisation (MSC) whose work was based on the documents presented by the member governments, the inter-government organisations and the non-governmental organisations of a consulting nature with the Organisation.

Among other measures, it elaborated the International Ship and Port Facility Security Code (ISPS Code) in force since 1st July 2004, which seeks to attain the following objectives:

1. "Establish an *international framework* that channels the cooperation among governments, governmental organisms, administrations and shipping and port sectors in order to *detect the threats to protection and adopt preventive measures against the events that affect the security of the ships and port facilities used by international business*." This means that, as far as Spain is concerned, the state and regional port authorities, harbour masters, Security Forces, harbour guards, private security agents, those responsible for the private terminals that operate with concessions or ship operators and maritime and port operators in general who are involved in a coordinated manner in a chain so that the information flows freely so as to detect and foresee the threats to the port sector in time to react. The ministries involved and the Regional Governments must provide adequate scenarios and the organs required for good coordination. An instrument of interest will be the content of the future Policing Regulation which shall profile a port security organisation with clear and specific missions in the areas of its competence, basically the preventive security that the new regulations and interests in presence demand.

2. "Define "*functions and responsibilities* of governments, government organisms, local administrations and the shipping and port sectors, at a national and international level, in order to guarantee maritime security." The Ministry of the Interior, through the Secretary of State for Security (SES), and the Ministry of Development, through the General Directorate of the Merchant Navy (DGMM), the Society for Maritime Rescue and Security (SASEMAR) and the Public Entity Ports of the State must be able to facilitate the implementation of these security measures in a coordinated manner, distribute them by levels of responsibility, establish an internal regulation framework that is capable of achieving the cooperation of all those involved by developing those precepts of the Law of Ports that require answers from the Ministry of the Interior in a standard that clearly limits the different competences and security demands.

3. Guarantee that *the information related to security is collected and exchanged quickly and efficiently*.

4. Offer a method to evaluate security in order to have *plans and procedures that make it possible to react* to the changes in the levels of security.

The following functional prescriptions are established in order to achieve the objectives of the Code:

1. Collect and evaluate information of the threats to maritime security and exchange it with the governments that are interested.

2. Require that communication protocols be kept for ships and port facilities.

3. Avoid unauthorised access to ships and port facilities and to restricted areas.

4. Avoid the introduction of unauthorised weapons, incendiary devices or explosives onto ships or into port facilities.

5. Provide the means to raise the alarm when there is a threat to security.

6. Require protection plans for the ship and for the port facilities based on security evaluations.

7. Require training, drills and practices to guarantee that personnel are familiarised with the security procedures.

All of the above is transformed into security plans in which certain levels of security are established and activated successively according to the risks and threats.

2.7 The Spanish port organisation

In recent years an important phenomenon of business concentration has arisen making it possible for private industry to take on works and services that in past times could only be managed by the State. This goes hand in hand with a process of industrial transformation and the privatisation of whole sectors of activity which means that private initiative has taken on a role that was unthinkable just a few years ago. This phenomenon is not foreign to ports where private terminals have sprung up to manage their own traffic through concessions in an independent fashion and without public participation.

Today we can say that the ports are, in effect, managed by the State, the Regional Governments and private citizens. These three regimes are very different, and in the matter at hand., manage security in very different ways.

It is appropriate to know their organisation and their way of operating.

Given the configuration of the State implemented by the CE of 1978, relating to ports, it was mandatory to establish a framework of distribution of competences between the State and the Regional Governments. Let's take a look at it, albeit briefly.

In its article 149.1 the Constitution states that among other competences the State has *exclusive* competence in the following matters:

> 20th. Merchant navy and ship flag registry, illumination of coasts and maritime signals, *ports of general interest*.

On the other hand, our supreme standard states in article 148.1 that the Regional Governments *may take on competences* in the following matters:

> 6.th Refuge ports, sports harbours and airports and in general those that do not have commercial activities.

Therefore we have a dual organisation in questions relating to ports, defining some of them as ports of general interest which evidently makes them the most important.

Chapter II of Law 27/92 of 24th November, on state ports and the merchant navy (LPEMM) modified by Law 62/97 of 26th December and by Law 48/03 of 26th November, relating to the economic regime and rendering of services of the Ports of General Interest, defines the different *ports* and *the maritime facilities*.

Article 2 defines the maritime ports, considering that:

The following are considered as a maritime port whenever they are located on the shore of the sea or of rivers and have the necessary physical, natural or artificial and organisational conditions that allow port traffic operations to take place and are authorised for the development of these activities by the competent Administration:

- Land spaces,
- Sea waters,
- Facilities

In order to be considered ports they must have the following physical and organisational conditions:

- A surface of water, with an extension of no less than half a hectare, with adequate conditions of harbour and depth, either natural or artificially obtained for the type of ships that have to use the port and for the maritime traffic operations that are to take place there.

- Berth areas, docks or docking facilities that make it possible for ships to approach and dock in order to carry out their operations or remain anchored or docked in adequate security conditions.

- Spaces to deposit and store merchandise or goods.

- Land infrastructures and adequate accesses for traffic that guarantee its connection to the major transport networks.

- Means and organisation that make it possible to perform port operation in adequate conditions of efficiency, speed, economy and security.

Port operations are understood as:

- arrival,
- departure,
- docking,
- undocking,
- stay and
- repairing ships in port, and
- transfer from them to land or to other means of transport, of merchandise of any type, fishing, stocking and passengers or crews,
- and the temporary storage of the materials in the port space.

Maritime ports can be commercial or non-commercial and may be considered of general interest according to the relevance of their function in the overall Spanish port system.

Port facilities are civil infrastructures and buildings and superstructures as well as mechanical facilities and technical service networks built or located in the territorial area of a port and aimed at facilitating port traffic.

Commercial ports are those that according to the characteristics of their traffic have the necessary technical, security and administrative control conditions for the commercial port activities to be carried our, with such operations being understood as being stowage, unstowage, loading, unloading, transfer and storage of merchandise of any kind in the volume or form of presentation that justify the use of mechanical means or specialised facilities.

The transportation of passengers, provided it is not local or in the river, and stocking and repairing ships shall be considered as commercial port activities.

For the exclusive effects of the Law of the Ports of the State, the following are not considered commercial port activities:

- Operations involving unloading and handling fresh fish excluded from the area of the civil service of stowage and unstowage.

- The docking, anchoring, stay, stocking, repair and maintenance of fishing boats and sports and military boats.

- The operations of loading and unloading that are performed manually as the use of mechanical means are not justified.

- The use of facilities and the operations and services required for the development of the activities indicated in this section.

For the purpose of this law, the following are not commercial ports:

- Fishing ports which are aimed exclusively or basically at unloading fresh fish from ships used for capturing them or used as a base for said ships, providing them some or all of the services required for docking, anchoring, staying, stocking, repair and maintenance.

- Those aimed at providing sufficient harbour for ships in the case of a store, provided that commercial port operations are not carried out there or if they are used sporadically or are not very important.

- Those that are aimed at being exclusively or mainly for sport or leisure boats.

- Those in which a combination of the uses from the above mentioned paragraphs is established.

In ports with a regional competence commercial activities must receive a favourable report from the affected ministries with regard to maritime traffic and the security of the navigation and if applicable, the existence of adequate customs, health and external trade controls.

The commercial ports that depend on State Administration shall include fishing spaces and docks in their unit of management, as well as those spaces aimed at sporting activities located within the service area.

At the same time they may include those spaces aimed at other non-commercial activities when these are complementary to the essential activity or to cultural or leisure equipment, fairs and exhibitions, provided that they do not interfere overall in the development of port traffic operations.

Maritime facilities are maritime quays, sea launching and repair facilities and other similar works or facilities which while occupying public land-maritime domains not included in the areas of port service, are aimed at the transfer of merchandise, passengers or fish, provided that they comply with the requisites established in the above articles to be considered as maritime ports and which are not the competence of the regional governments on the date this Law comes into force.

Their construction, authorisation, management and policing are subject to the regime of the use of land-maritime domain established in the coastal regulations.

2.7.1 Ports of General Interest

Ports of general interest are those that appear in the annex of the Law classified as such because some of the following circumstances are applicable to them:

- International commercial maritime activities are carried out in them
- Their area of commercial influence has a relevant effect on more than one Autonomous Community.
- They serve industries or establishments that have a strategic importance for the national economy.
- That the annual volume and the characteristics of their maritime commercial activities reach sufficiently relevant levels or respond to the essential needs of the general economic activity of the State.
- That because of their special technical or geographical conditions they constitute essential elements for the security of maritime traffic, especially in insular territories.

The change of classification of a port due to the alteration of the characteristics referred to in the previous section will be made by the Government, through a Royal Decree, at the proposal of the Ministry of Development and following the processing of the corresponding hearing with an audience with the corresponding Regional Government and the other Regional Governments that are affected by the area of commercial influence of the port as well as the Town Halls in which the service area is located.

The loss of the condition of general interest will imply changing ownership in favour of the Regional Government in whose territory it is located, provided that it has assumed the competencies required for said ownership.

2.7.2 Port spaces with regional competences

Article 16 of the Law of Ports of the State and the different Statutes of Autonomy deal with the port spaces that have a regional competence.

The land-maritime public domain spaces that are necessary for the Regional Governments to exercise the competences that correspond to them by statute in matters relating to ports must be assigned by the State Administration. Assignment is one of the empowering titles that make possible the exploitation of several activities on the state maritime public domain. As the port public domain is state, the autonomic ports are established on this domain through this title.

The extension of the service area of the ports with regional competence or the construction of new ports within their competence must have a favourable report from the Ministry of Development.

The report shall include the limitations of the new state public domain susceptible to assignment, the possible effect of the intended uses in those spaces on the protection of the land-maritime public domain and the measures that are necessary to guarantee said protection. Non-compliance with this essential requisite implies the non-approval of the corresponding project.

The final approval of the projects implies the assignment of the public domain in which the work is located, and if applicable, the delimitation of a new area of port service, which will be formalised through a document subscribed by the representatives of both Administrations.

Legislation on the coasts will be applicable in the regulation of the assignments.

Security is very de-structured depending on the Regional Government. Some are barely quays with small ramps of little interest. Other ports are important and many have international traffic affected by the Code, which means that security measures must be implemented. This is normally done with automatic access controls and security personnel.

The state organisation will also have to develop its own policing regulations which shall necessarily have to be adapted to the Security Plan in the respective ports.

2.7.3 Service area in ports managed under concession

In order to facilitate the optimisation of the exploitation of the port, the Port Authority may grant a concession or contracts for the exploitation of certain specialised services for which they might not have the speed, specialisation and stimulus required.

Article 17 of the Law of Ports deals with them. The service area of a port with a concession shall comprise the public domain whose occupation has been authorised and the spaces with private ownership included in them in virtue of the stipulations of the concession.

The concession in this case is the facilitating title for this type of commercial activities.

Security depends on the type of facilities with the most complex ones being petrol, gas, chemical product terminals and containers. For these cases the corresponding Port Facility Security Plans have been elaborated and the Port Facility Security Officers named.

Here the PFSP themselves will provide adequate response to the demands of the Code and the port authorities on which they depend shall explain the specific security measures both in the general list of requirements and in the specific conditions.

Provided that it is at one with the port, the Policing Regulation, will be a good vehicle to make possible the different controls to verify that the conditions agreed upon and the demands of the activity are being met.

2.7.4 Other ports and port facilities depending on State Administration

According to article 12 of the Law of Ports there are other ports, bases, stations, arsenals and naval facilities of a military nature and military port areas that are outside the area of application of the Law.

The affected public domain spaces are reserved for State Administration and the competences are exercised by the Ministry of Defence.

The Ministry of Defence shall also exercise the competences that correspond to it in virtue of the stipulations of the legislation regarding areas and facilities of interest for National Defence.

Given the important functions of the Civil Guard in the ports, article 13 states that the State Administration may reserve areas of land-maritime public domain to be used as naval facilities and port zones that are required for attaining the objectives established by the current legislation for the Civil Guard. These areas will be excluded form the scope of application of this Law.

We shall not go on with more considerations because they are outside the demands of the ISPS Code and therefore outside the Regulation of Exploitation and Policing.

2.8 The Public Service in the ports of general interest

In economical terms, in general and in the question of ports, in recent times the public service has taken on a secondary role and has been put into the background by the strong presence of the liberalism that advocates the virtues of the competitiveness of the private sector, efficiency, effectiveness, productivity, dividends and the struggle for higher market shares. The events of 11th September 2001 must make us reflect on security as a public service.

On the other hand, through collective negotiation, labour law has been drawing more stable and solid civil servant relationships towards this field and has given way to collective negotiations. This direction towards private law includes harbour guards who from the legal point of view are on the borderline between private and public.

Reading the text of the LPEMM and without wishing to go into excess detail, the following, among others, would be public services:

- Implementing the different port Contingency and Security Plans and checking on their compliance, and especially the implementation of the ISPS Code. (Obviously this function does not appear in the Law).
- Approving the projects for exploitation and capital budgets of the Port Authority and its pluriannual action programme (37.a).
- Managing the general port services and those of maritime signalling, authorise and control the basic port services and the operations and activities that require an authorisation or concession. (37.b)
- Ordering the uses of the port service area and plan and programming its development with the approved organisational instruments of the territory and urban planning (37.d).
- Writing and formulating special organisation plans for the service area of the port in development of the general urban planning or for the direct execution of infrastructure works and protection measures that are required as established in urban legislation and in the territorial organisation (37.e).
- Reporting on the project of the Regulation of Exploitation and Policing of the ports and elaborating and approving the corresponding Port Ordinances with the proceedings and requisites established in article 106, as well as checking on their compliance (37.i).
- Controlling, within the area of the port, compliance with the legislation that affects the admission, handling and storage of dangerous goods, as well as compliance with the obligations of the coordination of activities established in article 24 of Law 31/1995 of 8th November, on the Prevention of Industrial Risks, and on security systems and fire fighting systems, notwithstanding the competences that correspond to other bodies of the public Administrations specifically to sanctions for breaching labour legislation (37.j).
- Freely approving the tariffs for the commercial services rendered and proceeding to apply their application and collection (37. k).
- Granting concessions and authorisations, keeping the census and registers on the use of the port maritime public domain updated (37.l).
- Collecting levies for the concessions and authorisations granted, monitoring compliance with the clauses and conditions imposed in the act of concession, applying the sanctioning regime and adopting as many measures as necessary for the protection and adequate management of the port public domain.
- Inspecting the operation of the maritime signals whose control is assigned to them, in the ports of the competence of the Regional Governments, and reporting to them on the deficiencies detected for their correction.

Article 58 of Law 48/2003 of 26th November, relating to the economic regime and rendering of services of the Ports of General Interest deals with the concept and types of general services that we can consider as public services, within the public service which to some extent is offered by the ports.

Thus, general services of the port are those common services that belong to the Port Authority and of which the users of the port can benefit without the need to request.

The Port Authorities shall offer the following general services in the service area of the port:

- The service of organisation, coordination and control of the port traffic, both land and maritime.
- The service of coordination and control of the operations associated with the basic commercial port services and other activities.
- The services of signalling, buoying and other aids to navigation that help in the approach and access to the port as well as its internal buoying.
- The installation and maintenance of the facility buoys granted in concession or authorisation, including those aimed at marine cultivation and submarine emissaries will be carried out by the license holder or person responsible for the activity at their cost in accordance with the execution project approved by the Port Authority.
- The monitoring, security and policing services in the common areas, notwithstanding the competences that correspond to other Administrations.
- The service for lighting the common areas.
- The service for cleaning the common areas on land and in the water. This cleaning service does not include the cleaning of docks and open areas as a consequence of the operations to deposit and handle merchandise, nor of spillages and contaminating marine waste which is competence of the maritime Administration.
- The prevention and emergency control services, in the terms established by the regulation on Civil Protection, dangerous goods and other applicable standards, in collaboration with the competent Administrations, on civil protection, prevention and fire extinguishing, lifesaving and the fight against contamination.

Article 59 deals with the rendering of general services that will be manager by the Port Authority.

These services will be rendered in accordance with the standards and technical criteria laid down in the Regulation of Exploitation and Policing and in the Port Ordinances, by personnel of the Port Authority, notwithstanding the fact that they can be delegated to third parties in certain cases when security is not at risk or an exercise of authority is not involved.

Both the Regulation and the ordinances have part of their legal grounding here, which is ampler than the contents of article 106 of Law 27/92, reformed by Law 62/92 where the legal grounds for the Port Police Services are found. In the future, in the elaboration of these basic legal instruments, it will be necessary to extend the range of possibilities of development.

The port police services shall have their field of activity in these actions. Legally, it will be necessary to integrate the fact that these missions are carried out, on occasions, from interim labour situations subject to private law and by personnel that, to that date, had not been trained for these circumstances: this situation is not well understood with the exercise of authority that requires the performance of public functions.

This has been used to reform the groups of harbour guards, boiler operators and crane drivers in the port. This involves a risk in performing their functions. Their lack of knowledge in security matters could have serious consequences.

Thus, training becomes a particularly delicate requisite that cannot be ignored any longer. The Code has put emphasis on this and the Regulation of Exploitation and Policing must include these demands.

If the Civil Guard is in charge of the security of the coasts, ports and airports by OL 2/86 on Security forces and they have to be deployed in port spaces in a similar way to how they have done it in airports, the Port Police are destined to play an important role, alongside this group, in the security of the ports at the beginning of the XXI Century and the Policing Regulation which is pending elaboration and publication, is a good vehicle to deliver these demands for coordination.

The Regulation of Exploitation and Policing and the Ordinances, also pending publication, shall be applied to giving coherent future responses to these approaches, without forgetting that many of the security functions in the ports must be taken on by private companies when these have the concession for exclusive spaces within them in perfectly defined spaces or on certain goods or private buildings.

This network of the public security relations, with the special security represented by the harbour guards and private security needs more attention in the Regulation and in the port Ordinances.

2.9 Competences and powers of the Port Authorities

The competences and the powers of the Port Authorities that are affected by the Code and of our interest are precisely those that are related with public security, which will make them a preferential object.

The competences are established by territory or by matter. It is obvious that the scope of competences by territory are related, in general terms, to the area of services in the port and, by material, to the activities relating to the use of the port and the activities carried out there and everything relating to occupations of public domain in the port through authorisations and concessions, as well as the rendering of the basic port services.

The sanctioning regime is included in the Law of Ports. The successive projects of the Regulation of Exploitation and Policing do not include a sanctioning regime nor do they typify sanctions. Breaches and sanctions should be covered by the law, which is exactly what the Law of Ports does. Law 30/92 of Legal Regime of the Public Administrations and of the common Administrative procedure (LRJAPAC) states that according to the principle of legality, article 129: only breaches of the legal system laid down in a Law shall be considered as administrative breaches. And the same for sanctions, article 129.2: sanctions may only be imposed for administrative breaches, which in any case, shall be defined by a law.
But, at the same time, complementary regulation by regulations is allowed, article 129.3: the statutory provisions for development may introduce specifications or grading of the legally established table of breaches or sanctions, without creating new breaches or sanctions or altering the nature or limits of those contemplated by the law, to contribute towards the most correct identification of conducts or to the most precise determination of the corresponding sanctions.

It would be a serious mistake not to take advantage of the Regulation of Exploitation and Policing to give detailed answers to the application of the Law of Ports.

When dealing with access to the ship, section 9.11 of Part B of the ISPS Code recommends that the SSP shall include provisions for the systems of identification to be regularly updated and so that any abuse of them receives a disciplinary sanction.

On the other hand, when it addresses access to the port facility, in paragraph 16.12 of part B, it contemplates that for each level of protection the PFSP must indicate the means of identification required to gain access to the port facility and for people to remain there without being questioned. This could require the establishment of an adequate system of permanent or temporary identification for port facility personnel and visitors, respectively.

Any system of identification that is implemented in the facility must be coordinated, in so far as possible, with that applied on the ships that generally use the port facility. Passengers should be able to prove their identity with their boarding card, ticket, etc., but this will not give them access to restricted areas unless they are supervised.

The Regulation will be the vehicle that makes it possible to sanction these non-compliances adequately and proportionately.

The Regulation of Exploitation and Policing must include a detailed sanctioning policy, with the required adaptation and cover provided by the Law of Ports, in accordance with the principle of legality.

And there is no excuse for it to be otherwise. The experience of the old regulations of 1976, with a doubtful force regarding sanctions has enabled the Port Authorities to adequate the sanctions to the lesser non-compliances with less violence. The insignificant amount laid down in the sanctions also had its influence.

It is worth mentioning that the sanctioning competence and power laid down in the Law of Ports will correspond to:

- The Board of Administrators of the Port Authority for those cases of minor breaches relating to the use of the port and the exercise of activities offered in it.
- The Board of Administrators of the Port Authority, in the scope of its competences, for those cases of serious breaches typified in this Law.
- The Ministry of Development, at the proposal of Ports of the State, in the scope of its competences, for cases of serious breaches below two hundred million.
- The Council of Ministers, at the proposal of the Ministry of Development, in cases of very serious breaches with a quantity above that indicated in the previous section of this article.

Although this material will be studied in detail in preparation for the scope of application of the Regulation of Police and Port Ordinances, the key to the question being addressed in this study, it must be said that in the practical terrain the port authorities are not in favour of exercising the power of sanction nor do the circumstances in which they carry out their assignments favour the exercise of the sanctioning aspect such as authorities invested with public functions.

This is so because, as we see, this competence resides first and foremost with the Board of Administration where all the relevant port-maritime sectors that have interests in the port in question are represented.

In some way the alleged breaches are committed, to a large extent, directly or indirectly by personnel depending on themselves, which often conditions the application of the rule with the necessary rigour. Sometimes it is a dilemma and can be paradoxical to initiate a sanctioning process, for example, against a consignee who is on the Board of Administration, which is the body who has the power to sanction.

In short, it can be said that the sanctioning administrative action of the Boards of Administration of the Port Authorities is not excessively relevant for the reasons mentioned and. also because the old Police regulations from 1976 include minimum sanctions which were outdated with respect to the standard that covered it, namely the Law of Ports to which they are in no way adapted, regardless of the fact that their legal ground is to be found in the Law of Ports of 1928, replaced by Law 27/92.

The matter ought to be subjected to more specification in order to implement a sanctioning regime in accordance with the needs of the ports, especially in the field of public security. The vehicle is without doubt the Regulation of Exploitation and Policing which ought to be granted the rank of Royal Decree at least. Not that of an organisational Royal Decree, but rather an executive one, to submit it to the judgment of the State Council regarding its conformity with the Law of Ports and the ISPS Code, as well as other provisions affected.

2.10 The relationships between the National Directorate of the Merchant Navy and the public Entity Ports of the State

The previous legislation, prior to 1992, was very disperse, both in the area of port management and in that of maritime traffic. Some of these regulations date back to the XIX century.

The Laws of Port of 1880 and 1928 were written on a differentiation between the works and the activities of the ports themselves or "port services", as they were called in article 20 of the Law of 1928 and the private activities in the ports which were known as *work carried out by private companies.*

There were two types of port service:

- general movement of ships which was entrusted to the Marine Authorities,
- the service relating to the execution, conservation and use of works and buildings that included loading and unloading operations on the docks and the circulation on them which was the competence of the Ministry of Development (art. 20 Law of 1928).

Following Menendez Rexach, annexes were added to these services and to the ports, such as piloting, carried out by the Ministry of the Marine and maritime lighting and buoying carried out by the Ministry of Development (articles 32 and 33 of the Law of 1928).

We refer to the above because this dualism has been a constant that continues in the current law and differentiates between the Port Administration and the Maritime Administration. This is materialised in the existence of the General Directorate of the Merchant Navy and Maritime Captains in certain ports[5] which have boundaries within which a certain level of activity is developed or where, certain traffic or maritime security so require (article 88 LPEMM).

---

[5] RD 1246/95 regulates the constitution and creation of the Harbour Masters' Offices (BOE 01-08-95).

Current legislation in the matter of ports and merchant navy is kept unified in the same legislative block. Within the Ministry of Development, the General Directorate of the Merchant Navy, on one hand and the Public Entity Ports of the State on the other, share the competences. As for the management of these materials, this is translated into the existence of the Harbour Masters' Offices which manage the general movements of boats and of the Port Authorities which, depending on the general movement of the boats, organises the port spaces.

Merchant navy is understood as (Article 7 LPMM):

- The activity of maritime transport, excepting that carried out exclusively between ports or points of the same Autonomous Community which has competences in the matter, without a connection with ports or points in other territorial areas.
- The organisation and control of the Spanish civil fleet.
- Security in navigation and for human life at sea.
- Maritime security, including the empowerment to exercise the service of piloting and the determination of the services required for towing in the port as well as the availability of both in the case of an emergency.
- Maritime rescue in the terms established in article 87.
- Prevention of the contamination produced in boats, fixed platforms and other facilities that are to be found in the waters located in areas in which Spain has sovereignty, sovereign rights or jurisdiction and the protection of the marine environment.
- The technical and operative inspection of ships, crews and goods.
- The organisation of traffic and maritime communications.
- The control of the situation, flagging and registry of civil ships as well as their dispatching, notwithstanding the prior obligatory authorisations that correspond to other Authorities.
- The guarantee of complying with obligations in matters relating to national defence and civil protection at sea.
- Any other maritime service attributed by Law to the regulated Administration in Chapter III of Title III of this Law.

Merchant navy is not considered as the fishing fleet, in the areas of fishing and the organisation of the fishing sector or the inspection activity in these areas.

According to articles 92 and 93 of Law 48/2003, the management of the state port public domain will, while guaranteeing general interest, be aimed at promoting and increasing the participation of private initiative in the financing, construction and exploitation of the port facilities and in the rendering of services, by granting the corresponding authorisations and concessions, both in public concession and in public work, in accordance with the stipulations of the Law.

Providing and managing spaces and basic port infrastructures corresponds to the Port Authorities by promoting both the economic activity in the ports and the rendering of services from private initiative.

The management of the infrastructures and of the port public domain will be carried out with criteria of profitability and efficiency.

The ports of general interest are part of the land-maritime public domain and integrate the state port public domain which is regulated by the provisions of this Law and also by the coastal legislation.

The following belong to the state port public domain:

- Lands, works and fixed port facilities belonging to the state for the service of the ports.
- The lands and fixed port facilities that the Port Authorities acquire through expropriation as well as those acquired though a sale or through any other title when they are duly accepted by the Ministry of Development.
- The works that the State or Port Authorities carry out on said domain.
- Buildings erected by the concession holders of the port public domain, when they revert on the Port Authority.
- The lands, works and fixed facilities to aid maritime navigation, related to Ports of the State and to the Port Authorities for this purpose.
- The water spaces included in the service area of the ports.

3. The International Ship and Port Facility Security Code and port ordinances

3.1 Introduction: the context in Europe

This study is going to deal with the repercussions of the most recent maritime legislation in internal Spanish regulations relating to ports. The studies carried out in the heart of the IMO have led to the introduction of a series of amendments to the SOLAS Agreement and to the drafting of the new International Ship and Port Facility Security Code (ISPS Code).

The particular question now is what repercussion will arise from these demands, which are derived from Spain being a Contracting State, within the SOLAS Agreement and the ISPS Code, and how they will gradually be included in internal regulation. The ISPS Code comprises part A, whose stipulations are mandatory and part B in which the stipulations are recommendations. After a run through the maritime and port regulations we shall see how the publication of the future Regulation of Exploitation and Policing will be affected in its content.

Therefore, the first step is to situate Spain, its maritime traffic and its ports in the most immediate context: political, strategic and commercial and from there observe how the threats of terrorism might affect not only international legislation bur also our internal regulation.

The EU has adopted the Code but is also going to extend it to other areas through a Regulation that has already been published and a Directive.

In the proposal for communication from the Commission to the Council, the European Parliament, the European Economic and Social Committee and the Committee of the Regions on the improvement in the protection of maritime transport in order to elaborate a Regulation, which has now been published, on maritime security, certain data cane to light that give an idea of the extraordinary importance of port and maritime traffic for the EU.

Any ship can become a weapon if that is the objective, or in a weapon of mass destruction, or in an unconscious means of transport for harmful goods, unless adequate measures are taken in maritime protection and control. At the same time, it is possible to perpetrate a terrorist attack against a ship, for example, using another ship, or from inside by terrorists who take it by force or who were already infiltrated on it.

Passenger ships are especially relevant possible targets, due to the number of lives under immediate threat. Cargo ships are also vulnerable and can become dangerous vectors. For example, the nature of certain dangerous loads could induce terrorist groups to trying to make these ships explode in port areas, with easily imaginable human and environmental consequences. Finally, there is the illicit maritime transport of nuclear, bacteriological or chemical products to be used against the country of destination of the cargo.

3.2 The role of maritime transport in EU trade

Maritime transport is vital for the economic and commercial strength of the EU, as can be seen in the data below. Therefore, it is a top priority to improve its protection to conserve, and even increase, this role, as well as the confidence of its operators. The efforts required to enhance the level of protection of the ships and community ports must be considered in the light of the importance that the fleet and commercial trade have for the economy of the EU.

EU imports from other countries represent 17% of the world total. As an overall value, in 2001 EU exports amounted to approximately 981 billion euro and imports to 1027 billion[1]. Indeed, the EU is the leading commercial partner of two thirds of the planet. Evidently, keeping these markets and frontiers open is one of the main objectives of the EU's trade policy.

The EU's maritime logistic system, including the maritime transport of goods, ports and port facilities, intervenes in more than two thirds of all the trade between the Community and the rest of the world. Thus, it is important to improve the protection of maritime transport, by maintaining its competitiveness and facilitating trade.

3.3 Flag bearing fleets and fleets controlled by the EU

The proportion of the world fleet controlled by European shipowners has remained at around 34% of world tonnage in the last ten years.

The community fleet is comprised [2] of approximately 8,800 ships, among which there are 1,966 oil tankers, 1,104 container ships, 3,428 cargo ships of different types (classic cargo and Ro-Ro containers ships) and 685 passenger ships. In volume, it possesses a transport capacity of 257 million tons, including more than 3.15 million TEU (containers).

In tonnage, 67% of the fleet is registered outside the EU. An important proportion of the ships registered in Panama, Liberia, Bahamas, Cyprus and Malta is controlled by shipowners and operators from the European Union, which is hardly a surprise.

The flag bearing fleet in member States of the EU accounts for 13% of the total world tonnage, which is approximately 102 million tonnes and is composed of more than 4200 ships. This fleet employs 180,000 marines, 40% of which are citizens of other countries.

---

[1] Source: European Commission, DG TRADE.

[2] Data on 1st January 2001 on ships with a gross tonnage equal to or above 1000. Source: Institute of Shipping Economics and Logistics, Shipping Statistics, 2001.

3.4 The ports of the Community

The EU has 35,000 kilometres of coastline and hundreds of maritime ports. 2 billion tonnes of different merchandise go through the European ports every year. They are necessary for the European economy and trade with the rest of the world (hydrocarbons, solid fuels and minerals, manufactured products): We must remember that 90% of the oil trade with the EU is done by sea and almost 70% of imports pass along the coasts of Brittany and the English Channel. The volume of operations (in millions of tonnes/km) of the European Union ports registered the following figures in 1999.

Area	Trans-Ocean traffic	International traffic	Regional traffic	Total
Baltic Sea	53	101	50	204
North Sea	404	414	183	1001
Atlantic	153	219	10	382
Mediterranean	304	87	126	517
Total	914	821	369	2104

Table 1. Estimation of the volume of operations carried out in the ports of the European Union in 1999, broken down into areas, in millions of tonnes/km – DG TREN

The list of the 25 most important European ports in volume of traffic and evolution in tonnage during the period 1996-2000 can be seen in Annex I. It is worth pointing out the homogenous nature of the port services and the diversity of the ports included in the list (in category, ownership, size, function and geographical features).

It is hardly possible to establish a strict typology of the ports. Although there is a certain number of specialised ports in certain sectors, for example, the oil and chemical sector, the automobile sector or ferry services, the majority are open to all kinds of activities, even inside the port itself.

The growth of maritime transport is concentrated on containers, on ships that are getting bigger and bigger, in specialised port terminals and in regular ferry services. Since the beginning of the nineties there has been a growth in the number of transhipment hubs, a new type of port and system of warehouses.

The maritime vocation of the Community and the importance of sea trade for the strength of our economy make it recommendable to improve maritime security at a world level and especially in the EU in light of the current situation relating to terrorism.

On the other hand, the Directive that is being elaborated aims to go beyond the port security of the ship port interface to cover all the hinterland. Thus it considers that "the ports are delivery centres for dangerous loads and important poles of chemical and petrochemical production. Or they are in the proximities of town centres. It is obvious that a terrorist attack in a port could seriously disturb the transport systems and generate a chain of effects on the surrounding industry, as well as causing human victims in the port and among the neighbouring population."

The Directive has two clear objectives:

- To enhance the security of the areas of the ports in which the Regulation does not apply.
- To guarantee that the measures adopted in the Regulation benefit form the growth in the security of the adjacent port areas.

The Directive, which will need some type of transposition into Spanish legislation, must guarantee and monitor the success, at a community level, of a high enough level of port security, by completing and sustaining the security measures that are applicable to the ship-port interface. It shall guarantee a harmonised application and equality of conditions all over the EU, avoiding the appearance of differences among the commercial users of the ports and guarantee that the security measures required for the whole port (area of application of the ordinances beyond the port facilities) can be applied on the basis of the demands of the Regulation.

Given the diversity of the community ports and their different ways of organisation (public, private, concession), the Directive aims at introducing the flexibility required to attain the objectives established.

This will include defining the limits of the port with precision. The internal regulation will include the service area of each Port of General Interest, without forgetting that the Regulation and the Directive will also affect many other ports in the Autonomous Communities and of concessionaries of spaces of the port maritime public domain.

And from the moment of their publication there will be a period of one year to "put the legal, regulatory and administrative stipulations into force so as to comply with the Directive."

Based on this, the future Regulation and the Port Ordinances must, in their content and demands, go beyond the ISPS Code and go deeper into the most ample and important demands that the European legislation will apply in the immediate future. If the reforms are not made with an eye on the whole legislative block, we will be back into a series of partial reforms and submerged in a network of successive provisions that will create great confusion. The maritime and port administration must be applied in the coming months to finding adequate answers to the demands that are approaching.

3.5 Spain

For Spain the sea has been and is an enormous platform for the coming and going of most of the licit goods that are imported. Along almost 8,800 kilometres of coastline natural harbours have been transformed into ports which, because of their economic and commercial dynamism have built up cities around them over time, cities which are now strangling them.

Some illicit activities see the huge door that our coastline represents the chance to sneak past border controls.

These illicit activities, controlled by mafias and international drug dealers, smugglers and illegal immigration basically represent to date the huge threat and therefore the challenges to be met in the immediate future, not only for Spain, but for the Europe of which we are part and of the world in general.

In the dawn of this century, both national and international terrorism have been hitting the maritime sector, although with a relatively low intensity, except for some historical events to which we shall refer. Ports are an important part of this coastline.

Our geopolitical and strategic situation makes us the way to enter Europe for routes coming both from the African continent and South America with which we also share culture and language. In the south east, through the Mediterranean, we are Europe's geographical frontier with Africa and a cultural boundary with different civilisations in which, in certain sectors, the radical branch of Islamist terrorism has taken hold and which, like an enormous hydra, is reborn each time it attacks and threatens world stability. This globalised terrorism represents one of the big threats to the modern world.

Some of the most important maritime routes in the world touch our coasts, mainly those coming from the Mediterranean through the Strait such as those coming from America and Africa.

The transportation of goods by sea or river is used in more than three quarters of world trade. The world's merchant navy is made up of 86,000 ships with 100 or more gross tonnes.

The most important fleets by tonnage are those registered in the Bahamas, China, Cyprus, United States, Russian Federation, Greece, Japan, Liberia, Norway, Panama and Singapore which does not mean that behind them there are not others involved under different flags. Ships with these flags normally dock in our ports every day.

The phenomena of mass tourism and the "exodus to the coast" of the Spanish population means that our coasts are more and more built up which makes it easier for the organised mafias to find the ideal cover and easy accommodation for their perverse activities. Terrorism also finds the ideal hiding place while it awaits the opportunity or the order to perpetrate their criminal attacks.

The flow of immigration which increases in geometrical proportions, bring the bitter side of hunger and marginality to the Strait. It is here that the most radical fanaticisms are nurtured without too much difficulty.

Because of its design and destination the ship is very often an element of internationality. Its voyages frequently cross high seas or seas subject to the sovereignty of other states, which means that it is affected by circumstances and international legislation which are very profuse, changing and complex. In such a situation navigation involves legal uncertainties.

These circumstances make it easy for the radical wing of Islamic terrorism to hit the first world with attacks that go beyond all expectations.

As they congregate large numbers of people, the means of transport are themselves a preferential objective and may also become an ideal target to be used, once control has been achieved, as an instrument to attack sensitive and strategic targets. The most recent examples are, unfortunately, in the memory of everyone. Due to their nature, ports are not foreign to these threats as they are part of the system of maritime transport.

The above made all the alarm bells ring and has awoken sufficient awareness to put into place the defence mechanisms that are required to counter these hypothetical aggressions. The IMO has been the forum in which the measures to try to counter the possibility of these actions occurring, or at least their effects being diminished, have been debated and put into practice. Thus on 1st July 2004 the ISPS Code, which is part of the SOLAS, came into force.

The ISPS Code is a clear example of what has come to be known as *response legislation*. The free and democratic world has reached ample international consensus for its implementation. It is not an isolated measure. In other transport sectors, especially in the field of civil aviation, strict preventive measures have been imposed together with passenger, equipment and cargo control. In the light of the numerous attacks received, civil aviation as a means of transport, mainly of people, has been adopting measures for years, which means that its experience has undoubtedly influenced on the Code and will be of great help in this Project.

The speed of the implementation of the ISPS Code should not prevent us from reflecting on the threats. Thus, internal legislation related with the maritime transport sector must be revised to include the new demands of the Code.

As a consequence of its entry into the EU which was overlapped with the process of globalisation of the economy, the liberalisation of frontiers and a strong industrial growth, port security in Spain has probably been a secondary item in recent years. Ports have gone from a strong state intervention to a great liberalism turning them into competitive companies.

At the same time the Autonomous Communities have become increasingly important in the Ports of General Interest to the point where they designate the President of the Port Authority and determine the final composition of the Boards of Administration on which, with other representative sectors, the City Halls also sit. The LPMM and the reforms of 1997 and 2003 have tried to give answers to all of this. The process is not over. Some Autonomous Communities ask the State to transfer total control of the Ports of General Interest. Thus the ports have entered the field of political services.

The "*exodus to the coast*" that we referred to earlier on has had a unique incidence on the coastal cities which have grown at a very high rate in the vicinity of the ports. The ports have been strangled by the cities but at the same time the cities see the ports as a barrier to enjoy the sea and a focus of acoustic and industrial contamination. Public opinion has pressed for the ports to open to the cities in order to divert dirty and contaminating traffic and to break the barrier that the port has become for leisure and recreation.

All of this has influenced on the fact that port security had become weak. Accesses are no longer strictly controlled, at least in reference to pedestrians. Public establishments have been opened inside. If you pardon the expression, ports have been cornered in their activities right to the edge.

Globalisation and privatisation have been cutting down the sphere of activity of the Port Authorities. They have gradually stopped rendering port services (crane drivers, boiler operators, stowage companies) which have been taken over by private initiative. In short, it can be said that public service in the ports has been overshadowed and has been relegated to second place. The ports, in so far as they are perfectly limited spaces in the service area, seem to have disappeared.

As opposed to what happens in airports in which the traffic of people is the main traffic, in ports, for obvious reasons, it is the traffic of goods. This so obvious fact which needs no explanation is a recent phenomenon.

Before the generalisation of air transport in recent times, the history of navigation was the history of the transport of people and goods. Aviation, in a historical context, started yesterday. This is not a trivial matter because it has contributed, in terms of security, to a greater attention to airport traffic than to port traffic.

The port as a frontier and customs has also disappeared for several reasons. Thus, the Security Forces, which have the same competences in ports as in airports, have given more attention to the latter, in a Spain in which air traffic, which is the engine of the sun and beach tourist industry, and the huge industrial development in recent years, require an enormous police effort. The Civil Guard, as we will see in greater detail, is commissioned by law to custody ports and airports, but when it comes to facts their deployment and functions have been focused mainly on the airports.

Within the service areas, the ports had been carrying out public and other security activities, with the harbour guards acting as special police. Their functions have gradually lost entity as the functions and port spaces were liberalised. From being security guards with weapons they now offer their services unarmed and almost unnoticed. Although it may seem surprising, they have stopped carrying weapons because they agreed to do so in a collective agreement: they subjected the decision to whatever the governing authority would decide on the matter. As no decision has been made, it remains an undefined element which reflects the moments of change that the port model is going through.

The ISPS Code is not especially worried about port security. The concept of port as we understand it in Spain, given our organisational model is foreign to it. As we shall see, what it is concerned about are port facilities, much more reduced spaces, as it circumscribes the specific security measures that it implements to the ship-port interface.

Therefore, in what is known as the service area of a Port of General Interest, with security we will have several port facilities inside, perfectly defined by physical barriers, with their corresponding security plans and their Security Officers identified and responsible for their control and for their coordination with the Ship Security Officer when the ship is in the terminal.

Ship-port interface is understood as being the interaction that takes place when a ship is affected directly and immediately by activities that involve the movement of people or good or the rendering of port services to the ship or from it.

The port facility is the place determined by the contracting Government or by the designated authority where the ship-port interface takes place. This shall include, as required, areas for anchoring, standby docking and accesses from the sea.

The SSO and the PFSO take on similar responsibilities though they keep their distance. One in that which affects the ship and the other the port facility. An SSO with security will, on most occasions be a citizen who responds to the interests of private initiative and to the security of a commercial ship. It is not the same case with our Port Facility Security Officers who can respond to public or private interests, according to whether the port terminal to which we are referring is located inside the service area of a Port of General Interest, a port assigned to the Autonomous Community or on the other hand, a private terminal such as container terminals, oil terminals, cola terminals or gas terminals, to give a few examples.

Traffic that is generally reserved for the management of the port authorities are those which in essence are not susceptible to being privatised through an administrative concession, because they do not come on a regular basis or because the seasonal activity of the sector in which they are, such as the traffic of cruise ships or certain bulks.

At first glance, the most sensitive traffic from the point of view that we are analysing are cruises and the oil product traffic heading for oil terminals which in Spain are normally private.

Others of interest are the traffic of chemical and gas products. Cruise traffic is the objective of terrorists because cruises are vulnerable, due to circumstances such as the origin of the capital of the shipping company and of the nationality of the citizens being transported, due to the large number of passengers and crew on board. Oil, gas and chemical product traffic is vulnerable because they are strategic targets and because of the repercussion in public opinion of any incident with one of these ships and their repercussion on the environment. In any case, all of these ships can also be used as an instrument for a criminal action.

Oil is the most transported base product in the world. The EU occupies first place in the world in the trade of oil products. The imports of crude make up approximately 27% of total world trade, while the imports of the United States are about 25%. Around 90% of the oil trade with the EU is done by sea while the rest is transported in pipelines, by road or by navigable ways.

In traffic that has access to public facilities, as well as cooperating with in the security of the terminal just as in any private one, the PFSO also represent the public preventive security as they are personnel on the Port Authority payroll, which means that they must not forget where they are and their function of collaboration with the Security Forces and Corps in the face of any important safety related news. Thus, they have a double obligation to be diligent in security matters: to comply with the provisions of the Code that affect them and combine them with the duties of collaboration imposed by national legislation.

The fact that the ISPS Code focuses on port facilities located inside the Port of General Interest must not lead us to making the mistake of focusing on the obligations of the Code and forget the rest of the port spaces which normally surround them. In those spaces which are normally peripheral to the port facilities, there are other security obligations derived form many other international and national regulations. This area is still a customs office and other docks and terminals are dedicated to traffic not obliged by the Code, although many of them will be obliged in the future by Community legislation.

3.6 European Regulation

The Official Journal of the European Union dated 29th April 2004 published Regulation (EC) number 725/2004 of the European Parliament and of the Council on 31st March 2004, relating to enhancing the security of ships and port facilities that will gradually require security measures in this field which go beyond and have more rigour than those established in the ISPS Code. Therefore the scope of application will be extended to the ships that perform community piloting and to their port facilities, especially in the case of passenger ships due to the high number of human lives that this traffic puts at risk.

The Regulation, in its article number 2, requires the guarantee of maritime transport security at all times in the EU, as well as that of the citizens that use it and of the environment, against the threat of deliberate illicit acts such as terrorism, pirating and others. Therefore in its article 14 it requires the availability of means and the elaboration of a *national plan for applying the Regulation in order to achieve these objectives*. For this reason, new measures will be applied until 2007. These must not be overlooked when it comes to elaborating the national instruments. On 1st July 2005 measures were introduced for national passenger traffic.

The Regulation openly declares that deliberate illicit acts, and especially terrorism, are among the most serious threats to the ideals of democracy and freedom and the values of peace which constitute the very essence of the EU. Moreover, in accordance with article 9.3 each Member State shall adopt a national programme to apply the Regulation.

A Directive is also expected on the matter. It is currently circulating as a Proposal for a Directive. If the measures of the Code, in the port, are mainly aimed at protecting the ship-port interface, as a capsule of nearby security, the Directive and the transposition to the national regulation will be extended to the whole port which will mean that the port areas will be protected and what is understood as port will be defined, differentiating this concept from that of port facility. It shall also require that port security plans are elaborated, Let us say that the community regulation that has been published and the one that is forthcoming, extend the area of protection, beyond the ship-port interface and the port facility to all the defined port area. It extends the list of ships subjected to security plans and measures by the Code and in short aims at higher levels of security than those implemented by the IMO.

With all of this, and on a more immediate horizon, the development of article 106 of the Law of Ports, now known as the Regulation of Exploitation and Policing and their annexes with the corresponding ordinances, require a little fine tuning.

Thus the successive drafts of the Regulation of Policing, so often so close to being published, must be re-elaborated to contemplate and facilitate all of the above regulations and something which has not been done to date, to coordinate the harbour guards, as Security Agents, with those responsible for public security in the framework of Organic Law 2/865 of 13th March on Security Forces and Corps as the special police of the public domain that they are.

4. Policing regime in ports of general interest. Regulation of Exploitation and Policing

This chapter analyses the situation of maritime security at a world level and how the emerging forms of international terrorism can influence on the means of transport, especially maritime transport, to counter the threats that they pose to the extent possible.

First of all, faced with these threats, the answers at a national level are worth nothing, given the international nature of maritime navigation in its two basic elements, ships and cargos. Therefore, in the Concert of Nations reached an agreement of principle that was transformed into the ISPS Code within the SOLAS Agreement.

The Code imposes a series of demands, many of them mandatory, that are reflected in part A. As the obligations, without sanction for non-compliance, are of no value, once the security measures imposed by the Code have been implemented, it will be necessary to arbitrate legislative procedures to see how these demands are integrated into the Spanish legal regulations.

At the same time, and in a tangential manner, the EU, together with the US, feels especially threatened as it is one of the preferred targets of international terrorism; therefore, and with the intention of strengthening the measures of the Code, it has elaborated a Regulation and a Directive which will also have to be integrated into national regulation.

Both the Code and the Regulation are already in force although the latter will be brought into force step by step. The Directive will need development regulation in the bylaws clause.

These two instruments and the Directive, when it is developed, shall necessarily have repercussions on the national regulation because we know that, in accordance with article 96.1 of the Spanish Constitution "The validly formed international treaties once officially published in Spain, shall be part of the national regulation. Their provisions may only be cancelled, modified or suspended in the manner laid down in the treaties themselves or in accordance with the general rules of international Law."

Once it is in force the national legislation will have to be adapted to these demands in the interests of legal security and the better application of the regulations.

Law 48/2003 of 26th November, of the Economic Regime and Rendering of Services of the Ports of General Interest, which was elaborated after 11th September, taking into consideration the regulation of the Code that was being prepared, makes a reference to this new regulation in article 132, paragraphs 2 and 3, and especially the latter:

"2. Pursuant to the provisions of the current legislation on the prevention and control of emergencies, each Port Authority shall elaborate an internal emergency plan for each port that it manages, which, once approved in accordance with the provisions of the applicable legislation, shall be a part of the port ordinances.

3. Following a favourable report from the Ministry of the Interior and from the regional entity with competences in matters of public security on those aspects of their competence, each Port Authority shall elaborate a plan for the protection of ships, passengers and goods in the port areas against anti-social and terrorist acts which, once approved in accordance with the provisions of the applicable regulation, shall become a part of the port ordinances."

Continuing with this matter, the elaboration of the Port Facilities Security Plan (PFSP) which in some way respond to the provisions of paragraph 3 above is now complete, and will be even more specific if the legal term of the so often cited Sixth Final Provision of Law 48/2003 is completed as it will authorise the government to present a revised text of Law 27/1992, of 24th November, on Ports of the State and the Merchant Navy, within a year of the publication of this Law in the Official State Journal.

Given the serious changes that the international arena has undergone, this revised text and the numerous and successive reforms that have affected national legislation which is now being reformed, should not be long in coming. Indirectly its delay will have a repercussion on the publication of the Regulation of Exploitation and Policing.

This Regulation of Exploitation and Policing must be the immediate and logical consequence of the publication of the revised text, so that the publication of the law when it comes does not bring any constraints to it. Once the Regulation of the Port Ordinances has been published, it will be the appropriate vehicle for including the obligations of the ISPS Code and of the ongoing community legislation.

Maritime Administration must be diligent in responding to these demands and cannot be delayed in time, because the obsolete Regulation of 1976, apart from its arguable effect, is completely overburdened by the new security demands.

And it is no good doing what has been done until now in the various drafts and Projects of the Regulation, which is to say developing an articulated text which barely addresses the organisation of the police service and the regime to exploit the port, although they are essential. The Regulation must have a sanctioning regime. It is essential if it wishes to be consequential.

Moreover, this was the objective of Law 27/92 in its day and what has been maintained in successive reforms of the Law in article 114 which, when referring to minor breaches which they define as "the actions or omissions, which do not receive the consideration of serious or very serious breaches, due to their transcendence or to the importance of the damage caused, are typified in one of the following assumptions", is considering the breaches that refer to the use of the port and its facilities.

First of all, it states what will be a minor breach: "Non-compliance with the provisions established in the regulation of port exploitation and policing." In the following paragraph it states: "Non-compliance with the ordinances established or instructions given by the Port Authority regarding maritime operations in the area of the port."

So now we have the key to all the arguments and it is none other than seeing to what extent the Code and the EU regulations must be included in the Port Regulations and Ordinances.

If these instruments are not given a sanctioning regime, their application will require real experts in law to carry out a rational application when it comes to investigating non-compliances by delving through a complex network of exploitation and policing rules, of which there will be many. This is because, in accordance with this remission it will be necessary to look first in the Regulation and then in the Ordinances to find where certain conducts are forbidden or not. Then it will be necessary to argue the whole process of adapting the sanctions of the Law to specific conducts which is what the Regulation will have to do by particularising the application of the Law.

We shall now address the current state of affairs from the analysis of the current legislation, the functions of special police performed by the harbour guards, the current Regulation of Policing and its deficiencies, the different drafts and Regulation Projects, etc.

The Regime of Policing in the Ports of General Interest is included in Title IV, Policing Regime, chapter I, of Law 27/92 of Ports of the State and the Merchant Navy, under the epigraph of "Regulation of policing in the ports of the State".

Its legal grounding in article 106 of the Law of Ports, which it calls "Regulation of Exploitation and Policing" which literally says:

"1. Following the audience of the Port Authorities and a report from the General Directorate of the Merchant Navy, the public entity Ports of the State shall elaborate the General Regulation of Exploitation and Policing of the ports that will regulate the performance of the different services and operations. The Regulation shall include a model of port ordinances as an annex. The approval of the General Regulation and of the model of port Ordinances will correspond to the Ministry of Development.

The report from the General Directorate of the Merchant Navy will be binding with regard to the security of ships and of navigation, maritime rescue and the contamination produced from ships, fixed platforms or other facilities located in waters in the areas in which Spain exercises sovereignty, sovereign rights or jurisdiction.

2. The model of ordinances shall include the rules of the Regulation that are of general application to all ports and the points or matters that may be regulated by the corresponding Port Authority, in accordance with the criteria or principles established therein and those others of free regulation for which, failing them, there is the supplementary application of the Regulation.

3. With the binding report of the Harbour Master in the aspects of the competence of the General Directorate of the Merchant Navy, the Port Authorities shall elaborate and approve the port Ordinances following approval of conformity with the General Regulation of the public entity Ports of the State.

4. Both the General Regulation of the Exploitation and Policing and the Ordinances of each port shall be published, once approved, in the *Official State Journal*."

This legal matter, contained in article 106, has been restructured and improved, since 1992, the year in which the current Law of Ports was approved, in the legal reforms of 1997 and 2003. Notwithstanding this, neither the Regulation nor the Ordinances have seen the light of day, although there have been several attempts and the odd project that has been close to being published. The legal reforms are so close and successive in time that they have materially prevented the publication of the Regulation of Exploitation and Policing.

Moreover, it is now necessary to merge all the different legal texts relating to Ports to make their legal situation more complete. Thus, Law 48/2003, of 26th November, of Economic regime and rendering of services of the Ports of General Interest, which has partly reformed the Law of Ports, in its Sixth Final Provision, authorises the Government to dictate a revised text in the following terms: "The Government is authorised within one year of the publication of this Law in the Official State Journal to elaborate a revised text of Law 27/1992, of 24th November, on Ports of the State and the Merchant Navy and of this Law, into which the modifications produced by the following provisions are introduced:

- Law 62/1997, of 26th December, modifying Law 27/1992, of 24th November, on Ports of the State and the Merchant Navy.
- Article 47 of Law 50/1998, of 30th December, on tax, administrative and social order measures.
- Article 75 of Law 14/2000, of 29th December, on tax, administrative and social order measures.
- Article 4 of Royal Decree-law 4/2000, of 23rd June, on Urgent Liberalisation Measures in the Real Estate and Transport Sector.
- Articles 17, 33 and 79 of Law 24/2001, of 27th December, on tax, administrative and social order measures.
- Article 99 of Law 53/202, of 30th December, on tax, administrative and social order measures.
- Titles IV and V of Royal Decree-law 2/1986, of 23rd May, on the public service of stowing and unstowing ships.
- The authorisation referred to in this paragraph includes the power to rectify, clarify and harmonise the legal texts that have to be revised."

The deadline is very near so, if the order is completed, we shall soon have in a new revised Law all the legislation relating to Ports and the Merchant Navy.

The arguments that follow will be made from a critical perspective, in an attempt to analyse the current state of affairs and what they should be like in the future, in a world in which security is more complex every day and requires more involvement from everyone, each at the level and in the area that affects them. We should be aware of this because otherwise we will always be at the mercy of situations that surprise and overwhelm us.

Port regulations and organisation must take a step forward in the search for clear specific answers to the threats posed by a radical and indiscriminate globalised terrorism that seeks to cause the largest number of victims possible and the greatest repercussion of its criminal actions to foment hatred and the division of cultures and civilisation. This terrorism has started to become the main problem that democratic societies will have to face in the coming years.

Therefore, the Authorities of the Ministry of Development needs to implement the legal mechanisms and operative responses so that the Port Authorities can indeed implement all those preventive measures, provisions and demands that derive from the ISPS Code in the maritime terminals that are affected when a ship is docked in them.

The special measures that the requirements of the Code demand must reach their highest point of efficiency, basically, at the moment when the ship affected by the Code is docked in a port terminal, in what the Code calls *port facilities*. This specific moment of interrelation is known in the Code as *ship-port interface*.

The measures must have legal repercussions in the Regulation and in the Port Ordinances that are elaborated so that if due to the requirements of national regulations, these rules must refer to all the service area of the ports, they must, at the same time, contemplate and give an organisational response to the special demands of the maritime terminals included in the port space, according to the traffic that affects them and to the provisions of the corresponding protection plans.

In so far as the PFSP adopt a series of preventive measures in virtue of the evaluation of the risks that may affect security, they are an instrument that will become essential from the moment in which they are obliged to adopt a series of basically preventive and control measures, that make it possible to organise a secure area. Those responsible for security, especially the PFSO shall be in constant surveillance and shall make sure that these measures are applied in accordance with the provisions that that effect in the ISPS Code.

All of this will give the users of the facilities the necessary guarantees that their traffic is safe and that the risks for people, goods, facilities and ships are minimised.

But these measures implemented by the Code are very general and are aimed at being valid for all the countries that have entered the agreement, conscious of the threats of international terrorism and especially Islamic fanaticism.

For this reason the States have to do a bit more. They have to provide an organisation of human and material means that is serious, efficient and effective and is able to guarantee that these measures are fulfilled and that the port police organisation is able to adapt to the new demands.

The Ports of General Interest have an advantage over the other autonomic ports or private terminals which are housed in the port public domain by means of some operating permit that allows them to occupy the domain privately, especially in concessions: they have been capable of maintaining an organisation to carry out their port police activities which means that, if they adapt to the new demands by adequately training their harbour guards and if finally they are give a modern Regulation of Exploitation and Policing that is capable of making it possible to adapt to the new security demands of the Code within the port facility and of organising the rest of the port spaces, Spain will have secure ports with a modern port organisation and the necessary legal instruments to take actions in matters relating to security that modern times require.

The Regulation of Exploitation and Policing of the Port Ordinances can be an instrument of great interest in helping to achieve all of these objectives and to adapt the harbour guards once and for all to their appropriate functions, which are none other than those of performing public security duties that are required without thinking twice of any special police force.

4.1 The old Regulation of Services, Policing and Port Regime

No Regulation has been elaborated and published since Law 27/92 on Ports of the State and Merchant Navy came into force. In light of this objective fact which leaves a certain regulatory void is the defence, in a generalised manner, of the application of the old Regulation of Services, Policing and Port Regime, elaborated by the Port Board in May 1976.

This Regulation is abrogated. You just have to take a look at article 1, which addresses its legal grounding to see that it complements and develops the provisions of articles 31 of the Law of Ports, of 19th March 1928 and 63 of the Regulation for its execution in Law 27/68 of 20th June, on Port Boards and Statute of Autonomy and other provisions related with this Law and Decree 2357/75 of 11th September, on sanctions in port matters which are provisions repealed by Law 27/92 of Ports of the State and the Merchant Navy.

The regulation to which we refer is expressly abrogated and, therefore, its Regulation of Services and Policing. Despite this its sanctioning regime has been applied and even today it must be studied in order to participate in the public examinations made by the Port Authorities to furnish certain posts. It is systematically required in the programme for harbour guards. That is the way it is because there is no other regulation and the study is there, allowing an explanatory approach and a first contact with what will be the functions of the personnel who start a job for the first time in whatever port it may be.

It is a general rule and universally accepted that laws have to come before their executive and development regulations. This is the normal process for the legal production of regulations. In Spanish legal regulation there are few autonomous regulations left and they are used within the organisational area of the Administration for internal government and to define institutional relationships. In case of doubt and in order to verify that they exist a check is made as to whether they have been subjected to a ruling of the State Council. If they are merely organisational regulations this step is not necessary as there is no legal regulation on which to fall back.

The Regulation that we are analysing can either be connected to a later law saving its effect, with all the problems of application that that represents or it can be given its own effect, but as it contains a sanctioning regime that requires a law reserve it is impossible unless the application of the sanctioning regime is omitted. Despite all of these inconveniences, the Regulation has lived in a certain legal mist, it has been applied, and it has not been questioned too much in practice and has not produced serious consequences.

Another question is that its sanctioning regime is applied strictly from the point of view of legal security. It can be admitted without further ado that Law 27/92 of Ports and its modifications can act as regulations to cover part of their content as has been seen. This specific case of cover regulations comes about, paradoxically, when the law is after the regulation which, in theory, addresses its development. It is like going through the tunnel of time. In order to fill regulatory voids, this type of regulation is maintained because of what they represent in their organisational and sanctioning parts if the provisions of the Regulation find cover in the Law. That is to say, it is accommodated to it and does not go beyond its contents. The principle of legality makes this exception, which must not be abused, provided that we take into account that only breaches of the legal regulation so established in the law are administrative breaches. Our legal regulation requires a material or formal law reserve to typify breaches or impose sanctions in the administrative area. As we have insisted, autonomous regulations that that have their own basis have no place in this field.

These arguments are conceptual and complex but it is not necessary to bring them out them in a moment in which for security a new and complex legislation is being studied in matters of exploitation and policing to accommodate it with both the ISPS Code and with the upcoming community legislation, which will impose further demands on the port area and on the traffic of passengers and goods.

But at the same time and still with the sanctioning regime, in general, complementary regulation with rules is allowed: "The regulatory provisions of development may introduce specifications or adjustments to the legally established table of breaches or sanctions which, without constituting new breaches or sanctions, or without altering the nature or the limits contemplated by the law, contribute to the more correct identification of conducts or to the more precise determination of the corresponding sanctions." This is the role of the sanctioning regulations.

In accordance with this, while the provisions of the Regulation do not exceed the Law itself and the breach and sanction are within its cover these situations in which the regulations come before the Law, such as the case of the old Regulation of 1976, can be saved.

It is more doubtful and questionable when the Regulation of 1976 is applied without further ado and without establishing the legal grounds of the sanctioning proceedings in Law 27/92 which is where this cover should be provided, to impose meagre sanctions which, evidently, are not going to be contested by those sanctioned because otherwise the sanctioning regime of Law 27/92 would be applied and it is much more severe, so none of those involved would be interested in it. This can be a dangerous game though somewhat beneficial for the alleged offender as it hides a certain fraud. This is expressed as a critical comment with no other intention than that of encouraging, in so far as is possible, a rapid promulgation of the Port Regulation, which is so necessary at this moment in time.

The Regulation of 1976 is not a bad one, but time has passed and three port laws have been enacted which, to all effects, make it outdated.

It also presents other no less important inconveniences, such as the fact that it was only published in the Official Journals of the Provinces, which means that the principle of legality which has to be taken from the sanctioning regulations is also questioned.

These Regulations of 1976 are also specific for each port which means that in reality, despite their name, they are no more than ordinances for the port in question.

We transcribe part of article 5 which is of interest as it speaks of the jurisdiction of other ministries in the port area:

- The Marine Authorities, Customs, Work and Social Security, Health, Trade, Agriculture, Government Police and Civil Police have their own jurisdiction in the service area of the port on a permanent basis.

- The immediate and direct management of the surveillance and policing services on the docks and service area of the port will be exercised by the Director, who shall have the Police Chief under his orders who in turn will be in charge of the personnel of the harbour guard service, invested with the condition of Agents of Authority, in the role of Security Guard.

- The personnel of any guard service that could be established occasionally or permanently, apart from the direct surveillance of the goods in question, shall also make sure that their Regulation is complied with. (Referring to private security guards).

4.2 The legal grounding of the Regulation of Exploitation and Policing

All of the drafts that have been put into circulation by the sector for study and debate on the elaboration of the new Regulation of Exploitation and Policing look for its legal grounding, exclusively in article 106 of the Law of Ports and there have been doubts about the name of the Regulation itself and the content of article 106. The name of the Regulation and the content of this article have been modified in all legal reforms since 1992, the date the current Law of Ports was issued.

In citing some of the drafts of the Regulation we refer to the one of July 1999 which was elaborated as: "Project of regulation of service and policing in the state ports of general interest."

The Project of October 2000 is called "General regulation for service and policing in the state ports of general interest."

Law 48/03 of 26th November on the economic regime and rendering of services of the Ports of General Interest is now called the Regulation of exploitation and policing, making several references to it. They are transcribed later on.

It is difficult to understand at this stage the insistence on the name of the Regulation for a rule that must be executive and of development of a Law of Ports. The Laws are developed by Royal Decree and there is nothing stopping it being so in this case. The same contents can be implemented in a Royal Decree for the development and execution of a Law of Ports in questions of exploitation and policing. Moreover, it should be this way, as it is more modern and is better accommodated to the Spanish regulatory programme and to the current circumstances. Nor would it offer doubts regarding its regulatory rank and its connection with the Law of Ports.

Joining on the one hand *exploitation*, which is a mere organisation of a certain public service in the ports, with the concept of policing, could even cause problems in the elaboration of the future Regulation. Nowadays, *security* has sufficient entity on its own to justify a rule such as the Regulation of Policing, besides the other provisions such as those contained in a hypothetical Regulation of Exploitation. Here we support this formula.

An organisational regulation that does not require the imposition of sanctions is not very useful, if it does not require the ruling of the State Council as explained above. There would therefore be the possibility of elaborating a Regulation of Exploitation and another executive and development regulation of the Law of Ports in matters relating to Policing. The latter would have to be subjected to the ruling of the State Council and have a sanctioning regime for the breaches and sanctions in matters relating to ports. Nor is there any impediment to addressing the two matters in the same regulation, provided that both fields can be clearly defined, in separate chapters, give that the organisation is made from the inside or is delegated for the same purpose in external organisations and the policing cannot be delegated as it is a public function that requires the exercise of authority and has external effects.

In the world of globalisation the exploitation of the port requires formulas from private initiative which means that it can survive in an independent regulation which is more flexible and gives a better response to these demands. However, the repressive functions and those of authority must be tapered and require greater demands which means that a Regulation of Port Policing would make it possible to circumscribe a field with its own basis.

It is difficult to understand that the drafts referred to do not contemplate a sanctioning regime in the development of the Law of Ports, at least in the fields of exploitation and policing, as the old Regulation does. If a Regulation of Exploitation and Policing, or a Regulation of Policing opts for this regulatory development and it is not given a sanctioning regime in the Law of Ports, it will be difficult to respond to the demands of the Code when sanctioning non-compliances of the demands imposed, aw we will see later on.

The Law of Ports is highly sanctioning, if you pardon the expression. It contemplates an ample list of breaches and sanctions applicable by the Port Authorities and the Merchant Navy which has not been subjected to regulatory development since 1992. This does not help in the application of the Law, which, on the other hand, contemplates breaches that are linked to very important sanctions from an economical point of view and that a Regulation should moderate and particularise in its application. The breaches are so important that the very serious ones are usually devaluated to serious during the proceedings. Very few cases have been conducted as very serious breaches and less still have concluded and have executed with this classification. This is a sign of weakness in the regulation.

The range of sanctions is very ample in the Law of 1992 and requires a regulation of development and execution that particularises the application of the Law especially when it is full of blank provisions or of general formulas that in bureaucratic slang are known as a *bag of tricks* which is applied when they do not know which breach or sanction to apply. Regulations normally give legal security to this type of regulations or blank provisions.

In general terms a policing regulation should:

- organise the policing function in the ports and especially the missions, functions and responsibilities of the harbour guards.
- develop their legal status, given that the Law until its reform in 2003 did not even mention them;
- contain a series of provisions aimed at particularising the breaches and sanctions included in the Law of Ports referring to them;
- transpose a whole group of demands form the implementation of the ISPS Code and the Regulation and Community Directives regarding safety into the internal regulation.

When, all of a sudden, the ISPS Code surprises us with important and novel demands in security matters, the chance should not be missed to take advantage of the situation to give the Regulation a precise sanctioning system that makes it possible to typify the demands and prohibitions contained in its articles, besides the fact that an executive Royal Decree is needed to develop the sanctioning regime of the Law of Ports in a general manner.

An executive Royal Decree must be prepared in questions of port policing. It would provide many answers to the current demands without mixing organisational concepts, such as *exploitation, policing and functions of authority and security.*

We insist with these arguments and continue to do so because, in the application of the ISPS Code, given the administrative complexity of the Spanish port maritime system in which several ministries with different and fractioned competences are involved, at first another problem appears when the concept of *policing* is analysed from the point of view of the Security Forces and Corps and of Organic Law on the Protection of Public Safety.

In the matters being addressed here, any reform and regulatory elaboration must take into consideration other articles of the Law of Ports, beyond article 106, when establishing the legal grounds for the Regulation of Policing. One that seems unavoidable is article 111 which deals with the prevention of illicit activities and forbidden traffic.

In this way "in order to prevent the perpetration of illicit activities or the exercise of any forbidden traffic, the Government may prevent, restrict or condition the navigation of certain categories of civil ships in internal waters, the territorial sea or the adjoining area."

This article has been there, housed within the Law of Ports, without any practical application. It is certain that the contents are more within the field of responsibility of the Merchant Navy than in the activities of the ports, but is goes in the same direction and addresses the same answers and confronts the same port maritime security needs.

Regarding the sanctioning regime, the Regulation must go into the development of article 132 of Law 48/2003 and article 114 of Law 27/92 of Ports which has already been transcribed, but which we repeat here:

"Article 114. Minor breaches
"These are the actions or omissions, which do not receive the consideration of serious or very serious breaches, due to their transcendence or to the importance of the damage caused, are typified regarding the use of the port and its facilities, in one of the following assumptions:

- Non-compliance with the provisions established in the regulation of exploitation and policing of the port.
- Non-compliance with the ordinances established or instructions given by the Port Authority in relation with maritime operation in the port area."

Moreover, the legal grounding of the Regulation of Exploitation and Policing must be established in the recently published international regulation such as the ISPS Code, the Community Regulation and the Directive.

4.3 The Regulation of exploitation and policing and public safety

Security is structured into three large areas in Spain.

On the one had we have public safety which according to OL 1/92 of 21st February on the Protection of Public Safety, and in accordance with the provisions of the Constitution, establishes a generic attribution of competences to the State in matters of public safety (article 149.1.29) and it specifically attributes the Security Forces and Corps, which report to the Government, the task of protecting the free exercise of rights and freedom and of guaranteeing public safety (article 104.1). Its regulation affects the exercising of certain basic rights, such as the right to freedom, free circulation in national territory and entering and leaving Spain freely, or the right to meet.

This is then a first competence that is attributed generically, in all the national territory, to the Security Forces and Corps. It is exercised by the Ministry of the Interior and has necessary collaborators in the Police Forces of the autonomous Communities and of the Local Corporations.

Within this security organisation there is another special security, but public, which is basically focused in its activities in the field of administrative sanctioning but which has responsibilities in security matters in certain areas of limited action. They are known as special police and have a special obligation to collaborate with the Security Forces and Corps in the exercise of their public functions.

The police forces, among which is the Assistant Department of Customs Surveillance and the harbour guards, have their main base in Organic Law 2/86 of 13th March, on Security Forces and Corps and Organic Law 1/92 of 24th February, on the Protection of Public Safety, as well as other specific regulations. These special police have their own special fields of action, sometimes in a certain area of the territory or on a specific sector of activity. Harbour guards are limited in the exercise of their functions to the service areas of the ports.

The Regulation of Exploitation and Policing, especially in this second area of police action, must obviously develop the functions that are its own from the demands of the port regulations, both in an international area and a national one. It is obvious that it must respond to the demands of the ISPS Code in its references to security.

In the same way Regulation (EC) no. 725/2004, of the European Parliament and of the Council, of 31st March 2004, relating to the enhancement in the security of ships and port facilities, published in the Official Journal of the European Union on 29th April 2004, imposes greater and more extensive demands in the European area than the code itself.

The Regulation is obliged to enter into those public functions that are imposed by Law which means that its agents of authority, the harbour guards, must render assistance in collective security in the measure in which these two mentioned laws so impose.

Article 4 of OL 1/92, of 21st February, on the Protection of Public Safety, contemplates that:

"1. In matters subject to the administrative powers of special Police not specifically attributed to Entities reporting to the Ministry of the Interior, these may only intervene in so far as is necessary to guarantee the that the objectives laid down in paragraph 2 of Article 1 are attained.

2. Said Entities, through their agents, shall provide the necessary executive assistance to any other public authorities that require it to guarantee compliance with the Laws."

Paragraph 2 of article 1 clarifies that this competence includes the exercise of the administrative powers established in this Law with the objective of guaranteeing coexistence, the eradication of violence and the pacific use of the public roads and spaces, as well as that of preventing crimes and offences from being committed.

These measures are not less important than those others that the harbour guards perform as Administrative Police in accordance with the demands of the Law of Ports: to collaborate in public safety to guarantee coexistence, the eradication of violence and the pacific use of the public roads and spaces, as well as that of preventing crimes and offences from being committed, is understood as being within the service area of the port and is of huge importance given the current circumstances in which other threats have materialised.

The references to the special police in the laws on public safety are scarce. We found another reference in Organic Law 2/86 on Security Forces and Corps, In its article 4.1 it imposes on everyone the duty to assist the Security Forces and Corps as necessary in the investigation and persecution of crimes in the legally established terms.

In paragraph 2, it requires of people and entities that exercise functions of surveillance, security or custody, referring to personnel and assets or services of public ownership, the special obligation of assisting or collaborating at all times with the Security Forces and Corps.

Now we are in a position to define clear demands for these special police, among which we can include the harbour guards: some are derived form their obligations in the port area and others from their role of special police in the field of public safety.

Apart form collaborating with the Security Forces and Corps at all times within the demands of these two Organic Laws, which are extremely important, they must also do it in a very special manner, within their own functions and within the service area of the port.

These responsibilities, which are so important and which are going to make it possible to take on all the preventive functions required by the ISPS Code, must be specifically developed in the new Regulation and in the port Ordinances. Without a doubt, it will make it necessary to redefine the functions of the harbour guards which of late have been a little uncertain and confusing at the same time as they overlap with other obligations foreign to the responsibilities of public safety. The Regulation will be the adequate legal framework to establish these functions and responsibilities and to define a legal statute of functions and responsibilities for these security professionals.

It could be argued that in the ports there are other functions derived from exploitation that are not purely security ones. There is no doubt about it, but it is clear that a specific group from this sector will perform security tasks exclusively without harmonising them with any other. In essence, the Law of Private security itself imposes the requirement of the incompatibility of the security functions with any other.

It has to be thus, because the security functions are carried out in uniform, sometimes with weapons and are to a certain extent devaluated when they fall within the field of private or purely commercial activities.

4.4 Harbour guards. Historical evolution. Public function. Agents of Authority

When addressing the consequences that the publication and implementation of the ISPS Code will have for port security, the figure of the Agents of Authority must take on a special importance, at least in the Ports of General Interest which are competence of the State where, as special police of the public domain, they are going to carry out these duties. This makes it necessary to carry out a sturdy but in depth study of the figure and all it entails.

The harbour guards had been legally abandoned in the Law of Ports of 1992, which did not even mention them, despite the fact that the Law made several references to security and port police functions without mentioning their main protagonists, as we saw earlier.

The fact that the Law of Ports did not mention them left them in a certain legal uncertainty. On the one hand, the Regulation Projects did not define them and their functions seemed to be interchangeable with those of other civil servants and with private security. Thus, it was possible to join this group without too many demands and with little knowledge of security; moreover, they were one of the groups to which other port operators were assigned when the ports were restructured within the liberalising policy of port traffic and services.

There is an interesting fact in the "XI Collective Agreement for personnel working in the Port Boards, Autonomous Ports, Administrative Commission of Port Groups and Ports transferred to the Autonomous Communities that adhere to it" subscribed on 13th July 1991, which, when defining professional categories, reiterates the condition of agents of authority of the harbour guards[1], adding that they are in charge of monitoring and policing the port; for this personnel it is recommended to replace firearms with other means of defence that entail less risk and provided that the governing authority allows it, established the voluntary use of firearms, in accordance at all times with the stipulations of the Firearms Regulation.

The governing authority has said nothing to the effect, which means that at the moment they provide their services without weapons or other security elements, such as truncheons or handcuffs. From the point of view of security, it seems that the collective agreement cannot be the place for a group to decide whether or not to carry weapons as it falls outside of the field of this legal labour framework to enter such matters. The Agreement itself confirms this as it adopts the measure with a certain temporary nature as it may or may not be admitted by the governing authority.

On the other hand, when Law 27/92 led to the transformation of the regime for personnel working for the Ports of General Interest, acquiring the condition of non civil service staff (6th Additional Provision. Four[2]), has not affected the nature and functions of the port entities or the tasks carried out

---

[1] The current one does not contain these references. It is not be expected that the collective agreement be a valid vehicle to give the harbour guard the condition of agent of authority though they have a special consequence in the penal field.

[2] Four. 1). Civil servants assigned to Port Boards in services that are peripheral to the Administrative Commission of Port Groups and in the Autonomous Ports, may opt for the following, once this Law has come into force and until 31st December 1992:
    a) Join the Entities created as non-civil service staff that take on the competences that they are carrying out, with recognition of the seniority that corresponds for the effects of receiving the corresponding pay supplement, while holding the position of personal leave in their original Corps as established in article 29.3a) of Law 30/1984, of 2nd August on Measures to Reform the Public Function.
The periods of service accredited in the Regime of State Retirement Benefits may be totalled in the General Regime of the Social Security in order to calculate retiring rights, in accordance with the regulations contained in Royal Decree 691/1991, of

by their personnel, which in any case remain unchanged regarding the attribution of public functions in the service area of the port.

Having said this, in line with the position of the Ministry of the Interior, it would not be a bad idea if these functions were provided from the area of public function. Over the years and given these factual and legal precedents, their condition as agents of authority has been questioned.

A recent report of the General Technical Secretary of the Ministry of the Interior, analyses the figure both in its historical evolution and in its current problems. This will help us to see this transition of the figure, in recent times, in which they choose to abandon the use of weapons and the position of security guards.

1. The Regulation for the execution of the Law of Ports, approved by the Decree of 19th March 1928, referred to above, in the second paragraph of article 62, established:

"Harbour guards will report immediately to the Engineer in charge of the Service, shall be considered as Security guards, use uniforms and will be named by the Civil Governor of the Province."

2. By Order of the former Ministry of Public Works of 23rd July 1953, the Regulatory Statute was approved for administrative personnel, auxiliary technicians, auxiliary workers and minor officials of the Port Boards, Administrative Commissions and other port services. Article 12 included two different groups among the auxiliary personnel of the port Organisms, the first of which "*includes personnel invested with the condition of Agent of Authority because of their function*" and which was made up of the categories of "chief officers, petty officers, harbour guards and guards" which were unified as "harbour guards" by the Order of 24th June 1962. In turn, article 37 of the Order which defines the functions of this personnel added that "the service of harbour guard" was in charge of the "policing, conservation and surveillance of the docks, works and services of the Administrative Board or Commission of the port in question and its coastal area, as well as the custody of goods and merchandise deposited in the docks" and added that these auxiliary workers will be considered Agents of Authority, security guards and will have the right to use weapons within the service areas of the port."

3. The same situation is maintained in Decree 2356/1975 of 11th September, on sanctions in port affairs. Its article 5 determines that "the sanctioning proceedings will be instructed by the corresponding Port Director, on his own account, at the request of the interested party or from a public

---

12th April. For the purposes of calculating the indemnities due to the termination of the work contract following the acquisition of the condition of non-civil service staff, seniority shall begin on the date they take on this condition, except in the case that they expressly waiver the condition of civil servant in the moment they acquire said condition, with the scope established in articles 37 and 38 of the articulated text of the Law of Civil Services of the State, in which case seniority will be calculated form the moment they join the Public Administration.
    b) Continue in the administrative situation of active service, returning to the Department to which their Corps or scale is assigned.
2).The non-civil service staff of the above mentioned Organs and Entities shall join the corresponding Port Authorities with said condition.
3).The incorporation as non-civil service staff of the Port Authorities, resulting from the application of the above mentioned stipulations, will be in accordance with their working rights, and they shall be assigned the tasks and functions that correspond to their academic qualifications and professional capacity, in accordance with the organic structure that is approved and regardless of those that they were carrying out until the moment of their incorporation.

denouncement. Port workers, harbour guards and other agents of authority shall be obliged to report any breaches that they become aware of."

4. The figure of harbour guards is contained specifically in the Regulations of Port Services in similar terms. Thus, the Regulation of Services, Policing and Regime of the Port of La Coruña, similar to all the rest, of May 1976, in its article 6 "Surveillance and Policing of the Port" says:

"The immediate and direct management of the surveillance and Policing services in the docks and service area of the Port will be carried out by the Port Director who may delegate in the Chief Engineer of the Planning and Exploitation Techniques Section. He shall have the Port Commissionaire under his orders, who in turn shall be in charge of the personnel of the harbour guard service, invested with the condition of agents of authority in the role of security guards, with the mission of preventing, avoiding and reporting the breaches that may be committed with respect to this Regulation, maintaining due order, making sure that the works, materials or goods that are in the port come to no harm, complying with and making comply with the service orders transmitted by their superiors, as w ell as controlling the services rendered."

It seems clear that the legislation prior to Law 27/92 attributed the harbour guards with the condition of agents of authority.

4.4.1 Harbour guards in Law 27/92, modified by Law 62/97

Following the report of the General Technical Secretary of the Ministry of the Interior of 9th October 2000, it can be said that the current Law 27/92, modified by Law 62/1997, of 26th December, does not contain any regulation on the legal regime of the harbour guards, However, there are several legal provisions that make reference to the competences held by the Port Authorities in questions relating to policing and port surveillance.

In this sense, article 1 states, within the area that makes up the "purpose of the Law" of State Ports and of the Merchant Navy, that of "regulating", as well as other functions, that of "policing" the "ports that are of the competence of the State Administration." On the other hand, article 11 determines that the attributions on the ports of general interest "will be exercised by the Ministry of Development through the State Ports and the Port Authorities, notwithstanding the competences that correspond to other administrations or departments of the State Administration."

As for the legal regime that governs the activity of the Public Entity Port States and of the Port Authorities, the Law states that their activities shall be adapted to the "private legal regulation, except in exercising the functions of public power that the regulation attributes them (arts. 24.2 and 35.2) among which those relating to the "management and use of the public domain" , "the exacting[3] and collecting of public income" and "the impositions of sanctions" must be included.

Real characteristics of the functions of public power are the services of surveillance, security and policing of the port area referred to in articles 66 and 67 of the Law. Thus the final script of paragraph 1 of the first of the legal provision cited includes, within the concept of "port services", those of port

---

[3] Action and effect of demanding, applied to taxes, loans, fines, debts, etc.

surveillance, security, policing and civil protection notwithstanding those that correspond to the Ministry of the Interior or to other Public Administrations." At the same time, article 67, now eliminated, stated that the rendering of services may be done directly by the port authorities or through an indirect management, by any procedure recognized in the laws "provided that it does not imply the exercise of authority".

There is therefore, in line with the above mentioned report of the Ministry of the Interior, an activity of port surveillance, security and policing, for which they are invested with public power and whose exercise involves performing certain tasks or functions that the harbour guard has done historically.

Consequently, the Law of State Ports and the Merchant Navy has at no moment had the intention of depriving the port Entities of public faculties, but rather, they are assigned to the Port Authorities in an even more complete manner than the old Port Boards.

4.4.2 The position of the harbour guards relating to OL 2/86, of 13th March, on the Security Forces and Corps, OL 1/92 of 21st February, on the Protection of Public Safety and Law 23/92, of 30th July, on Private Security

An opinion on the matter has already been expressed. It almost literally follows the report of the General Technical Secretary of the Ministry of the Interior, of 9th October of 2000, signed by the General Technical Secretary Mr. Fernando Benzo Sainz. We do it because, although we do not agree with all of the legal arguments, we do share its basic line of argument and we believe that it has become, at least with respect to the organisation of the services, an instrument of interest. Many of the arguments have already been expressed in this study and if we repeat them it is with the intention of maintaining a coherent line throughout.

According to the report, Organic Law 2/1986 determines that the "Security Forces and Corps" are:

- The security Forces and Corps of the State that report to the Government of the Nation.
- The Police Forces that report to the Autonomous Communities
- The Police Forces that report to Local Corporations (article 2). In article 4.2 it establishes that the "people and entities that exercise functions of surveillance, security or custody referring to …… goods or services of public ownership,,,,, have a special obligation to assist or collaborate at all times with the Security Forces and Corps."

This means that the Law recognises the people and entities which have been assigned competences of the security, surveillance and custody of public assets apart from the general policing functions which correspond to the Security Forces and Corps.

Otherwise, the report continues, the functions of security and policing are currently regulated in two important Laws; OL 1/1992 and the Law of Private Security 23/1992[4].

a) Organic Law 1/92 regulates the exercise of what the doctrine calls, general police, whose competences are attributed to the Ministry of the Interior; however, despite all of the above, article 4 establishes:

---

[4] Law of private security.

"1. In matters subjected to the administrative powers of special police that are not attributed specifically to bodies that depend on the Ministry of the Interior, they may only intervene to the extent necessary to guarantee that the objectives laid down in paragraph 2 of article 1 are met. This competence includes the exercising of the administrative powers laid down in this Law, in order to guarantee public coexistence, the eradication of violence and the pacific use of the public roads and spaces, as well as that of preventing crimes and offences being committed, as already explained.

2. Through their agents, these bodies shall lend the necessary executive assistance to any other public authorities that require it to guarantee that the laws are complied with."

From what is written in the report we can unmistakably recognise the so called "special police" among which it is understood the "public police or public domain police" are included.

As for the Ports of General Interest, the policing faculties of the Port Authorities are expressly included in article 40.3j of the Law of State Ports and the Merchant Navy, among the functions of their respective Boards of Administration ("to exercise the faculties of policing attributed to them by the current Law, and which are necessary to meet their objectives"). The functions of inspection and surveillance attributed to the harbour guards who, as such, must be invested in the condition of agents of (port) authority to whom the serve, contribute to the adequate exercising of these faculties.

The Public Entity Ports of the State, another paragraph states, has insistently maintained that the group of harbour guards is invested with the condition of agents of authority in the exercise of their functions and it corresponds to the Board of Administrators of the Port Authorities to nominate them in accordance with the provisions of article 405j of the Law of Ports. Notwithstanding the fact that these harbour guards lack the quality of public civil servants, for this statement, by this Law all personnel of the Public Entity State Ports and of the Port Authorities have the condition of personnel subject to labour law.

The project of the new Regulation circulated as a "Project of regulation of service and policing of the State Ports of General Interest" in their most recent version of October 2000. We have taken a look at it and see that it still needs a few more detailed readings. We have made some comments on it in another part of the study, though that does not prevent a more detailed analysis here.

Its intention was to regulate the following matters:

- "The regulation and performance of the services rendered by the Port Authority.
- The general Policing of the service area of the port.
- The surveillance and control of the services rendered by people and entities other than the Port Authorities." (article 2)
-

The general policing of the service area of the port and the surveillance and control of the services rendered by people and entities other than the Port Authority seem (at least that is the intention that the Regulation seems to transmit on the date of its elaboration) to be going to make up the two most important areas of action of a harbour guard; one is a spatial area which is the service area of the port and another with an administrative content or on services and entities that operate in the port supplying services under any format of empowerment.

Article 3 of the draft deals with the scope of application.

"1º.- This Regulation will be applicable in the service areas of the Ports of General Interest of the State, defined in accordance with the provisions of article 15, now cancelled by Law 48/2003 and the First Additional Provision[5] of the Law of the State Ports and of the Merchant Navy and also in the spaces affected by the services of maritime signalling, whose management is assigned to the corresponding Port Authorities in accordance with article 38[6] of the Law of the Ports of the State and of the Merchant Navy, except for those provisions whose spatial or functional area are specific to the service area.

2.- All those people or entities who carry out any type of activity or render services in the areas indicated in the previous point of this article are subjected to this Regulation, as are the people, ships, floating devices, vehicles, machinery, facilities, materials and goods that are to be found in these areas, albeit circumstantially."

The exception referred to at the end of the first paragraph, "except those provisions that because of their spatial or functional area are specific to the service area", creates more doubts than it resolves and does not offer any clarity.

For our purposes there is no doubt that article 5 of the Project intends to regulate a kind of statute for the harbour guard, although the Law of Ports does not make any reference to the figure as expressed:

"Paragraph 1. The functions of the special police, stated in article 4.1 of the OL on the Protection of Public Security, attributed to the Port Authority by the Law of Ports of the State and of the Merchant Navy, correspond to the Board of Administration of the Port Authority.

These functions of the special police will be exercised by the service of harbour guards and other personnel of the Port Authority to whom the performance of the function is delegated in the service area of the port, in accordance with the orders and guidelines given by the Director of the Port Authority, in accordance with the provisions of Article 43 of the Law of Ports of the State and the Merchant Navy.

The rest of the policing and surveillance functions may also be carried out by other personnel to whom the Prot Authority delegates in the service area of the port."

This is an article that should be written with greater clarity. It corrects and improves the text written in previous drafts but still has important flaws. The intention here is to define and not clarify that there are functions that are for the special police and other functions that are not and that they are wrongly called, *policing functions*. In reality, it seems that these are functions that would fall into the area of

---

[5] Service Area. While no definition is made as established in article 15.1, the service area of the ports of state competence shall be considered as the group of spaces included in the service area that exists when this Law comes into effect and the surfaces of water included in areas I and II defined for each port for the purposes of applying tariffs, in accordance with current legislation.

[6] Article 38. Territorial area.
The territorial area of competence of the Port Authorities is that which is included within the limits of the service area of the port and the spaces affected to the maritime signalling service whose management is assigned to them.
If a Port Authority were to manage several ports which are competence of the State Administration, its territorial area shall be extended to the service areas of said ports and the spaces affected to the maritime signalling service whose management is assigned to them.

private security because its recipients can be individualised and the concept of *policing* is interpreted in a broad manner. In Spain, the term *police* has no adjectives and refers to the Security Forces.

Now Law 48/2003, of 26th November, of economic regime and the rendering of services of the Ports of Special Interest, has delivered us a new nuance which will undoubtedly make it necessary to give a new text to this precept in the future Regulation of Exploitation and Policing: the recognition of the harbour guards as agents of authority finally appears in the Law.

This is done in the Thirteenth Additional Provision which, when referring to the Port Police Service, states:

"1. The functions of special police, described in article 4.1 of Organic Law 1/1992, of 21st February, on the Protection of Public Safety, attributed to the Port Authority by the Law of Ports of the State and the Merchant Navy, correspond to their Board of Administrators.

2. These functions shall be exercised, in the manner determined by the Regulation of Exploitation and Policing, by the harbour guards and other personnel of the Port Authority, duly qualified and registered in the Police Service, to which effect they shall have the consideration of agents of authority of the Port Authority in exercising the powers of port police included in the Law of Ports of the State and the Merchant Navy, notwithstanding the obligation of collaborating at all times with the Security Forces and Corps."

The above confirms what we have been defending. This inclusion in the Law of Ports came from the insistence of a nationalist member of parliament from Galicia who had collected a petition from the group itself and especially the group of Port harbour guards from Ferrol San Ciprián.

It is curious that since 1992 this group has been working towards the privatisation of its functions and duties, seeking to distance itself from public functions on the crest of the wave of the privatisation of port services and liberalisation and that now they wish to take cover under the umbrella of the penal and administrative public function by claiming their condition as Agents of the Port Authority, which will give them greater protection against external aggressions as well as a bonus for aggressions suffered in the exercise of their functions.

It is not that they were not Agents of the Authority but that in the field of penal law quite a lot of sentences questioned this condition; others, on the other hand, accepted it without reservations.

In any case and getting into the details of the question, these functions are carried out "in the manner determined by the Regulation of Exploitation and Policing, by the harbour guards and other personnel of the Port Authority, duly qualified and registered in the Police Service, to which effect they shall have the consideration of agents of authority of the Port Authority in exercising the powers of port police," as stated in Law 48/2003.

The Regulation Project of October 2000 did not say exactly the same thing which means that it will have to be revised in its new draft. In article 5, which addresses the surveillance and policing of the port, it states that "these functions of special police will be exercised by the harbour guard service and other personnel of the Port Authority who are responsible for this function in the service area of the port, in accordance with the orders and guidelines established by the Director of the Port Authority, in accordance with the provisions of article 43 of the Law of Ports of the State and the Merchant Navy."

Article 43 says nothing in our favour as it is a simple Project without any legal importance that reflects certain aspirations of becoming a positive regulation with the content of Law 48/2003.

When analysing these concepts, there is a coincidence between the Law and the Regulation Project when they say "these functions of special police shall be carried out by the harbour guard service and the other personnel of the Port Authority" where there is an identity in the terms and in the concepts.

In any case, to extend the functions of special police to *other personnel of the port authority* is a very big risk, because OL 1/92, circumscribes these functions, as already seen, to those who as agents (of the port authority it is understood in this case) perform their duties by exercising a competence that includes, according to article 1.2 of said OL, "the exercise of the administrative powers established in this Law, with the objective of guaranteeing coexistence, the eradication of violence and the pacific use of the public roads and spaces, as well as preventing crimes and offences from being committed."

These agents must be the harbour guards for all the reasons argued above and because security should be a specific duty of uniformed people, a public function, with a certain stability and permanence. Without a doubt this is what OL 1/92 refers to when it commissions the special police. It is an error to extend this concept of special police to an undetermined group of people in general because in any case this condition of special police will depend on the personnel who make up the Port Authority. Security in general and public and port security especially gain nothing by this lack of clarity, apart from the fact that it is doubtful that the Law of Ports could make any member of staff and Agent of the Authority, simply because they belong to the port authority. In dealing with agents and public security it seems that the Law of Ports should not exceed the more specific Law which is the OL on public safety or, to a certain extent, article 4 of OL 2/86 on Security Forces and Corps, as seen elsewhere.

Along the lines of our argument, Law 48/2003 explains who are going to be agents of authority and requires that they are "duly qualified and registered in the Police Service, to which effect they shall have the consideration of agents of authority of the Port Authority in exercising the powers of port police." This somewhat specifies what the Project intended, in article 5, that is that these functions could be carried out by anyone "who is charged with performing the function in the service area of the port, in accordance with the orders and guidelines established by the Director of the Port Authority." Now, the Law at least requires that they be part of the Police Service; a police service that will have to be given an adequate organisation and statutory legal framework so that entering and leaving it is something more than just a question of organisation in the port area.

It is to a certain extent the case now in the Law of Ports but it is still an error that simply being registered can, as if by magic, convert any member of the Port Authority, firstly into a harbour guard, and then into an Agent of Authority.

Being an agent of authority involves a little more. To start with, exercising public functions exclusively. As for the harbour guards, if they are to become part of the group which from now on is going to be called Police Service according to Law 48/2003, it is not sufficient to register them: it has to be done within a rigorous selection process, with defined knowledge and training in port matters (as is being done) and also in the field of public safety and that of collaboration with the Security Forces and Corps. This training will be appropriate and will serve as a basis for the performance of the functions of special police, always defined in the security laws with regard to public security, although evidently in the case of port security, in the administrative sense it has a n extraordinary importance for this group, especially in the area of sanctions, as they are in a position to make reports that could lead to the investigation of the corresponding sanctioning proceedings in accordance with the Law of Ports and which, in future legislation, will appear in the Police Regulation if it is decided to include a sanctioning administrative procedure in the content that includes the development of breaches and sanctions and the particularisation of the breaches and sanctions established in the Law of Ports, as is being defended here.

In paragraph 2, the Project states that "the faculties of policing attributed to the Port Authorities include, among others, the following functions:

- Control, inspection and coordination of the port services and assistance to navigation, offered directly by the Port Authority or through indirect management.
- Control, inspection and coordination of the operations and activities that require their authorisation and concession.
- Monitoring compliance with the clauses and conditions in the act of awarding concessions and authorisation.
- Control and inspection of the works, facilities and equipment located in the port area within the scope of their competences.
- Control and inspection of the goods and containers located in the port area in the scope of their competences.
- Control in the port area of compliance with the regulations regarding dangerous goods and health and safety, as well as the security and fire fighting systems, notwithstanding the competences that correspond to other organs of the Administration.
- Control access of people to buildings, works, port facilities and areas of restricted access or cordoned off areas within the service area of the port.
- Ensure compliance with the rules of the current General Regulation of Service and Policing and the rest of the regulations applicable to the port service."

Paragraph 3 states that they will have the consideration of Agents of Authority.

- Those who carry out the functions of special police attributed to the Port Authorities by the Law of Ports of the State and of the Merchant Navy and those referred to in article 4 of the OL on the Protection of Public Security, whether it be permanently or circumstantially.
- Those who have been assigned the execution of the agreements adopted by the Board of Administrators in the exercise of their public powers.

It is not very clear that simply because a person executes the agreements of the Board of Administrators, they can become an agent of authority. These will be agreements referring to public functions because, as we all know, the activities of the ports today are closely related to private law in most of their decisions. The definition of agent of authority has to be found in the security function that they perform.

Besides, this ample interpretation of the condition of agents of authority in the port area is surprising when the tendency of the courts is to circumscribe it, on an increasingly more frequent basis, to the Security Forces and Corps. Today this concept is not even defined in the Penal Code although there is a reference to it and it is implied in several types of criminal offence to demand further responsibilities in the exercising of public functions and at the same time to offer a greater legal protection against the aggressions to which they may be subjected in exercising their functions.

The mention of their condition of security guards that appears in the Regulation of 1976 has disappeared which means that by virtue of the omission they lose the chance to carry weapons along the lines adopted in the Collective Agreement, although in certain ports they are reconsidering the idea of at least carrying them. This is due, once again, to the increasing insecurity in these port areas surrounded by cities, sometimes badly lit and where petty crime finds a haven for its illicit and violent acts in the flexibility of access control (especially pedestrian) which has grown in recent years.

Whether they carry weapons or not will be a requirement of public safety and of the regulations and agreements that affect the port facilities. The Code neither proposes nor rejects it, although it is significant that it considers the question and comments on it, as this is not the case in the national legislation of port matters. A position of excess security should be defined once and for all, as we insist here, regarding the legal statute of this group which at this moment is moving towards legal uncertainty and towards the systematic doubt as to what its functions are to be. In the light of the lack of provisions in security matters to regulate the situation it is being shaped in the collective negotiation, although it is only fair to recognize that the trend is changing and the ISPS Code could be a turning point in this crossroads. For the moment the Law has recognised their condition as agents of authority, which had previously been questioned.

According to part B of the ISPS Code, the use of firearms on board ships, or in their proximities and in port facilities could represent special and important risks for security, especially with regard to certain dangerous or potentially dangerous substances and must be considered with utmost care. Should a Government decide that it is necessary to have armed personnel in these areas, then that Government must make sure that such personnel is duly authorised and that they have received the adequate training for the use of weapons and is aware of the specific risks for security that exist in such areas. If a Government authorises the use of firearms, it must give specific security guidelines on their use, The PFSP must contain specific indications on this matter, especially regarding its application to ships that transport dangerous or potentially dangerous substances.

Here the Code deals with security in the ample sense and in a generic fashion as the recipients of its provisions are States with a very complex and different port organisation as there are countries in which the port facilities are completely in private hands and others in which they are very controlled. The port organisations throughout the world are as many as countries and possibilities to render port services exist, including both public service and private service. We need go no further than to study the European ports.

According to Gonzalez Laxe and Gabriel and Pablo de Llano in their "*Economic analysis of the port system in Galicia*" there are the following types of ports in Europe:

   a) ports managed by the State,
   b) ports managed by municipal authorities,
   c) ports managed by autonomous authorities,
   d) entirely private ports.

The above mentioned authors refer to the difficulty of establishing a uniform organisational system within European policy. "The reasons are clear, the administration systems of the German. Belgian, Dutch and English ports are neither uniform nor are they regulated by Law, while the administrative regime of the main Spanish and Italian ports is maintained in a Law."

"...In the Netherlands most of the ports are municipal ports, administered directly by the City Hall or by a municipal body (such as in the case of the ports of Rotterdam and Amsterdam). In Belgium the ports of Anvers, Gand and Ostende are administered by the city halls either with a direct formula or through port authorities, while the port of Zeebrugge is managed by a private company made up of representatives from the region (65%), the town (31%) and a minority of private agents (3.6%). In Germany most of the ports are administered by the Länders (for example the ports of Emden, Cuxhaven, Hamburg or Bremen) and/or the city halls (Lubeck and Kiel) and there are no public entities in charge of the tasks that must be carried out by Port Authorities. Finally, in the United Kingdom there are three different categories: the ports managed by the local authorities (normally small ports with the exception of Portsmouth) and the oil ports of Sullum, Voe and Flotta; those managed by Trust (which are about one hundred independent establishments under the protection of a Law, a Royal Charter or a decision of a local authority) and are ports managed by the owner, the local community or the administrators of the Trust. They have the same independence as if they were managed like a private port but they are limited with reference to their capacity of debt. There are currently six ports managed by Trust, Clyde, Dundee, Forth, Medway, Tees & Hartlepool and Tilbury; and the third group are the private ports, whose main group is ABP (Associated British Port) which currently has 22 ports among which we can mention, Plymouth, Southampton, Hull, Grimsby, Cardiff, Newport y Lowestoft."

Once we have made this small digression as an example, the fact that harbour guards in Spain carry weapons or not does not mean that they are not carried in the Ports of General Interest, as the Security Forces and Corps are present and the harbour guards play a subordinate role to them in the field of public safety. But there would be no obstacle to this being so. Moreover, as the ports have started to carry out private security surveillance services under Law 23/92 of 30th July and that this trend is growing because of the ever growing number of private activities inside the docks through concessionary titles, many harbour guards have been shunned in this field by those who carry them and who are in similar fields of action.

If the Civil Guard gives service in the ports they must be aware of the obligations and preventions of the ISPS Code in this matter.

Paragraph 4. "The harbour guards and other personnel to whom the Port Authority entrusts policing functions within the service area of the port shall lend the Security Forces and Corps the assistance required to obtain the security objectives established in article 1 of the OL on the Protection of Public Security."

The Port Authority may not entrust policing functions to people who are not harbour guards, or pushing the same concept to the limit, personnel from the Port Authority itself but functions of another type, especially in defence of private property within the framework of the Private Security Law, but not of the police. This text needs correcting for the future.

Paragraph 4 continues: "In the same fashion, for the compliance of these objectives, the Port Authority may require the help of the Security Forces and Corps in accordance with article 4 of the mentioned Organic Law of the Protection of Public Safety."

It is obvious that this is the way it should be, but it would be necessary to establish a channel of communication and given that the Law does not provide for it, or for a better understanding, from the perspective of the ISPS Code and its demands, an action Protocol should be signed between the Civil Guard that has the functions of custody in the Ports and the Public Entity Ports of the State for this purpose.

It seems totally illogical and rather unreasonable that in the process of elaboration of the Port Facilities Security Plan at a local level, the organisations that have collaborated with the Public Entity Ports of the State and/or the Entity itself, have not taken into consideration the opinion of or involved the Civil Guard Forces deployed in the Port and its senior officers in the matter when, if there were a crisis of any kind, and especially one provoked by terrorism, they would be the first to take charge of the situation ignoring the provisions of the PFSP. At the moment this study was elaborated, many Civil Guards deployed in the ports did not know or were not aware of the existence of these Security Plans and they did not know the Port Facilities Security Officers in the Port.

The above is not just the responsibility of the Public Entity which took some initiatives in the matter through meetings; the Ministry of the Interior has also taken the matter of the Code with great calm and is taking its time in giving instructions in the matter. The Secretary of State has elaborated a Communication Protocol of Levels of Protection that it has sent to the port maritime organisation, but to date this has not reached those responsible for the custody of the ports.

Paragraph 5 states that, "notwithstanding the orders and instructions that the President of the Port Authority may issue, the immediate and direct management of all the surveillance and policing services in the service area of the port, will be exercised by the Director of the Port Authority. The Port Ordinances may regulate the regime of organisation and performances of the services."

There is no evidence that the Presidents or the Port Directors have received training in special police matters or in public safety, at least in general matters, although there are exceptions in the most elementary preventive levels. The figure of a person responsible for safety shall be created within the ports. This person shall have knowledge in the matter and shall be able to coordinate the PFSO of the different port facilities located in the Ports of General Interest.

Continuing with the Regulation Project, paragraph 6 states that:

"In accordance with the provisions of the Law of Ports of the State and the Merchant Navy and within the limits established in the current legislation, the harbour guards and other personnel authorised by the Port Authority may access the different facilities, ships or platforms located within the service area of the port, in order to carry out the inspection, surveillance and control tasks that the Law attributes to the Port Authorities."

This paragraph, without any further comments, could cause problems when the areas to be inspected could be the address or dwelling of a citizen. On many occasions certain parts of a ship constitute the home of an individual and the intimacy of the home constitutes a basic right which can only be removed with a legal authorisation or with the consent of the owner, as established in article 18 of our Carta Magna when it consecrates the inviolability of the home. The Spanish Law of Civil Procedure states in its article 545 that no-one may enter the home of a Spaniard or foreigner resident in Spain without their consent, except in the cases and in the manner specifically expressed in the laws.

Besides, due to their condition of merchant ships, subjected in many areas of activity to the legislation of the state of their flag, they must observe other provisions established in International Agreements on the matter and in our Spanish Law of Civil Procedure. In this manner, for the purpose of the above articles, article 554 considers national merchant ships, among others, as home. Article 561 states that "nor may they enter and register foreign merchant ships without the authorisation of the Captain or, if refused by the Captain, without that of the Consul of their country.

In foreign war ships, the absence of the authorisation of the Commander will be replaced by that of the Ambassador or Minister of the nation that they belong to."

These are always delicate questions of sovereignty although nowadays the concept of sovereignty is disappearing, in defence of the interests of the Port State, in many recent regulations, particularly in the area of the EU and related with the environment and port maritime security *Flag state control* is being replaced with *Port State Control* (PSC),

"Paragraph 7. The personnel of any surveillance and security service that can be established by the users of the port, either temporarily or permanently must have the prior authorisation of the Director of the Port Authority and as well as complying with its specific tasks, must ensure that this Regulation is complied with and lend their cooperation to the harbour guards and other agents of authority."

More than cooperation, which is between equals, perhaps the word *collaboration* should have been used as those who are in possession of the public function, by extension and order of the Port Authority are the harbour guards and the other private surveillance services carry out their activity subordinate to them.

We have reached the point in which the regulation becomes flexible in order to include private security in the field of security in matters relating to ports. On the other hand private security has been present in the port areas for several years. The possibility of these security services being contracted by companies that operate in the service area, and even by the Port Authorities themselves is regulated insofar as they are not given special police missions referred to in the OL of Protection of Public Safety.

If this is so, at least it seems that way in the text, it will be necessary to require that these private services have specific training and it will be necessary to specify which functions they are going to perform and how the coordination mechanisms are arbitrated; in any case if they must ensure that the Regulation is complied with it would be a good idea to be trained for the purpose and to require that they have knowledge about it. Private security personnel will normally carry out their duties in the limited areas of the concessionaries, looking after their facilities, goods and merchandise. To impose the obligation of ensuring compliance with the Regulation should be understood as being circumscribed to their area of action, because otherwise it would create more problems with this generic obligation that it could resolve.

4.5 Agents of Authority. The Doctrine

Following Rodríguez Devesa, the so called agents of authority can be of two types, as the CP of 1928 so correctly recognised. Some were auxiliary civil servants and subordinates and were not differentiated form those mentioned today in article 24.2 of the CP of 1995 regardless of the rank of the functions that they perform. "A public civil servant is considered as anyone who through an immediate provision of a Law or by election or when named by a competent authority that participates in the exercise of public functions."

"There are others who lend assistance to the authority, whether it be circumstantial or spontaneous or by obligation in virtue of their profession, without retribution from the State, to collaborate in a special way with the Police or security forces. In order to give them the penal tutelage that is granted to civil servants and the responsibilities they have to account for, it will be necessary to investigate whether, case by case, the circumstances required by paragraph 2 of article 24 of the CP have appeared and it will not suffice that in a Regulation or provision, with a lower rank than the Law, they are considered agents of authority.

The concept and the nature of the agent of authority of the harbour guards, which we defend here at this present moment, seeks a clear definition:

- between the extension of their public functions and their private functions,
- among the contradictory jurisprudence regarding said nature,
- in their contractual regime subjected to labour relations and not civil service ones
- to carry weapons or not.

4.6 Jurisprudence

However, the Courts have been recognising this penal protection on quite a frequent basis. Since Law 48/2003 was issued it is understood that, with the requisite of its recognition by Law removed, there should be no doubts in this respect. The acceptance of their condition as agents of authority should now be explained without conditions

Although it is prior to the recognition of Law 48/2003, we now comment a recent sentence of the Fourth Section of the Provincial Court of Valencia, of 30th June 1999 which, transcribed in its legal groundings for the purpose, states:

"THIRD.- Based on article 24 of the CP it must be concluded that the Port Authorities have control or their own jurisdiction in Law 62/97 and the previous 27/92 of Ports of the State and the Merchant Navy that attributes exclusive functions in relation with the port activity and in relation with matters subject to administrative powers, recognised by the Law of Protection and Public Safety. This is no more than the affirmation of the existence of authorities of a different nature, but of a common kind, and each of them has their own agents. And the harbour guards are those of the Port Authority.

FOURTH.- The consequence of this is what the accused did to them and which has been classified as offensive language deserves, as the appellant states…., the classification as a public order offence for not respecting and giving due consideration to agents of authority and in application of article 8 of the CP, should be sanctioned by article 634 of the CP…"

Another sentence of 9th July 1999, of the Third Section of the Provincial Court of Cadiz in resolving an appeal, denies them this condition, though we must say that the sentence is not very clear and does not analyse the question in depth. The facts, in summary, are as follows. An individual was inside the quay collecting abandoned fish when he was surprised by a harbour guard who asked him to abandon the premises. At the control gate he was told that he would have to leave the bag he was carrying with the fish. He refused and in the ensuing struggle he head-butted the harbour guard in the face. The guard fell to the ground and was briefly unconscious as a result of the violent contusion and suffered a 1 cm lacerated contused wound to the forehead from the impact of a tooth, a traumatic avulsion in the first left incisor of the upper arch and a fracture of the fifth metacarpal when falling on his hand. The wounds took 40 days to cure, during which time the harbour guard was unable to perform his usual work and required medical or surgical treatment consisting of exodontics and a dental implant immobilising the ferula for a month. Following the incident the accused showed remorse.

The Public Prosecutor lodged an appeal claiming the consideration of agent of authority for the harbour guard in order to obtain a stronger sanction, but the Court rejected it arguing that the concept of *agent of authority* has not to be compared with that of authority or that of public civil servant, as they are not a third type in the category which must be limited to the Security Forces when they are acting in the exercise of their functions as the High Court has repeatedly indicated. In sentence 13.12.93 it stated that there is no doubt in recent jurisprudential doctrine, even before Law 30.07.92. The negative doctrine of the condition of agents of authority has been maintained thus through a triple argument:

- the principle of law reserve
- the private nature of the function they perform
- the consideration of their functions as that of rendering complementary or auxiliary services of the state, regional or local Security Forces.

This sentence is severe, worrying and distressing for our interests in times when the wind that blow for public safety and the threat of terrorism should give the agents and their actions a minimum legal protection in the exercise of their functions because they are representing the coercive power of the State. These agents are its final cog and are faced, on a daily basis, with the most delicate, most violent and most visceral situations and must have protection from the institution and the laws. The sentence is even more worrying because it is based on another sentence of the High Court.

Specific recognition, recently included in Law 48/2003, must force a reconsideration of this position and criteria of the Courts with respect to the Special Police in general and to the harbour guards, in particular.

The sentence of 18.11.92 states that "agents of authority are people who, by legal provision or when named by someone with the competence to do so, is in charge of keeping public order and of the safety of people and objects. This task is reserved mainly for the State Security Forces…"

The sentence can be criticised because it does not differentiate harbour guards from private security and does not consider that they offer public services. In our opinion it does not differentiate the three large areas of security; public safety, special police and private security. The harbour guards should be found a place among the special police.

4.7 Security Forces in the Port. Functions

When we stated that the harbour guards, as special police, performed security functions in the field of the service area of the Ports of General Interest, we tried to establish the limit of these duties. Evidently the requirements of public safety clearly go beyond the functions of the harbour guards and must be performed by the Security Forces and Corps as can be easily seen throughout this document.

a) The Civil Guard in the ports

Organic Law 2/86, of 13th March, on Security Forces and Corps, entrusts the custody of coasts, ports and airports, among other missions, to the Civil Guard. In the future, the Civil Guard must consider increasing their current presence which is very limited to the fiscal missions (reduced today by the suppression of the internal frontiers within the EU) that they carry out in the ports and take a step forward as they have done in the airports to strengthen and take on the port security missions which the Law undoubtedly assigns them, notwithstanding the missions of the port police that have to act as auxiliaries to this Force in the duties they perform.

The Law does not differentiate the custody missions in ports and airports when assigning them to the Civil Guard. Perhaps the large volume of travellers that our tourism produces led those responsible in the Civil Guard, given the limitations of their staff for new duties, to giving preferential treatment to the airports which is logical and especially in recent times in which the activity of the ports, with a few exceptions, has not been so high.

In the immediate future those responsible for the police forces must not forget that the ports are not only the destination of most cargo but that in this modern day of leisure activities cruise traffic will become very important in these early days of the century. This traffic will require police response in the field of the struggle against radical terrorism, the custody of the facilities, the security of people and of goods, the struggle against irregular immigration and against the huge threats posed by drug dealing and to a lesser extent by smuggling.

Faced with the serious threats of the most radical Islamic terrorism,, a National Security Plan for Civil Aviation was elaborated for the airports. It was issued in February 2004 though, being a security plan it was limited in its distribution in order to preserve its confidentiality. This document could be an example. The ISPS Code can now be the opportunity to advance regulations in the port area, regulations such as the Regulation of Exploitation and Policing, leading to the elaboration of a global regulation that addresses the development of the global security functions based on the Law of Ports, the OL of Public Safety, and OL 2/86 of Security Forces.

Having said that we move on to briefly analyse OL 2/86 on which the above arguments are based and in so far as it is applicable here.

"Public safety is the exclusive competence of the State. Its maintenance corresponds to the Government of the Nation (1º.1)"

The Constitutional Court has made several declaration on this matter, and admits the existence of Regional and Local Police Forces as the only exception to this statement, when the corresponding Autonomous Statutes so establish.

"The members of the Security Forces and Corps shall adapt their action to the principle of reciprocal cooperation and they shall be coordinated through the bodies that this Law established for this purpose (3)."

"They all have the duty of lending the necessary assistance to the Security Forces and Corps for the investigation and persecution of crimes...(4º.1)"

"The people and entities that exercise functions of surveillance, security or custody referring to the personnel and goods or services of a public or private nature have the special obligation to help and collaborate, at all times, with the Security Forces and Corps. (4º.2)"

The Port Authorities, especially through the harbour guards, exercise functions of security, surveillance and custody referring to the goods and services of a public nature such as the Points of General Interest and the goods and facilities contained in them in certain cases.

b) Competences. Security Forces and Corps.

The State Security Forces and Corps shall exercise their competences in accordance with the following territorial distribution (Art. 11.2):

> "The National Police Force (hereinafter NPF) in the capitals of provinces and in the municipal areas and urban areas that the Government determines.
>
> The Civil Guard shall exercise them in the rest of the national territory and in its territorial sea."

A first assignation of spatial competences is contemplated, preserving the missions of criminal investigation and obtaining information that any of the Corps might carry out in all the national territory.

For an optimal use of the means, the Ministry of the Interior may order any of the Corps missions assigned to the other Corps. These decisions will be adopted most of the times by the Government Delegates.

But, apart from this spatial distribution, a *material* distribution of competences is established (Article 12). They will be exercised by the NPF.

> Controlling Spanish nationals and foreigners entering and leaving national territory. Those established in legislation regarding immigration, refuge and asylum, extradition, expulsion, emigration and immigration.

In our port environment, surveillance should be strengthened on the incipient trickling of the selective irregular immigration of people who travel in merchant boats and who, in a reduced number and sometimes in coexistence with some component of the ship crews, arrive in the ports.

This is also an easy way for the introduction of terrorist elements or to disembark secretly in our ports on a stop over. This would make it necessary to increase police control, always according to the availability of budgets and staff.

It is known that the internationalisation of maritime transport in recent years has come about with the changes of property and the management of the ships, the creation of new registrations, technical advances and contracting crews from different cultures that do not always speak the same language.

More than 1.2 million marines work on ships with more than 100 tonnes or expect to embark on them. Two thirds of them are form Asia, There is a clear tendency to contract seafarers from developing countries. Among the main countries that provide people to go to sea are China, the Republic of Korea and the Philippines.

A growing number of marines are also being contracted from Poland and the Russian Federation. Many seafarers work on board ships that are not registered in their country of origin which means that on occasions there are problems of communication and misunderstandings among them that can put the security of the ship or the cargo in danger. The accessibility of Western countries for these crews is no less important with it being the main destination of their cargos and the ease with which they can skip controls once they are in the port on board the ship.

The Security Forces undoubtedly do the best they can in their missions but they must give priorities according to the assigned human and material resources. The missions will have to be profiled, as will the human and material resources, and police units and methods will be developed to be efficient to give reasonable responses to the policing problems in the Ports in a general manner and the port facilities affected by the Code in particular, by linking cooperation systems that make it possible to take advantage of all the elements of security available including the harbour guards and the private security guards.

According to OL 2/86, the following missions, among other, will be exercised by the Civil Guard:

- Preserving the State Prosecution and actions aimed at avoiding and persecuting smuggling.
- Custody of the means of communication on land, coasts, frontiers, ports, airports and centres and facilities whose interest require it.

The Civil Guard is assuming the responsibility of surveillance and custody in security matters in the ports which, due to the different circumstances and in line with the rhythms they may impose, has to be developed in the future. This will probably happen because of the final deployment of their Maritime Service and the re-adaptation of the coast guard services and of the old tax services in the ports in one single unit. To combine and coordinate these services and to have the aerial surveillance tools for a best possible use in the maritime area, will mean that all those organs with a power of decision will be kept busy over the coming years, This task will be undertaken in the short / medium term by the new Civil Office for Tax and Frontiers and we hope and wish that they do it successfully.

4.8 Maritime Service of the Civil Guard

On the other hand, RD 246/91 of 22nd February regulates the Maritime Service of the Civil Guard and assigns it functions in Spanish maritime waters of legal police, of a governmental nature, of public order. and of tax and administration, as well as those military functions that are established. The Ports of General Interest are located in internal waters, surveillance area and are the responsibility of the Civil Guard of the Sea.

As for the functions of the Civil Guard at sea and in the ports, article 13 of the LPEMM, in compliance with the stipulations Organic Law of Security Forces and Corps states that:

"Reservation of areas.- The state Administration may reserve spaces of maritime-land public domain for the purpose of naval facilities and port areas that are required to comply with the objectives that the current legislation attributes to the Civil Guard that will be excluded from the scope of application of this Law."

Article 26, paragraph e) states that the following functions correspond to Ports of the State in order to meet general objectives:

"To define the technical and economical criteria for the application of the general provisions in security matters, tariffs, works and acquisitions, exploitation of the port services, concessions and authorisations relating to port space and of the economical and commercial relationship with the users. All actions in matters regarding security will be carried out in collaboration with the Ministry of the Interior."

Following these references, and others that could be made to the effect, if the Regulation Project is approved, as it appears in the draft of December 2000, we will have lost a great opportunity to address what Port security should be, of how to link the different responsibilities, of which channels there are and how to deal with the co-operation, co-ordination and collaboration among the different police in exercising their functions, from an understanding of what the specific missions of each police force are and of those that correspond to the harbour guard.

In relation to the collaboration among ministries, paragraph 2 of the 4th Additional Provision of the Law of Ports states that:

"The Ministry of Public Works and Transportation may request the collaboration of the Ministry of the Interior in its maritime services[7] when so required by the general interest needs of the civil marine, of the security of people or objects or of maritime transport."

An agreement in this respect must be reached in the not too distant future between the Ministry of the Interior and the Ministry of Development to find a final design for the model of police in the sea once the deployment of the Civil Guard in Coasts and Ports is concluded. This will provide a better position to attend the responsibilities that the legislation attributes to this Corps in the Ports and in Spanish maritime waters.

Insofar as the ports are customs areas, other missions correspond to the Customs Services assisted by the Civil Guard as State Tax Guard and for the control of goods subject to clearance.

4.9 Public safety. Public Order

We should not forget that the large ports are mainly inside the cities that surround them which means that for practical reasons in these places the NPF normally takes care of public safety in the strict sense of the expression inside the port areas, though in this respect nothing from a legal point of view prevents the Civil Guard from carrying out these competences. In any case they will have less agents dedicated to public safety and at times although these competences are very important or are not well

---

[7] Today the maritime service of the Ministry of the Interior is the Maritime Service of the Civil Guard.

defined it is necessary to attend certain criteria of efficiency or effectiveness given that when it comes down to it, what the citizens and the institutions really want is a solution to their problems.

We sincerely believe that the distribution of competences on the Ports is a pending subject and that some day the Ministry of the Interior will have to resolve it. All of this goes without citing the possible competences of the Local Police which they claim in some way and which are not clearly defined, given that the ports are the balconies of large cities and an integral part of the towns.

The idea, which has hardly been exposed, would make for a monographic study. We believe the moment has come to define and clarify the different police competences in Spanish ports of general interest, especially in the service areas, as the current ambiguity has led to each port, in practice, developing a different police model and it will continue to do so.

Some ports have developed and encouraged port police to the point that, in fact, they have been compared to the State Security Forces; in others, on the other hand., the police function has been absent in recent years and the Agents of Authority (as recognised by almost all of the obsolete Port Ordinances and the Projects of the future Regulation and Ordinances) with the title of security guard have been performing merely administrative functions, controlling unloading activities, acting as water carriers, controlling the entrance to the service areas, etc.

Legislation, including the most recent, insists on attributing the Civil Guard with the custody and surveillance of the ports. RD 1599/2004 of 2nd July which develops the basic organic structure of the Ministry of the Interior established that, reporting to the General Director, the General Deputy Directorate of Operations, in the person of a General Officer of the Civil Guard in the situation of active service, is responsible, in accordance with the guidelines issued by the General Director, for the management, promotion and coordination of the service of the units of the Civil Guard. The following units report to the General Deputy Subdirectorate of operations:

"The Civil Office for Tax and Frontiers under the orders of a General Officer of the Civil Guard in the situation of active service, to whom it corresponds the organisation and management of the State tax security, the actions aimed at avoiding and persecuting smuggling, drug dealing and other illicit traffic, the custody and surveillance of the coasts, frontiers, ports, airports and territorial sea, and in this area, the control of irregular immigration."

4.9.1 Private security and the Ports of General Interest

Throughout this document we have discussed the Spanish port organisation model. The main worry here is security in the Ports of General Interest but we must not forget other public terminals that are affected by the ISPS Code. Thus, many ports assigned to the Autonomous Communities are affected because their port facilities are affected by the requirements of the Code, which as we know, is applied to ships which are dedicated to international voyages:

- Passenger ships, including high speed passenger ships,
- Cargo ships, including high speed ships, with a total tonnage equal to or above 500.
- Mobile drilling units at high sea
- The port facilities that render services to such ships dedicated to international voyages.

This does not apply to war ships, auxiliary naval units or other ships dedicated to governmental services that are not of a commercial nature.

Some coastal Autonomous Communities have maintained figures similar to the harbour guards to perform certain regional port administrational functions.

The figures will not give the response required by the Code in matters of security and will offer a more precarious security though it is true that the traffic that enters and leaves the ports assigned to the Autonomous Communities is steady traffic, which at first sight do not appear to be the preferential targets of international terrorism, but the moment things are taken for granted, the likelihood of them becoming a terrorist target increases.

These ports must have a security system, either directly or through concessionaries, to give an adequate response to the needs of the ISPS Code. Thus a PFSP had been elaborated and its PFSO has been nominated.

Apart from those which have completely autonomic police that decide to use them in these duties with a specific nature, which is quite unlikely, the normal thing is that they contract the services private security companies. These formats of security and surveillance are not new in the port area: the Ports of General Interest themselves have often contracted them or have imposed their contracting on certain concessionaries. We have already seen that the Regulation Project opened the way to this security format on certain occasions.

Other port facilities, concessionaries of port public domain spaces, manage large volumes, normally of liquid bulks, such as the traffic of ships with oil, gas or chemical products which could potentially be sensitive targets for terrorism in general and radical Islamic terrorism especially. These port facilities handle enormous volumes of inflammable or dangerous products that make the PPs or the POs essential elements for security. This security is normally contracted from private companies at the same time as they keep standby specialists in matters relating to fires or to the fight against emissions or uncontrolled waste.

These surfaces and facilities which are normally operated as private spaces must not be separated either from the Regulations of Police Port corresponding to the port in which they are located and to a greater extent if they are all rolled into one.

The Regulation of Exploitation and Policing must include a chapter dedicated to the terminals *managed* by concessionaries that consign certain private ships and goods, but which being strategic objectives, may be attacked by terrorism and must be subjected to a special surveillance, not only a specific surveillance but one carried out by all those responsible for safety matters. As an example we could quote the large oil platforms as they represent a threat, especially those that are located right in the heart of cities, because of the enormous repercussion of the management of these materials as dangerous goods.

The Port Ordinances will make it possible to adapt the provisions of the Regulation to the specific terminal and its problems. In any case everything related to the use of the public domain must be regulated, in the Regulation of Policing: this includes the arrival, departure and manoeuvring of ships and everything related to their anchoring, any type of movement that is required inside the port areas, loading and unloading operations and docking and stays if they have a repercussion on the operation of the port or if they interfere in their traffic, underwater work and provisions relating to the prevention of contamination in the marine environment and provisions on the handling of dangerous goods.

Very frequently the anchor areas will be controlled by those responsible for the port and the Security Forces who shall also render the services they consider appropriate according to the threats and the factors that are being contemplated in each specific case and its initiative.

Further attention will be paid to the Law of Ports and Law 48/2003 in another part of the document to specify other special obligations.

4.10 Training and practices in port security matters in the ISPS

Given the specificity of the services not only in the ports in general but in the port terminals as well as in the requirements of the provisions of the Code, it seems inevitable that it will be necessary to train all security professionals, no matter what kind they are and regardless of whether they carry out private or public functions that the Code does not distinguish.

One of the tasks and responsibilities of the PFSO will be, by order of the ISPS Code, that of guaranteeing that the personnel responsible for the protection of the port facility has received adequate training.

The PFSO and the security personnel of the port facility must have adequate knowledge and have received training, taking into account the guidelines that appear in part B of the Code.

The personnel of the port facility that carry out specific security tasks must know their functions and responsibilities, as they appear in the PFSP and have the capacity to carry out the tasks assigned to them.

In order to guarantee the efficient implementation of the security of the plant facility drills will be carried out at adequate intervals.

The PFSO shall guarantee the efficient coordination and implementation of the PFSP through an adequate participation in the mentioned drills, taking into consideration the guidelines given in part B of the Code.

There is no doubt that it will be an added requisite within the conditions for contracting those responsible for providing the service, normally security guards, that they know these specific missions in port security matters or otherwise, make a commitment to do so before starting the service.

On the other hand, the PFSO must have the required knowledge and receive training related with some or all of the following aspects, as appropriate:

- The administration of maritime protection.
- Related international agreements, codes and recommendations.
- Related governmental legislation and regulations.
- Responsibilities of other security organisations.
- Port facility security evaluation methodology.

- Recognition and inspection methods for the protection of ships and port facilities.
- Operations and conditions of the ship and the port.
- Security measures for the ship and the port facility.
- Preparedness and response to emergencies and contingencies.
- Teaching techniques for the training and instruction in maritime security including security procedures.
- Processing of confidential information on security and channelling all the information on security.
- Knowledge of trends and current threats to security.
- Recognition and detection of weapons and dangerous substances or devices.
- Recognition, without any discrimination, of the characteristics and behaviour patterns of the people who could be a threat to security.
- Techniques used to avoid security measures.
- Security equipment and systems and their operational limits.
- Auditing, inspection, control and observation methods.
- Methods to perform physical checks and non invasive inspections.
- Security drills and practices, including those drills and practices coordinated with the ships.
- Evaluation of the security drills and practices.

All the personnel of the port facility (including the security guards as well of course, which is extensive to the harbour guards that have security tasks assigned to them) must know about and receive training related to some or all of the following aspects:

- Knowledge of trends and current threats to security.
- Recognition and detection of weapons and dangerous substances or devices.
- Recognition of the characteristics and behaviour patterns of the people who could be a threat to security.
- Techniques used to avoid security measures.
- Techniques for crowd management and control.
- Security related communications.
- Equipment performance and security systems.
- Equipment testing and maintenance and the security systems.
- Inspection, control and observation techniques.
- Methods for registering people, their personal belongings, equipment, cargo and the ship's supplies.

The rest of the personnel of the port facility shall have sufficient knowledge of the provisions corresponding to the PFSP and be familiar with them, with respect to some or all of the following aspects:

- Meaning of each of the levels of security and subsequent demands.
- Recognition and detection of weapons and dangerous substances or devices.
- Recognition of the characteristics and behaviour patterns of the people who could be a threat to security.
- Techniques used to avoid security measures.

5. The Law of Ports and the Regulation of Exploitation and Policing. The future.

5.1 Law 48/03 of Economic Regime and of the Rendering of Services in the Ports of General Interest and the Regulation of Exploitation and Policing

Law 48/03, of 26th November, of Economic Regime and the Rendering of Services of the Ports of General Interest, males several references to the Regulation known as the Regulation of Exploitation and Policing, which we transcribe below:

In the "Statement of Reasons" it states that "chapter V is dedicated to the authorisations of occupation of the port public domain by the Port Authority, establishing two classes of authorisations. On the one hand, the use of fixed port facilities by ships, passengers and goods which will be governed by the Regulation of Exploitation and Policing and the Port Ordinances. On the other hand, the occupation of the public domain of the port with removable buildings or facilities, or without them, for a period of no more than three years."

These relate to what we could call the organisational part which would correspond to the exploitation and to the public domain of the port.

However, in so far as it will be regulated, in the future, the objective will be the use of the permanent port facilities by ships, passengers and goods, these regulations would be necessarily affected by the demands of the ISPS Code and must make it possible to reconcile everything in the regulations with the contents of the corresponding PFSP. This will be dealt with in more detail in another part of the study.

Article 24 refers to the fee for goods and states that "in the exceptional case that the occupation of the goods handling area is authorised, the quantities established in this paragraph will be applicable.

The definition of the transit and handling areas, into which the areas of commercial use are divided, which will be carried out in accordance with the stipulations of the Regulation of Exploitation and Policing and in the Port Ordinances, will be approved by the Board of Administration of the corresponding Port Authority."

To legally define the transit and handling areas has to be one of the contents of the Regulation in its organisational part of port exploitation. Commercial uses, when they refer to occupying port spaces and the movement of goods, supplies and provisions, are within the application of the Code which makes it necessary to integrate the stipulations of the future Regulation with this activity and more specifically the PFSP must give an answer to all of this.

According to article 58 general port services are those common services carried out by the Port Authority and which the port users can enjoy without the need to request them.

In the service area of the port, among others, the Port Authorities shall provide the surveillance, security and policing services in the common areas, notwithstanding the competences that correspond to other Administrations.

Article 59, when referring to the rendering of general services states that they will be managed by the Port Authority and that "these services shall be provided in accordance with the technical regulations criteria established in the Regulation of Exploitation and Policing and in the Port Ordinances, by Port Authority personnel, notwithstanding that they can be delegated to third parties in certain cases when security is not put at risk or when they do not involve the exercise of authority."

Continuing along the lines of the argument at hand, it seems that it can be deduced that the general services that involve safety related activities or the exercise of authority cannot be delegated to third parties. Despite everything, the circle of people involved in the security activities or those that imply the exercise of authority must be limited to the Services of the Port Police and to those directly responsible in the line of command, as agents of authority, act in representation of the Authority because that is where they receive their name and in whose name they act. This type of services must respond to the demands of hierarchy and order. The word order is used in two meanings, that of "establishing order" and that of "issuing an order."

In another part it was commented that compliance with the regulations and orders, when they are required by the agents of the Port Authority, imply more demands and responsibilities for the those subjected to these requirements or orders, than if the instructions were demanded of them by other port personnel who is not invested with this authority, or if they were, when the people subjected to the requirements were not aware of such a circumstance. The uniform, in principle, is an important sign of the presence of an authority or of an agent of authority.

The external signs of the functions of authority generally predispose the citizen towards obedience provided that said authority is exercising its functions; on the other hand it makes citizens aware that if they contravene the indications they will incur more severe administrative breaches, and can even become involved in penal offences or crimes such as disobedience, insults and resisting authority which are offences that are specifically reflected to protect those who exercise public functions.

Those affected by and subjected to regulations are all those people or entities that carry out any type of activity, or who render any kind of service in the service area of the Ports of General Interest, as well as people, ships, floating devices, vehicles, machinery, facilities, materials and goods that are to be found, albeit in transit, in the areas affected.

Article 62 deals with the use of the basic services:

"1. The Basic services shall be provided at the request of the users by authorised companies.

However, the use of the service of piloting will be mandatory when so determined by the maritime Administration in accordance with the provisions of the applicable legislation. Besides, the Regulation of Exploitation and Policing shall, for the purpose of maritime security, establish the obligatory use of other techno-nautical services in accordance with the conditions and characteristics of the port infrastructures, with the size of the ship and the nature of the cargo being transported, as well as the weather and sea conditions.

2. For operational and security reasons, the port ordinances approved by the Port Authorities shall establish complementary regulations and specific conditions of use of the basic services as well as the geographical area to which they extend.

3. When the use of the service is not obligatory, the Port Authorities may impose the use of techno-nautical services if because of exceptional circumstances they believe that the operation, operability or security of the port is at risk. Nevertheless, in such circumstances and for maritime security reasons, the Harbour Master may declare that the services are obligatory."

Article 64 contemplates the regime for access to the basic services in order to establish the conditions of access to the service laid down in the conditions. They must be transparent, non discriminatory, objective, adequate and proportionate and must guarantee, among other objectives, the protection of the interests of the Port Authority and of public safety.

On the other hand, in addressing the regime of use of the port public domain, article 95 explains that "the use of the port public domain shall be governed by the provisions of this Law, of the Regulation of Exploitation and Policing and of the corresponding Port Ordinances, which shall establish the areas open to general use and if applicable, free. Anything not covered in the above provisions shall be governed by coastal legislation."

The message transmitted by this article implies a huge innovation with respect to the previous regulations. Its content must be agreed upon, at least during its regulatory development, with other organisms and entities that have their own jurisdiction in the port. One gets the impression that the most recent reforms of the Law of Ports ignores the fact that a port is also a customs, a frontier, an area where services such as external health, Security Forces and Corps, etc. carry out their activity. Opening the ports to the cities is something that is generally accepted. It is true that the limits, which were stricter in the days when there was more intervention in the ports, are disappearing. This should not lead us to the mistake of thinking that it suffices to keep certain areas safe, required now by the ISPS Codes, areas that we call port facilities and which we give a Plan (PFSP) and a responsible officer (PFSO) and that the rest of the port is an open area free from any control or where security controls are very lenient.

There are ships that do not meet the required tonnage and other international and piloting routes that reach ports that are not subjected to the ISPS Code, at least for the moment because new demands will be coming from the community Regulation and Directives which are close to publication. The open areas should not be the result of a mathematical operation that consists of subtracting the port facilities defined with fences from the whole surface area of the port.

We wish to insist on this point in the light of the rapidly changing port legislation that we have perceived in recent times; the request for more competences for the Ports of General Interest, if not their transfer, by the Autonomous Communities once they have designated the President of the Port

Authority and have determined the final composition of the Board of Administrators; increasingly stricter security rules for certain port spaces at the same time as the ports are opened to the surrounding spaces. Security Boards should be created in the Ports in which all public interests are present with responsibilities, attributed by Law for them.

In this ever changing environment, everything goes so quickly that some Port Authorities, with the best of intentions but due to the pressures and the speed of the changes, open and close accesses, define areas for pedestrians, etc., without seeking the opinion of the other institutions involved especially regarding that which affects security. In matters of security, a body is required for exchanging ideas and reflecting and reaching common ground where all the interests present can contribute with their different points of view. A Security Board would respond to all of these needs and could, without reducing the flexibility of the operation of the port areas, coordinate other very important demands and responsibilities.

Article 99 refers to the types of authorisations of the Port Authority: "the use of permanent port facilities by ships, passengers and goods, which shall be governed by the Regulation of Exploitation and Policing and the corresponding Port Ordinances."

Several comments have already been made on this subject as a reference is made to these matters in the "Description of Motives" of Law 48/2003.

Paragraph 5 of Article 106 states that the concession or authorisation of docking facilities shall include that corresponding to the corresponding handling area, notwithstanding the fact that, exceptionally and for reasons derived from port exploitation or that insufficient port facilities are available, when the Port Authority grants the corresponding administrative title or afterwards, it shall impose the obligatory use of the facilities in concession or authorisation in favour of third party basic port service suppliers. In this case, the beneficiaries shall pay the corresponding tariff to the holder of the concession or authorisation. This must be established with criteria of objectivity, transparency and without discrimination and may not exceed the maximum amount approved by the Port Authority in the corresponding title: "The Regulation of Exploitation and Policing shall determine the objective reasons derived from port exploitation or from the availability of insufficient docking facilities that justify the obligatory use in favour of third party basic port service suppliers."

The Twelfth Additional Provision also addresses the Regulation of Exploitation and Policing:

"The mentions made in Law 27/21992, of 24th November, on State Ports and the Merchant Navy to the Regulation of Service and Policing of the ports will be understood as being made to the Regulation of Exploitation and Policing of the ports."

It seems that this definition of the Regulation is consolidated after several attempts to give it a title. The Thirteenth Additional Provision acquires an extraordinary relevance when, in reference to the Port Police, it states that:

"1. The functions of special police, described in article 4.1 of Organic Law 1/1992 of 21st February, on the Protection of Public Safety, attributed to the Port Authority by the Law of Ports of the State and the Merchant Navy, correspond to their Board of Administration.

2. These functions shall be carried out in the manner determined by the Regulation of Exploitation and Policing by the harbour guards and other personnel of the Port Authority, duly qualified and registered in the Police Service, for the purpose of which they shall be considered as agents of authority of the Port Administration in exercising the powers of port police as established in the Law of Ports of the State and the Merchant Navy, notwithstanding the obligation of collaborating at all times with the Security Forces and Corps."

There are other references to the ordinances in Law 48/2003. In article 129, it states that "the previous contingency plan shall form part of the port ordinances.

The availability of these means shall be required by the Port Authority in order to authorise the rendering of the services and the operation of the port facilities included in the previous paragraph."

Paragraphs 2 and 3 of article 132 make reference to the ordinances:

"2. In accordance with the provisions of the current legislation on the prevention and control of emergencies, each Port Authority shall elaborate an internal emergency plan for each port that it manages, which, once approved in accordance with the provisions of the applicable regulations, shall form part of the port ordinances.

3. Following a favourable report of the Ministry of the Interior and of the autonomous body with competences in matters relating to public safety on those aspects that are of its competence, each Port Authority shall elaborate a plan for the protection of ships, passengers and goods in the port areas against antisocial and terrorist acts which, once approved in accordance with the provisions of the applicable regulations, shall form part of the port ordinances."

Here is the crux of the problem that we are addressing which, in short, is going to make it possible to transfer the demands of this generic plan and of those more specific ones required by the ISPS Code to the Port Ordinances. With respect to the protection of ships resolutions will have to be made that are compatible with the demand of the ships and compatible with their respective Ship Security Plans (SSP). These measures shall be complemented with the coordination between the Ship Security Officer (SSO) and the Port Facilities Security Officer (PFSO) in those cases of traffic required by the Code.

The above is written such that it could lead to confusion. Previously the port security plans were reported by the Civil Guard and by the National Police Force when they were affected, in accordance with the distribution of competences that corresponds to each force in the port area. Law 48/2003 when including this precept, especially in paragraph 3 is undoubtedly thinking about the forthcoming provisions of the ISPS Code.

The interlocutor of the Port Authorities should not be the Ministry of the Interior. The interlocutor of the Ministry of the Interior should be the Ministry of Development. The interlocutor of the Port Authorities should the Chief Commander of the Civil Guard and if applicable, the Provincial Police Chief. The favourable report of the Ministry of the Interior which is understood should be the local police authorities mentioned in the argument being presented here should not be prior. The competences in public safety matters correspond exclusively to the State and are held and exercised by the Ministry of the Interior, which means that in any case its intervention on matters of security will not be prior, but shall be to revise the contents of the plans: not altogether of course but in the part that refers to security. The situation is such because article 4 of OL 2/86 and 1/92 say so.

The local port authorities must be in a position to provide useful points of view for the safety plans. This is especially the case of the Chief Commanders of the Civil Guard, thanks to their geographical proximity and knowledge of the current problems, as this Corps has offices inside all the ports and the responsibility for their custody and surveillance falls on them aside from performing their duties as State Tax Guard in the customs offices.

When in the hypothesis of the most dangerous work, which we all hope will never happen, the Ministry of the Interior, through the Secretary of State for Security, will have to adopt a level 3 in a port facility, it might be that the forces that have intervene in the first place to cordon off the area or neutralise a threat are those that are nearest the port. According to this article they will not know the provisions of the Plan, or those of the PFSP which seems rather pointless and unreasonable.

This Plan, which will have many similarities with the PFSP, has more content and a more ample space of application, as it will affect all the surface area of the port, while the others will be limited to the interface of the ship with the port facility and there could be several of them. This Plan will be unique. It will have to include the different specifications of the various PFSP that are affected by the measures of this Plan which will obviously contain more generic provisions.

5.2 Law 27/92 and the Port Regulation

Most references to security and to the Regulation are in Law 27/92 so we shall proceed to analyse it.

Article 26 addresses the function of the Port Authorities. We refer to those of interest for our objectives regarding security.

"e. To define the criteria for the application of the general provisions in matters regarding security, works and acquisitions and economical and commercial relationships with the users.

Actions related to security matters will be carried out in collaboration with the Ministry of the Interior and when applicable, with the corresponding organs of the competent Autonomous Communities for the protection of people and goods and for maintaining public safety.

m. Having completed the process established in article 106, elaborate the General Regulation of Exploitation and Policing and subject it to the approval of the Ministry of Development, and report on the conformity of the Port Ordinances with the Ordinance model included in said Regulation."

This precept insists on placing the interlocution of the Port Authorities with the Ministry of Development (considered excessive). The proximity to the ships and to the problem will mean that the Security Forces and Corps are in an ideal situation to respond to these needs. Otherwise, the Ministry of the Interior will have to delegate these functions in the General Directorate of the Civil Guard which has Offices in the proximities of all the Ports of General Interest. This is how it used to be, but since the implementation of the requirements of the Code, to date these necessary co-ordinations have not yet been distributed locally.

The expression that brings in entities from outside the Ministry of the Interior with the formula "when applicable, with the corresponding organs of the competent Autonomous Communities for the protection of people and goods and for maintaining public safety" is quite precise because, although the Civil Guard is in charge of the custody and surveillance of all the Ports of general Interest in Spain, other integral police forces are present around the port areas and they have duties relating to security, especially in the Basque Country and in Catalonia.

With regard to paragraph m), it would be equally interesting to listen to the Security Forces, both in the Regulation and in the Ordinances, not in matters of exploitation but in those regarding policing.

The collaboration required by the regulation of the harbour guards and other personnel that provide security services in OL 1/92 and 2/86 with the Security Forces and Corps makes it recommendable to specify how far they should go in these security missions and in the prevention of crimes and offences.

According to article 37.i the Port Authorities shall "report the general Regulation project of exploitation and policing of the ports, and elaborate and approve the corresponding port ordinances with the proceedings and requisites established in article 106, as well as make sure they are complied with."

Article 114 typifies minor breaches:

"Minor breaches are those actions or omissions which do not have the consideration of serious breach or very serious breach because of their importance or the extent of the damage caused and are typified in one of the following cases:

1. Regarding the use of the port and its facilities.
Non-compliance with the provisions established in the regulation of exploitation and policing of the port."

Traditionally and for practical reasons, the Law of Ports, at least in questions of sanctioning, has several blank precepts and several rules of remission. Law 27/92 has been in force for 14 years now but to date no General Regulation of Ports has been developed in a Royal Decree which means that the amplitude of some precepts, remissions to other rules and regulations and ambiguities may go against legal safety. In matters relating to sanctioning, and without breaching the principle of legality, they may particularise and moderate the application of the regulations and this is their main function.

When article 114.1 refers to the breaches relating to the use of the port and to the activities that take place therein, a very wide field of activities, it remits to non-compliances with the requirements of the Regulation.

The power of issuing Regulations, Ordinances and Orders that some authorities retain and which is very significant in the area of local Administration, for the better performance of their functions and is attributed by the legislation of the sector, must not be ignored and less still allowed to be lost. It is an instrument that is usually applied in the field of the most common minor breaches and allows the immediate Authority, in this case the Board of Administration, to exercise a power and a competence in sanction related matters on a daily basis, for small non-compliances or requirements without much violence and to act in a firm manner in preventing more serious breaches.

In light of the wide field of activity of the Regulation of Exploitation and Policing and the Ordinances in matters relating to ports, if as we have defended in this document because we consider it would be useful, the Regulation is given the status of Royal Decree and if, in order to highlight the non-compliances referred to in the Law, a detailed and extensive process for typifying minor breaches related to the expected behaviours is included, this would enable the Port Authority and its agents, the harbour guards, who are in charge of controlling and monitoring these typified breaches, to have at hand a precise and detailed list, a table of breaches and sanctions, for all those foreseeable actions and their possible legal consequences, which would in turn enable them, following the corresponding processes, to impose small sanctions.

Insisting on the fact that the Regulation and the Ordinances should have their own sanctioning regime may seem a little like a personal campaign. Every port Regulation to date has had a sanctioning regime and what is more, the current Community Regulation 735/2004, whose provisions have a direct effect and immediate applicability, states in article 14 that: "the member States shall guarantee that efficient, proportionate and dissuasive sanctions are introduced for not observing this Regulation." Article 18 of the Directive Project, requires that the member States apply efficient, proportionate and dissuasive sanctions in the case of non-compliance with the provisions of the Directive.

The port area is a working space which means that the sanctioning regime is there to try to avoid non-compliances that interfere in the everyday life of the rest of the users, deteriorate installations or which imply non-compliance with the clauses and conditions of the powers granted to concessionaries therein. On many occasions it will suffice to issue a simple recommendation to redirect behaviours that are not accepted or are prohibited by the Regulation, but there will be other times when a small sanction does not constitute a serious problem and it can be seen as an exemplary correction because of the obvious effect that any action of this type will have in such a small area where everyone knows each other. In any case, the sanctioning power in the ports requires a prudent use of coherence, balance and opportunity.

For more serious non-compliances, there is the list of serious and very serious breaches within the Law itself. In this aspect it would be convenient for it to have its own sanctioning Regulation, apart from the powers of ordinance of the Regulation of Exploitation and Policing that have their own area:

"2. With regard to the activities subjected to prior authorisation or concession or provided under contract.

Non-compliance with the regulations of exploitation and policing of the port, of the General Regulation of Piloting and other regulations that regulate port activities."

The other regulations will be related to dangerous goods, the environment, quality,.. that are in force or which are to be put into practice in the future.

"5. Breaches relating to the contamination of the marine environment. Non-compliance with the regulations or the non observance of the prohibitions contained in the policing regulations for ports or other waters on keeping the waters clean or common uses of the maritime environment."

This has always been a matter that some port Authorities have not really understood. The Regulation ought to be a good opportunity to define it. On some occasions in the areas of their responsibility the Port Authorities have let the Harbour Masters incur in breaches that fall within the area of their competences and powers. Regardless of whether they are liked or not, these competences are there to be exercised. The Port Authorities have the competence to sanction all of the waste produced inside the port area, unless their importance or impact constitute a penal offence because of their repercussion on the health of people or other external circumstances, except for those which are produced on ships or platforms, which in all logic should also be sanctioned, but for which the Law has no provision and for which there is no opposition. An extreme case, which could help to understand the competences of the Harbour Masters and logically the General Directorate of the Merchant Navy and of the Boards of Administration of the Port Authorities, Public Entity, etc., often comes to light when fuel is being supplied to a ship: if the hose slips out and spills gas oil into the water the competence to present the case belongs to the Port. If there is an overflow because the chabolero[1] is not paying attention the competence is of the Harbour Master. This is not final, indeed it is arguable, but it helps to understand the competences in the extremes. In the first case it is a spillage from land to water, and in the second case, from a ship to the water.

Fourth Additional Provision. Collaboration among ministries

1. The Departments of the State Administration and other Organisms of the Public Administration may request the collaboration of the services of the Ministry of Development when general interest needs so require.

At the same time, the Ministry of Development may request the collaboration of the services attributed to the mentioned Departments or Organisms that carry out functions in the port or maritime area, provided that they involve general interest needs.

2. The Ministry of Development may request the collaboration of the maritime services of the Ministry of the Interior when the general interest needs so require in the area of civil marine, the safety of people or objects or maritime transport."

This provision reminds us of the more general principle of collaboration among administrations established in Law 30/1992 of 26th November, on the Legal Regime of the Public Administrations. Article 4 of the Common Administrative Procedure addresses the principles by which the relationships among the Public Administrations are to be governed.

"1. The public Administrations act and are related in accordance with the principle of institutional royalty and consequently, shall:

- Respect the legitimate exercise of other Administrations in their competences
- In the exercise of their own competences, weigh up all the public interests involved and specifically those whose Management is the responsibility of other Administrations.
- Facilitate information that the other Administrations require on the activity being carried out in the exercise of their own competences.
- Give cooperation and active support, in their own area, when other Administrations request it for the efficient exercise of their competences."

---

[1] Name given in port slang to the person on land who is in charge of the elementary maintenance and custody of the ship.

6. The International Ships and Port Facilities Security Code (ISPS Code) and the obligations derived from it for the contracting governments

Throughout the whole argument of this document, the focus is intentionally on security. A Regulation of Exploitation and Policing has many other areas of action and organisation, such as the Regulations for dangerous goods, for occupational risks, contingency and security plans, etc.

The fact that all of this is developed with a focus on security is due to two basic reasons:

- that the ISPS Code is a security Code,
- that other sectors of activity are already well known in the maritime port area by all the professionals in the sector.

International terrorism of an extreme radical nature has been marking several milestones that indicate their significant presence and implantation worldwide with indiscriminate and bloody terrorist actions. Following the tragic and devastating events of 11th September 2001 which caused thousands of deaths in an unprecedented attack, the twenty-second Assembly of the IMO agreed to implement new legal mechanisms to elaborate new measures related with the protection of ships and port facilities which would be able to respond and counter the potential threats against maritime security.

Among other things the above was crystallised in the elaboration of the International Ship and Port Facilities Security Code (ISPS Code) in force since 1st July 2004 which strives to meet the following objectives:

1. To establish an international framework that channels the cooperation among Governments, governmental organisations, administrations and shipping and port sectors in order to detect the threats to their security and adopt preventive measures against the events that affect the security of the ships or port facilities used for international trade.

    Within this framework of action, considering that Europe is, together with the USA, the preferential objective of this type of criminal organisation, it seeks to develop its own legislation which, in assuming the Code in its entirety, extends it to broader traffic and spaces within the ports. This is why the Regulation has been published and why the Directive to which we are referring is about to do so. It is clear that greater commitments are reached in the international area when the number of countries is lower and the community of interests and similarities between them is greater.

The Green Paper and the White Paper contemplate European transport policy for 2010, in which maritime transport must be aware to develop the so called highways of the sea, offer innovative services, help to launch intermodal operations within the Marco Polo programme, encourage the appearance of forwarding agents and standardise containers and mobile boxes.

The above, which is indicated as an example and does not cover the reality of the future of maritime transport in Europe, must be accompanied by safety procedures and verification protocols.

2. Define functions and responsibilities of the Governments, the governmental organisms, the local administration and the shipping and port sectors, at a national and international level in order to guarantee maritime security.

Local administrations in Spain shall be understood as the Autonomous Communities, as local entities have very few competences in port matters; these are limited to actions in matters related to urbanism and sometimes, indeed in controlling noises, although this competence is doubtful, given that the environment inside the port is the competence of the Port Authority and that noise forms part of what is known as *acoustic environment*.

City halls are also entering the ports through the control of premises, used for leisure purposes when certain areas of the ports begin to be used as areas for nightlife and clubs as a response to pressure from the citizens to move them away from the urban areas. In any case they are open areas that will only be a port space insofar as they are of public domain until they are de-authorised which will without doubt be the final destination of these spaces when they become urban land.

This is the other bone of contention for public safety to be controlled in the future. Leisure areas are being attracted to the vicinity of the most sensitive port facilities, such as the cruise terminals. These bring large concentrations of people at certain hours, both on land and on board in a small space. Indeed in a few ports we will have the paradoxical situation of passing form a totally open area, such as the leisure area to a restricted one, such as the maritime cruise stations without being able to continue, and all of this separated by small walls or metal fences.

3. Guarantee that the information relating to security is gathered and exchanged promptly and efficiently.

In Spain, it seems that to date and from the perspective of the ISPS Code this function is not being managed adequately. At least the channels of communication do not seem the most useful, the most agile and the most ideal. Given the current organisation of the Ministry of the Interior and the Ministry of Development, any relevant data from the point of view of information, captured or detected in the port maritime area that could be important for safety and which does not require immediate responses is channelled through the vertical conduits through the General Directorate of the Merchant Navy, SASEMAR, and the Public Entity Ports of the State and from there to the Secretary of State for Security. Apart from the fact that the channels of communication are slow and that this is information related with antisocial acts, evaluations and conditioning factors will be introduced at each level of the port maritime area which could adulterate the information.

The communication of information must be done at a local level where it can be verified, compared with other police data and be subjected to a first analysis by professionals from the Security Forces and Corps.

4. Offer a method to evaluate security in order to have plans and procedures that make it possible to react to the changes in the levels of security.

The Code establishes the following functional prescriptions to achieve these objectives:

1. Collect and evaluate information about the threats to maritime security and exchange it with the interested Governments.

2. Require the maintenance of communication protocols for the ships and port facilities.

3. Avoid unauthorised access to the ships and port facilities and to their restricted areas.

4. Avoid the introduction of unauthorised weapons, incendiary devices or explosives into the ships or port facilities.

5. Provide the means to raise the alarm when there is a threat to security.

6. Require security plans for the ships and the port facilities based on the evaluations of the security.

7. Require training, drills and practices to guarantee that all personnel are familiarised with the security procedures.

All of the above is transformed into security plans in which certain levels of security are established to be implemented according to the risks and threats.

As the risks and threats become more evident and credible the Ministry of the Interior should take on a more leading role in the management of the crisis.

The Government establishes the levels of security and gives guidelines against the events that affect maritime security. Higher levels indicate a greater risk.

The following are among the factors to be taken into account to establish the level of security:

1. To what extent the information regarding the threat is credible, whether it is corroborated or not and whether it is specific or imminent.

2. The consequences of the event that affect maritime security.

When they establish a security level of 3, the Governments shall give instructions and facilitate information regarding the security of the ships and the port facilities affected.

Security level 1: the adequate minimum means of security must be maintained at all times.

Security level 2: adequate additional means must be maintained during a period of time, as a result in the increase of the risk of an event affecting maritime security.

Security level 3: specific means of security must be maintained during a limited period of time when an event that affects maritime security is likely or imminent, although the specific target cannot be determined.

Radical Islamic terrorism dealt another blow to the transport sector when it attacked the local train network in Madrid on 11th March, 2004 causing numerous deaths (192) and numerous injuries.

If airplanes have been used as instruments for terrorism and trains caused the massacre in Madrid, no moderately experienced analyst can fail to notice that a ship offers important possibilities to be used as an instrument for a large scale criminal action.

Now more than ever security is a question for everyone and everyone should get involved, at least, in preventive security. The increase in maritime security has been a growing demand in relatively recent times[1]. The truth is that recent events have exceeded even the most alarming predictions.

6.1 Obligations of the contracting Governments

It is worthy of mention that the Code encourages the Contracting Governments to adopt as a priority the necessary measures to complete the process of required legislative and organisational development as soon as possible at a national level for the application of the prescriptions of the amendments to the Agreement (and to the Code), relating to the certification of the ships that have the right to raise their flag or of the port facilities located in their territory.

For Spain, as a member of the European Union, the legislative and administrative proceedings include integrating, together with the requirements of the Code, the important decisions and regulations that are occurring in this area and which have already been given a brief mention.

With the whole regulatory block derived from the implementation of the ISPS Code, the community Regulation and Directive and the necessary adaptations that the Law of Ports requires, and when the mandate contained in Law 48/2003[2] is fulfilled in all the disperse regulation and the different laws are revised in a single text, it will be possible to elaborate the Regulation and the Port Ordinances. It is not an easy task but it is very important to have a clear and defined legal framework.

In the functional prescriptions of the Code it is stated that the information on the threats to maritime security should be collected and evaluated and exchanged with the interested Governments.

---

[1] See foot notes numbers 1, 4 and 5 of Chapter 2

[2] Sixth Final Provision. Authorising the Government to issue a revised text..

6.2 Responsibilities of the Contracting Governments

There are several ministerial departments in Spain with responsibilities in the marine world and in the maritime land and port maritime public domain which does not help when it comes to implementing any measure and less still when it come to security measures.

Moreover, if we take into account the territorial organisation of Spain, which is a territorially and functionally very decentralised country, the difficulties increase as there is a growing presence of the Autonomous Communities with competences in this matter. If we add to this the complexity of the Spanish sport system, with public ports at both a regional and state level and ports managed by concessionaries we can begin to understand the maze of relationships that come to the fore when a measure is to be implemented.

When dealing with security we have seen that we are in the presence of two state bodies with competences in the port area, the special police such as the harbour guards and private security, which is the instrument that all the concessionaries of the private terminals have to attain their objectives and respond to their security demands.

The Government must implement a system of coordination and create entities for this purpose at the same time as it develops legislative measures that clearly define who is who and what their competences are in the ports in security matters.

According to the ISPS Code, the Government establishes the levels of security and gives guidelines to protect against the events that affect maritime security. Higher levels indicate a greater risk.

"When they establish a security level of 3, the Governments shall give instructions and facilitate information regarding the security of the ships and the port facilities affected.

It is understood that the Governments act through the Ministries of Security and Interior. In the case that a security level 3 is declared, those who have to assume the leading role will be responsible for public safety. The measures taken will correspond to the entity of the event or events that provoked such an extraordinary level of security and shall provide the response measures. It will be, in short, the Security Forces and Corps who, as professionals of public security and specialists in terrorist events, take on the leading role in the crisis.

In this study we have indicated the need to organically establish Security Boards in the ports where all those responsible for port security will be represented.

In the case of a crisis of vital importance, with those responsible forming the first crisis cabinet, they will be in a position to ponder all the interests present in both maritime and port security and public safety, under the management of the Delegates or Subdelegates of the Government. We have also seen that the community Directive points in this direction when it refers to the "port security committee that advises the responsible authority."

The fact that in the first place the Code wishes to establish a generalised preventive security for all the port maritime operators, practically from the implication of security as a cost for the users, with a few exceptions, this should not lead to the Government abandoning certain tasks that include public functions of authority in private managers.

The Governments may delegate some tasks in a recognised security organisation, with the exception of:

- Determining the applicable level of security.
- Approving an evaluation of the security of the port facility and later amendments to an approved evaluation.
- Determination of the port facilities that must be designated a PFSO
- Approval of a PFSP and later amendments to an approved plan.
- Execution and compliance of the control measures.
- Definition of which cases require a declaration of maritime security.

6.3 Declaration of maritime security

The Governments shall determine when a declaration of maritime security is required through an evaluation of the risk that an operation of ship-port interface or a ship to ship activity implies for people, goods or the environment. A ship may request that a declaration of maritime security be completed when:

- The ship operates at a higher level that the port facility or another ship with which it has the interface.
- There is an agreement on the declaration of maritime security between Governments that regulates certain international voyages or specific ships in those voyages.

The declaration of maritime security shall be completed by:

- The captain or the chief officer in the case of ships.
- In the case of port facilities, the PFSO or if the Government otherwise declares any other organism responsible.

6.4 Ship security

Ships are obliged to act in accordance with the levels of security established by the Governments.

The SSP are not subject to the inspection of the officers authorised by a Contracting Government, but if they have reasons to believe that the ship does not comply with the prescriptions and the only way of verifying non-compliance is to examine the prescriptions pertaining to the SSP, limited access of an exceptional nature will be granted to the sections of the plan relating to the non-compliance, but only with the consent of the Government of the ship in question, or of the captain.

The SSP becomes a crucial element and is subject to reservation, except for the State Authorities of the flag and the Captain himself and the SSP. Extraordinary measures are required to justify lifting the obligation of reservation, and access to the whole SSP is never granted but only rather to the part affected by the event at hand, that is, a partial and justified access. It seems logical that it be so.

6.5 The port facility

The PFSP must be approved by the Government in whose territory the port facility is located and shall take care of the following as a minimum:

- Measures to prevent weapons, dangerous substances and devices from being taken on board a ship to be used against people, ships or ports.
- Measures to prevent unauthorised access to the port facility, to docked ships and to restricted areas.
- Procedures to address threats or a failure in the security measures.
- Procedures to respond to any instruction regarding security that the Government considers security level 3.
- Procedures for evacuation in the case of a threat to security or the failure of the security measures.
- Tasks for port facility personnel that are assigned security responsibilities and the rest of port facility personnel with regard to security.
- Procedures for the interface with the activities of ship security.
- Procedures for the periodical revision of the plan and its updating.
- Procedures for reporting events that affect maritime security.
- Identification of the PFSO and his/her round the clock contact data.
- Measures for protecting the information contained in the plan.
- Measures for guaranteeing the efficient protection of cargo and equipment for handling the cargo in the port facility.
- Procedures for verifying the PFSP.
- Response procedures in case the security alert system is activated on a ship in the port facility.
- Procedures for granting shore permits to ship personnel, personnel turnover, visitor access to the ship.

6.6 International security certificate

An *international ship security certificate* will be issued following an initial verification or a renovation of the initial verification. The certificate will be issued or approved by the Administration by a recognised security organisation.

A Government may, at the request of the Administration, have the ship subjected to verification and if in its opinion the provisions are met it shall issue or authorise the issue of an international ship security certificate and if appropriate shall approve or authorise the approval of the certificate for the ship in accordance with the Code.

6.6.1 Responsibilities of the contracting Governments

Some of the responsibilities of the Governments are listed below:

- Determining the applicable level of security.
- Approving the SSP and the amendments to a previously approved plan.

- Verifying that the ships comply with the provisions of chapter XI-2 and with part A of the Code and issuing the international ship security certificate.
- Determining which port facilities should designate a PFSO, responsible for the preparation of the PFSP.
- Make sure that the evaluation of the port facility security and any following amendments is carried out and approved.
- Approve the PFSP and any later amendment to the plan.
- Execute the control and compliance measures.
- Subject the approved plans to tests.
- Communicate information to the IMO and to the shipping and port sectors.

6.6.2 Determining the level of security

The Governments are responsible for determining the level of security. The Code defines 3 levels of security for international use:

- Security level 1 (normal): level at which the ships and port facilities operate normally.

- Security level 2 (reinforced): level which will be applied if the risk of an event occurring that affects security is increased.

- Security level 3 (exceptional): level that will be applied during the period of time in which an event that affects security is likely or imminent.

The ship is subject to supervision inspections by the State that manages the port although these inspections will not normally include the examination of the SSP, except in very specific circumstances. The ship may also be subjected to additional methods of control if the Government that executes the measures has reason to believe that there is a danger to the safety of the ship or the port facility being used.

The ship is also required to carry information on board which, upon request, shall be available to the Governments. This information shall indicate who is responsible for the decisions relating to the use of ship personnel and other aspects related with the use of the ship.

6.6.3 The port facility

Each Government must guarantee that the security evaluation of the port facility that gives service to ships dedicated to international voyages is carried out. The evaluation may be made by the Government, a designated authority or a recognised organisation and shall be approved by the Government or the designated authority. This authority may not be delegated.

The port facility security evaluation is basically a risk analysis of all the aspects of the operations of the port facility in order to determine which elements are the most susceptible and are most likely to suffer an attack. The risk is proportionate to the threat of an attack occurring, together with the vulnerability of the target and the consequences of the attack.
The evaluation shall include the following:

- Determination of the threat for the port facilities and infrastructure.
- The identification of possible vulnerable points.
- Calculation of the consequences of the events.

Once the analysis has been completed, a general evaluation of the level of risk is carried out. The evaluation helps to determine which facilities should designate a PFSO and prepare a PFSP.

The port facilities that are obliged shall designate a PFSO. Part A of the Code establishes the tasks, responsibilities and training requisites of such officers and the drills and practices they have to carry out.

The PFSP shall indicate the security measures that have to be taken in the port facility to be able to operate permanently at security level 1. The plan shall also indicate the additional or intensified security measures that the port facility may adopt to go to security level 2 and to be able to operate if said level so requires. The plan shall also indicate the preparatory measures that the port facility shall take to respond promptly to the instructions that it may receive from those in charge of addressing an event that affects maritime security at security level 3.

The port facilities that have to comply with the Code shall have a PFSP approved by the Government or by the designated authority and operate in accordance with said plan. The PFSO shall implement the provisions of the plan and ensure that they are complied with.

The ships that use the port facilities may be subjected to an inspection and be supervised by the State that manages the port as well as to additional control measures. The corresponding authorities may require that information is given about the ship, the cargo, the passengers and the ship's personnel before it enters the port. In some circumstances access to the port may be denied.

6.6.4 Information and communication

The Governments shall facilitate information to the IMO and the information shall be available to enable efficient communication between the Governments, and between the SSO or the CSO and the PFSO.

6.7 Responsibilities of the Contracting Governments

6.7.1 Protection of the evaluations and the responsible authority

The Governments shall guarantee that measures are taken to avoid the unauthorised distribution of confidential material relating to security and may name an authority to carry out the security functions related to the port facilities.

6.7.2 Recognised security organisations

Governments may authorise a recognised security organisation (RSO) to carry out certain activities, including:

- Approving the SSP in the name of the Administration.
- The verification and certification that the ship complies with the stipulations, in the name of the Administration.
- Carrying out the required evaluations of the port facilities.

An RSO may advise the companies or port facilities in security matters, including security evaluations, SSP, port facility security evaluations and the PFSP.

If an RSO has carried out the evaluation or SSP, it should not be authorised to approve the SSP:

When an RSO is authorised, Governments should take their competence into account. An RSO must be able to prove the following:

- Specialised knowledge relating to security.
- Knowledge of the operations of ships and ports, of ship projects and construction, if it offers services to ships and of port projects and construction if it offers its services to port facilities.
- Capacity to evaluate risks related to the security of the operations of ships and port facilities, including ship-port interface and the way of reducing such risks to a minimum.
- Capacity to update and perfect the specialised knowledge of their personnel.
- Capacity to control that their personnel are trustworthy.
- Capacity to maintain the appropriate measures to avoid the unauthorised distribution of confidential material.
- Knowledge of the Code and of national and international legislation and prescriptions on security.
- Knowledge of the trends and threats related to security.
- Knowledge about the recognition and detection of weapons and dangerous substances or devices.
- Knowledge about the recognition, without discrimination, of the behaviour characteristics and patterns of people who might pose a threat to security.
- Knowledge of the techniques to avoid security measures.
- Knowledge of security and surveillance equipment and system and of their operational limitations.

A recognised organisation may be designated as an RSO if it possesses the corresponding knowledge in security matters.

A port, a Port Authority or the operator of a port facility may be designated as an RSO if they possess the corresponding knowledge in security matters.

The figure of the captain keeps his powers intact. At all times, the captain of the ship is the person responsible for the security and protection of the ship. Even at security level 3, he may ask for an explanation or modification of the instructions issued by those responsible for addressing an event that affects maritime security if he has reason to believe that they could in nay way put the ship in danger.

The CSO or SSO shall contact the responsible PFSO so that the ship is prepared to apply the security level applicable to the ship in the port facility.

Once contact has been established with the ship, the PFSO shall notify it of any change on the security level in the port facility and shall facilitate all the corresponding information regarding security.

Although there may be circumstances in which the ship operates at a higher level of security than that of the port facility that it is using there should never be a case in which a ship has a lower security level than that of the port facility it is using.

If a ship has a security level above that of the port facility, the CSO or the SSO shall notify the PFSO immediately. The PFSO shall make an evaluation of the case in collaboration with the CSO or the SSO and shall agree the security measures with the ship, including those of completing and signing a declaration of maritime security.

Governments:

- Shall study the way to quickly distribute the information regarding the changes in levels.
- May use NAVTEX messages or warnings to sailors to notify ships and the CSO and SSO and other means that provide similar or better speed and reception.
- Shall prepare the means to notify the PFSO of the changes in the levels of security.
- Shall collect and update the contact data of the list of people who have to be informed of the changes in the levels of security. Although the information on the level of security does not need to be considered confidential, the information on the underlying threat might be confidential.
- Shall study the type and degree of detail of the information transmitted and the method to transmit it to the SSO, CSO and the PFSO.

6.7.3 Points of contact and information on the port facility security plans

When a port facility has a PFSP, it must inform the Organisation about it and shall make it known to the CSO and SSO, Only the existence of the plan shall be communicated without going into any further detail about it. The Governments shall examine the possibility of establishing central or regional points of contact in order to facilitate the updated information. The existence of these points shall be distributed. Information shall also be given on the recognised security organisation designated to act in the name of the Government, with the details of the responsibilities delegated in the organisations and the conditions of the delegation.

In the case of the ports that do not have a PFSP, the central or regional point of contact must be able to designate a competent person on land who can organise, if necessary, the adequate security measures for the time that the ship is in the port.
The Governments shall facilitate the contact data of the civil servants that the SSO, the CSO or the PFSO may report security concerns to. These civil servants shall evaluate the information before taking measures.

The problems reported may be related to security measures that fall under the jurisdiction of other Governments, which means that the Governments must examine the possibility of contacting their counterpart Governments to analyse the need for corrective actions. For this purpose, they should provide the IMO with the contact data of the government workers.

6.7.4 Identity cards

The Code recommends that the Governments issue adequate identity cards to those civil servants who have a right to go on board or to enter the port facilities in the performance of their duties and that they create procedures to verify the authenticity of the cards.

The term *civil servant* must be interpreted in the ample sense of the word and includes any agent of authority, which means that it also includes the harbour guards and the rest of the personnel registered in the Police Service of the Ports of General Interest.

It will be difficult to issue these documents in Spain because of the variety of organisms involved in security that can go on board, even beyond the requirements of the ISPS Code. From the General Directorate of the Merchant Navy, inspectors go on board to control waste and security measures and to verify the different requirements. Those responsible for security in the Port Authorities go on board to coordinate the security measures of the ship with those of the port facility.

From the Ministry of the Interior, the Civil Guard goes on board to check security measures, make boarding inspections and check fiscal documentation. This Corps can at the same time, according to their function of fighting against drug dealing and terrorism which they share with the National Police Force, make several inspections of the ship or of the ship's hull on the underwater body.

Besides, this Corps has the prime responsibility in the control of equipment, goods and provisions, although their controls are sporadic and at their own initiative. The National Police Force goes on board for matters related to illegal immigration, stowaways and the control of documentation. Other organisms, such as external security, Cites, etc., may access the ship or the port facilities.

In any case, this recommendation is well founded and a single document for all those who are authorised to go on board a ship or to enter a facility or a port would be very useful and beneficial for security.

Besides, if it had a magnetic band, it would be possible to differentiate the various levels of access to the different spaces of port security, such as the port facilities, restricted areas and would be very useful for controlling automatic access.

This has been achieved in airports. In any case it would be the Public Entity Ports of the State, together with the General Directorate of Police, who would have to issue an identity card which, at least in Europe, would have to have identical characteristics, given the international nature of the composition of maritime navigation.

6.7.5 Ship which do not have to comply with part A of this Code

Governments should examine the possibility of establishing adequate security measures to increase the security of the ships affected by the Code and to guarantee that each provision on security that is applicable to ships enables their interaction with the ships to which part A of the Code applies.

On this point it can be said that the EU has elaborated its own regulations which go beyond the requirements of the ISPS Code.

6.7.6 Threats to ships and other events at sea

Governments must offer general guidelines on the measures to reduce the risks for ships that fly their flag when at sea. They should offer specific guidelines on the measures to be adopted in accordance with levels 1 to 3, if:

- there is a change in the security level applicable to the ship while it is at sea, for example, due to the geographic zone in which it is navigating or related to the ship itself.
- if the ship is caught up in an event, or threat, that affects maritime security while it is at sea.

Governments must define methods and procedures for these cases. If an attack is imminent, the ship must try to establish a direct communication with those responsible for dealing with the events that affect the maritime protection in the flag State.

Governments must also establish a point of contact that offers guidance in safety matters for all ships:

- that have a right to fly their flag
- that is operating in its territorial sea or has communicated its intention to enter it.

Governments must offer guidance to the ships that operate in their territorial sea or which have communicated their intention to enter it. This could include the following recommendations:

- modifying or delaying its passage,
- following a certain direction or going to a specific place,
- report on the availability of the personnel or equipment that could embark on the ship,
- coordinate its passage, the arrival in and departure from the port, in such a way that there is the possibility of a patrol escort with ships or aircraft (airplanes or helicopters).

Governments must see that the ships that operate in their territorial sea or communicate their intention to enter it, shall diligently implement any security measure recommended by the Government for the protection of the ship and those ships that navigate nearby.

The plans prepared by the Governments for the purpose of paragraph 4.22[3] must include information on a point of contact including the Administration that is available 24 hours a day. These plans must include information on assistance with neighbouring coastal States and a procedure for the coordination between the PFSO and the SSO.

6.7.7 Equivalent measures for port facilities

In the case of certain port facilities, in which limited or special operations are carried out, but in which traffic is not occasional, it might be adequate to guarantee compliance using security measures that are

---

[3] 4.22 The Contracting Governments shall also establish a point of contact that offers guidance in security matters for all ships:
- that have a right to fly their flan; or
- that are operating in its territorial sea or have communicated their intention to enter its territorial sea.

equivalent to those prescribed. This may be the case for terminals near factories or docks that are not used very frequently.

6.7.8 Approval of the PFSP

The PFSP must be approved by the corresponding Contracting Government which must establish the appropriate procedures for:

- The presentation of the PFSP to the Government.
- Examination of the PFSP
- Approval of the PFSP with or without amendments.
- The examination of the amendments presented following approval.
- The inspection or auditing that makes it possible to verify that the approved PFSP is still valid.

The appropriate measures must be taken in every stage in order to guarantee the confidentiality of the contents of a PFSP.

6.7.9 Declaration of compliance of a port facility

The Government in whose territory the facility is located may issue a declaration of compliance of the port facility (DCPF) which indicates:

- The port facility in question.
- That the port facility compiles with the provisions of the Code.
- Period of validity of the DCPF, specified by the Contracting Governments but which shall not exceed five years.
- The provisions of the subsequent verifications established by the Government and a confirmation when these are carried out.

The declaration of compliance of a port facility must be adjusted to the model that appears in the appendix of the present part of the Code. If the language used is not Spanish, French or English the Contracting Government may include a translation to one of them if it considers it appropriate.

6.8 Communication protocol of the security levels in Spain

6.8.1 Determination of the level of security

The Governments are responsible for determining the level of security to be applied in a give moment to ships and port facilities. The Code defines the three levels of security for international use.

In Spain, the Ministry of the Interior (SES) is responsible for determining the levels of security applicable to ships (with national flag) and (national) port facilities.

The SSP shall indicate the security measures, both physical and operational, that must be taken for the ship to be able to operate at all times at security level 1. The plan must also indicate the additional or intensified security measures that the ship may adopt to pass to security level 2 and to be able to operate in said level, when so ordered.

Besides, the plan must indicate the possible preparatory measures that the ship would have to take in order to respond quickly to the instructions that they might receive form those responsible for dealing with a security level 3 event that affects maritime security or threatens it.

It will normally be someone from the police who will be responsible for giving these instructions. Taking the definition of the community Regulation which calls it a *deliberate illicit act*, due to its nature or context an event is understood as being capable of jeopardising those ships used in both international and national maritime traffic, their passengers or their cargo or the port facilities associated with them.

National traffic is included because the definition was taken from the Regulation; for the purpose of the PFSP Code it would only affect international traffic. Although the PFSP Code withdraws its instructions and puts them at the disposal of public safety at level three, those responsible for the maritime ports are ready to receive instructions.

The PFSP must comply with the same guidelines as the SSP and act in a similar way in security levels 1, 2 and 3.

6.8.2 Procedure for determining the level of security

When determining the level of security, the Contracting Governments shall take into account all the information relating to the threat, both general and specific.

The general information relating to the threat is that which does not determine the port facility, the ship or the moment or type of threat.

The specific information relating to the threat is that which refers to a specific port facility, a specific ship or a specific type.

In general terms, level 2 will be applied when the threat is general in the sense that the following is determined in the following cases:

- Undetermined threat against ships with a national flag
- Undetermined threat against Spanish port facilities
- Undetermined threat against a specific ship.
- Undetermined threat against a specific port facility.
- Undetermined threat against undetermined ships or port facilities

Security level 3 is generally applied when the threat is specific. This type of level is only established as an exceptional measure if there is credible information that an event that affects security in any of the following cases is likely or imminent.

- Specific threat against a national ship.
- Specific threat against a specific port facility.
- Threat against national ships in a specific port.
- Conflictive area.

In the application of a certain level of security, the circumstances of national or international risk of the time and place shall be taken into account together with the accuracy or reality of the threat.

Security level 3 will only be maintained during the time that the identified threat or real event that affects maritime security lasts.

Although the level of security may pass from level 1 to level 2 and from there to level 3 there is also the possibility that it goes directly form level 1 to 3.

There may be circumstances in which the ship operates at a level of security that is higher than that of the port facility it is using, but a ship shall never have a level of security that is lower than that of the port it is using.

6.8.3 Communication of the levels of security

a) Methods used for communication:

- System to communicate alerts used by the ship or the port facilities (NAVTEX messages or warnings to sailors).
- Any other system that offers a similar speed and cover.

b) People to whom the changes in the level of security are communicated:

- The Ship Security Officers (SSO)
- The Company Security Officers (CSO)
- The Port Facility Security Officers (PFSO)
- Those people or Departments that have an interest in knowing about it (General Directorate of the Merchant Navy, shipping company, etc.)

If a ship has level of security that is higher than that of the port facility that it wishes to use, the CSO or the SSO shall notify the PFSO without delay. The PFSO shall perform an evaluation of the specific case, in collaboration with the CSO and the SSO and shall reach an agreement with the ship on the adequate security measures, including completing and signing a declaration of maritime security.

As soon as possible the CSO and the SSO shall contact the PFSO responsible for the port facility that the ship expects to use, in order to determine the level of security applicable to this ship in the port facility.

Once contact has been established with the ship, the PFSO shall report any further change in the level of protection of the port facility and shall facilitate all the corresponding information relating to security.

6.8.4 Response to a specific and determined threat

- Determine the applicable level of protection.
- Communicate the level of security to the ship, port facility and interested entities.
- Apply the adequate response procedure to the threat received.

6.8.5 Procedure for communicating threats and levels of security

1.- The threat will be communicated to the Secretary of State for Security (CEPIC)[4], through SASEMAR or Ports of the State, to any of the media mentioned in Annex 1.

2.- The Secretary of State for Security shall communicate the corresponding level of security to SASEMAR or Ports of the State through the media that appear in Annexes II and III, who shall transfer it to the corresponding port authority (PFSO) or ship (SSO).

6.9 The Ministries and Organisms involved in its implementation

The implementation of the security measures required by the new regulation involves certain entities in Spain. We could state that in normal situations the role is taken on by the Ministry of Development through the General Directorate of the Merchant Navy, the Public Entity Ports of the State and SASEMAR.

When it is necessary to adopt extraordinary measures within level 3, the main protagonist will be the Ministry of the Interior, through the Secretary of State for Security and the General Directorate of the Civil Guard and the Police who carry out specific duties in matters relating to prevention and the fight against terrorism. In Spain, the existence of Autonomous Communities with full competences in matters of terrorism, especially the Basque Country and Catalonia, in certain operational interventions, could require their participation.

The Spanish Police Forces have also shown their efficiency and professionalism in the fight against the terrorism of ETA and other criminal groups, many of them practically disappeared, such as GRAPO, FRAP, etc, although GRAPO reappears from time to time.

The fact that two Ministries, such as Development and Interior, are involved, and in line with the arguments defended in this study, it should be used as a corollary to establish a Board of Coordination in matters relating to port maritime security at a national level, above the highly praised Port Security Boards,

On the other hand, the existence of two Ministries should not imply the existence of sectioned off compartments. Aside from the preventive measures required in the Code and that are implemented by those responsible for port security (harbour guards) private security (security guards) etc., the Security Forces, especially the Civil Guard apply certain measures to complement maritime and port security,

---

[4] Telephone: 915 371 883, 915 371 884, 915 372 056, 915 372 057, 915 372 058
Fax: 913 191 645, 913 191 228, 913 197 389
E-mail: cepic@ses.mir.es

in virtue of their obligations of custody exposed elsewhere. These other means of public safety such as the investigation and surveillance of terrorist elements and extortionists in general are of a more general nature but are extremely important.

If we could classify the characteristics of the requirements of the ISPS Code as preventive and more general within a concept of horizontal safety which is manifested in passive means, controls, protocols, etc., the requirements of public safety implemented by the Security Forces and Corps are more specific and concrete but they keep all their competences such as those carried out before the implementation of the ISPS Code. We must not forget this.

Therefore on certain occasions they will consider it appropriate, always at their own initiative and because they have the relevant information or are led to it by objective circumstances that have arisen on a specific ship or in a specific port, to inspect the hull of a specific ship or the docks of a specific port facility.

On other occasions the Special Groups of Underwater Activities of the Civil Guard (SEAS) will inspect the submerged part in the docks. The Maritime Services of the Civil Guard will also escort certain cruise or oil ships, for example, on a daily basis. But these measures do not go against those that they must adopt from the Code: they are an extra for safety on a different level of requirement not circumscribed to the Code.

Having said this, the Regulation of Exploitation and Port Policing and the Ordinances must contain the exact provisions for those responsible for port security to know their channels of communication and the responsibilities of the Security Forces and Corps of the State, especially the Civil Guard, present in all the Ports of General Interest and with direct responsibilities over them in matters of surveillance and custody.

Through the Civil Guard, the Ministry of the Interior should also make an effort to coordinate and invest in matters relating to port security. Article 13 of the Law of the Ports has included the reservation of areas, so that the State Administration can "reserve spaces of land-maritime public domain for the use of naval facilities and port areas that are required for compliance of the objectives that the current legislation attributes to the Civil Guard and which are excluded from the scope of application of this Law."

The Civil Guard must redefine its missions in the ports by giving priority to the question of safety which has been left in the background in favour of their obligations as fiscal guard of the State. There must be maritime bases in the Ports and modern facilities to be able to carry out the most important services that OL 2/86, of Security Forces and Corps, assigns them.

Thus public safety must be guaranteed in the Spanish port areas in general and especially in those port facilities located in our ports within the requirements of the ISPS Code. The coordination of the efforts of this Corps with the Harbour Guards will without a doubt bring about a better, more modern and safer image of our ports.

The Ministry of the Interior needs to implement the regulatory development of the distribution of competences between the Civil Guard and the National Police Force. As many years have elapsed it should also look into a profound reform of Law 2/86 on the understanding that the security requirements of today are not the same as those of almost 20 years ago.

In accordance with the above, the surveillance of the coasts, when talking about European maritime police and the maritime frontiers of the EU, the surveillance and custody of its ports, require personnel, facilities and boats that are appropriate for the objectives that the Civil Guard must attain in compliance with the Law.

6.10 Towards a new port police

The growing uncertainty around public safety in a modern world in which the differences in people's buying power, the mobility of the population, marginality, etc., are all present with a large repercussion on the ports which have been affected because they provide the perfect site: barely lit, if at all and stuck right in the heart of the surroundings of the cities. In this way they have become a haven for indigents who take advantage of any slip to move into them or into abandoned ships or ships with very little surveillance.

The group of harbour guards has been gradually "devaluated" in its public functions, which means that the status of the figure has fallen into a crisis affected by the sweeping changes in the port system: it has lived through the transition form an interventionist system in the port area to a liberal system: from being closed in a regime of civil service to a non-civil service one; form carrying weapons to not doing so: from being security guards to not being so, etc.

The reality is that the subjectivity of the harbour guards has suffered from these changes. The fact that this group has been of little use in the retraining of unemployed workers has not helped either: self-esteem has been lost and this seems to be the clear impression of many of its members who appear to have gone on a round trip without even moving.

They have started to need a legal statute and more protection in the laws for their functions and have made vehement claims for them to be mentioned in the Law of Ports which did not even do so until the recent reform of Law 48/23, and that they are doing this simply for their name to be specifically recognised, and more importantly, their condition as agents of authority as there were several doubts depending on which courts or judges intervened in the cases and in which part of Spain the events took place.

In light of all these circumstances, this figure has tottered in an unstable equilibrium between its functions as special police and as a port worker, collecting taxes, providing water to ships, etc.

The trend has been inverted. This figure now claims its full recognition as the special police officers that they are. Circumstances have also helped this.

It is now the desire of the group of harbour guards to be more involved in matters regarding security.

6.10. 1 Legal labour stature that seeks the recognition of policing function

In the resolution of 22.12.1999, of the General Directorate of Work, BOE number 15 of 18.01.2000 issued the I Framework Agreement of Labour Relations of Ports of the State and the different Port Authorities[5].

We shall analyse this text, because the status of the figure of the harbour guard, which is scarcely mentioned as the other special police in ordinary laws, needs to dig deep into their different areas of action in order to try to define content and functions.

It can be said that this Agreement prefigures a kind of scale, albeit for working purposes from the point of view of the collective negotiation, which defines a series of functions:

a) Harbour guard chief

He is assigned the category: Chief Foreman (level 10). As regards security, he is the Service Head of the harbour guards in such a way that there can only be one per Port Authority, and he shall be *responsible for complying with the different Regulations applicable to the Corps, by exercising the authority invested upon him.*

The Agreement has two references which are worthy of mention: the first that it remits their functions to the Regulation (we understand that it is to the Regulation of Exploitation and Policing primarily, as is logical) and, on the other hand, it refers to the functions of authority which are none other than those of special police invested in public functions in the service area of the port.

Their responsibilities include the following, with special reference to those related to security or policing:

- the complete organisation of the service,
- performing the surveillance rounds to check the correct cover of the service,
- assigning posts (access control, dock, quay, office, maritime station, parking areas, etc.)
- control of the compliance of these missions to those assigned and the preparation of those relationships with services carried out by each of those people reporting to them,
- relationships with Port Exploitation and Public Order Forces (Civil Guard, Municipal Police),
- the incidences elaborated by the harbour guards

Through its collective negotiations, this group takes on important security and surveillance functions as can be seen through the missions assigned to the person who takes on the role of Manager.

b) Another figure that the Agreement defines is the Harbour Guard Chief, who shall control and supervise in a shift or geographical area:

- the duties of the harbour guards in the service area of the port,
- being responsible for compliance with the different Regulations applicable to the Corps
- exercising the authority invested in it.

The references to prime concepts of public safety in their area, such as controlling, supervising, complying with Regulations and exercising the authority invested in them are constant.

The responsibilities are:

- the partial organisation of the service (on a shift or geographical area),
- performing the surveillance rounds to check the correct cover of the service,

- assigning posts (access control, dock, quay, office, maritime station, parking areas, etc.) and control of the compliance of these missions to those assigned,
- the preparation of those relationships with services carried out by each of those people reporting to them, and the relationships, in absence of their superiors, with Port Exploitation and Public Order Forces (Civil Guard, Municipal Police),
- incidences elaborated by the harbour guards and their transmission in the turnover to the Surveillance Foreman.

c) The harbour guard. Team Leader.

He is responsible for applying the different regulations that correspond to him and verify the reality of the operations that are carried out in the service area of the port, in his shift and/or geographical area, exercising the authority invested in him.

Apart from his functions as harbour guard he coordinates a group of between four and fifteen harbour guards.

His responsibilities are the surveillance and control of the service area both on foot and in a vehicle: The mission may be specified in:

- the control of arrivals and departures of people and vehicles,
- the security of merchandise
- the control and regulation of traffic in the dock and in the parking areas and reporting any breaches that may be committed,
- controlling road safety,
- the surveillance of compliance with the regulation and reporting and proposing sanctions in the case of non-compliance.

We are talking about the typical functions of port administrative police and special police in the area of security which is why they have been under scrutiny. The harbour guard can perform other extraordinary services (such as escorting Army convoys) in accordance with the specific needs of the Port Authority.

d) Harbour guard

He is responsible for applying the different regulations in his competence and verifies the reality of the operations that are carried out in the service area of the port, on his shift and/or in his geographical area, exercising the authority invested in him.

His responsibilities are:

- the surveillance and control of his service area both on foot and in a vehicle,
- the control of access of people and vehicles, offices, maritime station, quay, etc.
- the security of goods,
- the control and regulation of traffic in the dock and in the parking areas, reporting any breaches that may be committed.
- controlling road safety

- the surveillance of compliance with the regulations and reporting and proposing sanction in case of non-compliance

However it is true that they carry out other duties not specifically related to security, though there are only a few, within the performance of the functions of their competence. This needs no further comment and goes in the direction of the provisions of the Projects of the Regulations of Exploitation and Policing.

We have already studied elsewhere the function that the draft of the Regulation makes with respect to his functions with the clarifications introduced by Law 48/2003 from the perspective of security regulations.

6.10.2 The position of the unions

Between 26th and 28th March 2004 the Spanish union "Comisiones Obreras" held a workshop in Barcelona where they listened to the demands of the group of Harbour Guards in which they expressed their concern for the training, qualification, competences and professional qualification with the coming into force of the so often mentioned Law 48/2003 which, for the first time in a legal regulation, recognises this group with the status of agents of the Port Authority.

As a result of the workshop a draft was drawn up to unify criteria regarding the professional responsibilities and claims, the draft was sent around the ports as a document to be debated among the different members of the group.

The group is now referred to as the Harbour Guard-Port Police Force. After this, in the second paragraph, it addressees security directly as an essential part of maintaining the public image of the ports, it makes reference to the recent problems that could be caused by international terrorism and insists on the need to increase efficiency in the control of the detection of criminal acts.

It analyses the uncertainty produced by the fact that all the Police Forces should do "everything". It asks for a definition of functions so as to assume responsibilities. It literally assumes the content of article 1.2 of OL 1/92 on Public Safety, in that they are functions for the protection of public safety in order to guarantee coexistence, the eradication of violence and the pacific use of public spaces as well as preventing crimes and offences being committed.

This documents claims and assumes a whole array of police functions from the administrative area (and at the same time as special police in the port public domain) as functions of public safety included in the Law.

Point 2.4.3 is worthy of mention for its extraordinary interest as it claims the need for a service in a vessel which is an essential need defended in this document in so far as modern cruise traffic has to be controlled from the water side.

Some ships, especially cruise ships, have tried to lower their own boats with personnel from the ship which, although it does not pose a legal problem if the ship has a Spanish flag, it does in the case of foreign ships as it would be unacceptable to have a foreign security service exercising the exclusion of navigation in the vicinity of the ship in question.

It would be normal for this service to be carried out by the Guards or if not by those contracted by the Spanish security companies within the framework of private security and which should not pose any problems, at least legal; their coordination with the Harbour Guards is another question altogether.

On the other hand, the Code requires that accesses, approach paths, anchoring areas and manoeuvring and docking areas be specially protected areas. This is the same with the waters adjacent to the port facility.

This mission should not be left outside of the scope of action of the harbour guards who must have vessels in order to be able to carry out their duties. It is, without a doubt, a pending matter, though it is true that the Port Authorities could get by by contracting private security companies trained in these matters.

Sometimes, among general duties, these functions are sporadically carried out by the Civil Guard of the Sea. However in security level 1 it should be a normal measure of preventive security.

Moreover, having vessels would make it possible to issue sanctions in the water itself, sometimes inaccessible to this group, for breaches such as dumping contaminants from ships because, although it is the competence of the Harbour Master, nothing stops these actions being taken by this Authority, which in the long run would lead to cleaner waters.

The draft dedicates quite a lot of attention to uniformity, to distinctive signs,... which means that it is claiming greater competences than those exercised to date and that they are exercised in an exclusive manner.

It is a document which should be analysed because it transmits the position of an important sector within the group of harbour guards.

6.11 Private security

The growth of private security in Spain and Europe is spectacular, due to the privatisation of entire sectors of commercial activity, of infrastructures, high voltage networks, the gas and oil sector, etc. On the other hand the accumulation of wealth and the concentration of companies have influenced on the strong development of the private sector and on the size of companies. Economical development has been very important and has also had its influence on the strong development of this security sector.

Private security is regulated in Spain by Law 23/1992, of 30.07.1992 developed by RD 2364/1994 of 9th December, which approves the Regulation of Private Security.

6.11.1 Security guards

Security guards will only be able to carry out the following functions:

- Carry out the surveillance and protection of movable and immovable goods as well as the protection of those people who may be there.

- Carry out identity checks at the access to or inside certain buildings, without being able to withhold personal documentation at any time.
- Prevent criminal acts or breaches from being committed within their task of protection.
- Immediately hand over delinquents together with all the instruments, effects and evidence of their crimes to the members of the Security Forces and Corps within their task of protection. They may not interrogate these people.
- In relation with the operation of alarm centres, provide the services of response to any alarms that occur which do not correspond to the Security Forces and Corps.

For the function of the protection of the storage, handling and transport of explosives or other objects or substances that are determined in regulation, they will need to have obtained special authorisation.

Such functions will only be able to be carried out by the guards who belong to the security companies, who wear a uniform and the distinction of the position they occupy. Within the entity or company to which they belong, the guards shall have exclusive dedication to the function of security in accordance with their position and may not carry out other missions simultaneously.

In general terms they shall carry out their functions exclusively inside the buildings or properties that they must watch over. These functions may not be carried out on public roads or on those which though not public roads, are for common use. However, in the case of industrial parks or isolated urbanisations, surveillance services may be implemented as specifically authorised.

Once they have been granted the corresponding licenses, security guards may only carry weapons for those functions so determined in the regulation which as well as the protection of the storage, counting, classification and transport of money, values and valuable objects, include those of surveillance and protection of factories and deposits or the transport of weapons and explosives, of industries or dangerous establishments that are in deserted areas and any others of a similar importance.

The weapons that are appropriate for these security services, whose category will be determined by the regulation, may only be carried while on duty.

6.11.2 Chiefs of Security

When the number of security guards, the organisational or technical complexity or other circumstances that are determined in the regulation make it necessary, the functions of the guards will be carried out under the direct orders of a chief of security who will be responsible for the operations of the guards and of the security systems, as well as of the organisation and execution of the services and the observation of the applicable legislation.

6.11.3 Private security on foreign ships

On the other hand we have the complicated problem of watching over a stowaway on board in the port. This matter is the exclusive responsibility of the captain. According to the interpretation of the General Technical Secretary of the Ministry of the Interior "The surveillance of ships – docked in port – carried out by personnel that are not members of their crew, is an activity that without doubt corresponds to articles 5.1 a) and 11.2 a) of the Law of Private Security[5], which means that it can only be done by security guards belonging to security companies." "Even when the ship has a foreign flag, in accordance with international regulations, it must be subjected to the laws and regulations of Spain."

It is argued that whenever the ship is in territorial waters, we are in the presence of an object located in an area of Spanish sovereignty and therefore subject to the specific laws and regulations. We understand these conclusions to be correct provided that they abide by international law.

6.11.4 Private security in ports

There is a growing presence of private security in port areas thanks mainly to the concession holders, but also the Port Authorities, all of which is arousing susceptibilities among the harbour guards. Article 5 of the draft of the regulation of 2000 states that other personnel may perform the functions of surveillance on the understanding that private security agents cannot perform public duties, that their functions are limited to specific areas of the Ports of General Interest and that they will be under the control of the Group of Harbour Guards or police in charge.

In any case, private security has grown so much and has increasingly taken on so many functions that it is taking over more and more areas of activity in place and functions that until recently were quite unthinkable. There is nothing stopping them providing their services in port sites exploited under concession which means that a gap has been opened when it comes to creating these spaces due to requirements of the ISPS Code inside the ports.

This will have its consequences as until now the ports were a more or less patrolled single surface, but at the end of the day just one space. Now, in the Ports of General Interest, there are sectioned and fenced off areas, known as *port facilities* in the ISPS Code, some of which are state owned and others in the hands of concession holders who evidently must bear the expense of the private security required by the corresponding PFSP.

This will be a matter to be resolved within the Policing Regulations. The concern is how to combine the general surveillance of the port by the State and carried out by the harbour guards and the Civil Guard at different levels, with these fenced off and sectioned spaces under the direct responsibility of the concession holders.

This will be one of the hobbyhorses in the elaboration of the Policing Regulation that must be dealt with in the text so as to avoid mutual interferences while creating systems for the collaboration between private and public security.

---

5 Law 23/92, of 30th June, on Private Security.

7. The Code and the Security Plan for port facilities

7.1 Introduction

The PFSP is a plan that is elaborated in order to guarantee the protection of the port facility and the ships, people, cargo, units of transport and provision of the ships in the port facility from those risks that affect maritime security.

A port facility is understood as being the place in which the ship-port interface takes place: this shall include, when required, areas such as anchor areas, waiting docks and accesses from the sea.

A ship-port interface is understood as being the interaction that takes place when a ship is affected directly or immediately by activities that include the movement of people or goods or when providing port services to the ship or from the ship.

The PFSO is the person designated to respond for the elaboration, implementation, revision and updating of the PFSP and for coordination with the SSO and with the CSO.

Before going into details it is worth mentioning that the European Regulation, which has already been published, and the Directive, which is in the process of elaboration, will lead to an extension of security to greater areas of application and to more specific measures to increase the security of maritime transport and of the port facility. Therefore the measures that are taken in complying with the requirements of the ISPS Code, included in the SOLAS are not sufficient to complete the reforms in internal regulations, it is essential that from now on these legal European instruments are taken into consideration in order to integrate all the requirements relating to safety that may arise in an internal legislation and especially in the Port Regulations and Ordinances.

With regard to this European legislation, in a report dated 24th October 2002 and which should be read, the Economic and Social Committee makes a serious analysis of the problem posed by terrorism, of the costs of implementing security measures, of how the insurance industry reacts against terrorist acts, etc. Part 1.3 of the introduction makes a valid point by stating:

"The need to pay more attention to security in the whole world is imperative and has been recognised by both governments and industry. Perfect security is an impossible goal.

In times of a deep crisis the tendency is to try to plan all possible contingencies and to speak of ways that these hypothetical cases could be avoided. However, aside from the seriousness of the threats to security, these intense security measures cannot be maintained over periods much longer than a few days at a time. In order to make a value judgment as to when to apply these security measures and to establish their level of intensity it is necessary to better understand the types and likelihood of the risks that the transport network faces.

As a result of the event of 11th September, the maritime and air transport industry gave their full backing to the need to defeat terrorism and other threats to the security of ships and aircraft. Security is a question in which, as a general rule, all the links in the chain should participate in order to achieve specific results. Each part of the chain should have its share of responsibility; otherwise, the weakest link would become the target of the terrorists who intend to infiltrate the system."

In Spain, public ports are decidedly moving towards a privatised management, although the Ports of General Interest are still in the hands of the State, despite the fact that in recent times the interventions of the Autonomous Communities have grown and they have an ever growing role in them. The obligations implemented in the Code in matters relating to security are going to create a new area in the ports which the Code now calls *port facilities*.

This sectioning, which will indeed take place as a result of the application of the regulation to which we are referring, will, for the purpose of security, transform docks which were being managed by private companies into perfectly defined and closed port terminals with their corresponding access control. This will mean that they will become really privatised. In any case, their management, organisation and operation will be private, through a concession and private security will be present in these spaces. However, certain rules from the Regulations and Ordinances will be applicable to both the concession holders and the users of certain public services.

On the other hand, other spaces defined as public and the rest of the spaces without delimitation will remain under the competences and responsibilities of the Port Authorities. In this case public means shall be implemented for their surveillance and custody. Some processes and spaces may admit and require the presence of private security in which case, if this option is taken, these guards will act as auxiliaries to the agents of the port authority as has occurred in the airports, which are ahead in security matters and can be used as a reference, especially in passenger and cruise ships as they represent the movements of people in a similar manner to those of civil aviation.

Although it has already been expressed elsewhere, the successive reforms of the Law of Ports of 1992 have attracted and allowed other leisure activities in the ports at the same time as important port areas were opened for the citizens who live nearby to enjoy.

The practical result is that now, a typical port could have these features:

- Half open surfaces

A series of spaces open to the public, with certain limitations, in which surveillance is scarce because there are hardly any commercial or dangerous activities in them. Cycle paths or walk paths have been installed in some of them. Some of these areas are usually closed at night. It is not unusual for bars and restaurants to be opened in these areas. With the pretext of giving a service to the users of the port, in practice they are open to the general public, because the controls, and especially of people, are very lax. Goods are not normally deposited in these areas although it is not unusual. They are open to the traffic of the port and occasionally crossed by railroad tracks. Little by little they are getting free from the public domain easement and are providing urban land for leisure activities, hotels, congresses....

We could venture an opinion that these areas are in transition to be converted into public urban spaces and their final destination is a more or less imminent release form public domain[1].

These areas usually house the facilities that give service to fishing, such as the quays, exporters, ice facilities, car parks for large vehicles, etc. The moment has come to make important and brave decisions in this matter, without being dragged along by events and disconnect these areas, traffics and services from the easement and risks of international maritime trade.

Nowadays, an international commercial port with important requirements in all areas, including security which is going to be reinforced even more in the future, cannot be jointly managed with the activities of the prime sector related to fishing. They are not even similar. The time has come to separate those spaces dedicated to fishing activities and transfer them to the Autonomous Communities when they are not capable of managing their own interests, in the form of a concession, through organisations of producers.

The same can be said for sports harbours. Together with the sector of cruise ships and containers these are the activities with the strongest growth. The leisure industry is the driving force behind the growth of the sporting fleet. The increases are around 12% per year. It is by far the most numerous of the fleets in numbers. On 31.12.2003 we had

- 286,482 leisure boats (List 6+ List 7+ Old List 5),
- 18,789 jet skis.

Fishing and leisure should be left out of the scope of management of the Ports of General Interest. They are activities that due to their nature do not concern them and which represent the normal activity of a Port of General Interest. Besides, the movement of people and small boats in fishing and sailing are a very important obstacle and hinder the implementation of security measures.

The segregation of these activities to control the ports is not going to jeopardise these sectors either because they are often necessarily affected by measures and controls that are foreign to them simply because of the fact that they are located inside the port.

- Controlled surfaces

These are areas that provide commercial services to traffic that is not affected by the Code, internal piloting and small merchant ships although they make international crossings but which in the immediate future will be affected in a large number by the European legislation. Their boundaries with semi-open surfaces are diffuse and are at the entrance to specific docks, where the goods that generate this traffic is handled in operations of loading, unloading, stowage, quite close to the edge.

Some of these areas will become subjected to greater security requirements, as the European legislation and the Directive start to be implemented in the immediate future.

---

[1] A necessary step to rid the public domain of its condition of inalienability, unattachability and inprescriptibility

- Restricted surfaces

Areas which, since the beginning of July 2004 have been forced to respond to the demands of the ISPS Code which is applied to ships dedicated to international voyages:

- Passenger ships, including high speed passenger vessels.
- Cargo ships, including high speed vessels, with a gross tonnage equal too r above 500.
- Mobile off-shore drilling units.
- The port facilities that provide services to such ships dedicated to international voyages.

These last surfaces shall have specific plans, predetermined people in charge and action protocols according to the evaluations and risk analyses.

All of this puts the Spanish port system into a situation of crisis as it had allowed an important relaxation in the field of security services in recent years. When talking about public safety this includes that which is the competence of the Ministry of the Interior (the Civil Guard is almost exclusively dedicated to its fiscal duties) and that which depends on the Port Authorities (the harbour guards have withdrawn a large part of their duties in security matters and focused on providing services).

In security matters they will now have to make an effort to adapt to the new demands given that the threats are real and that we have already suffered their most severe consequences. Unfortunately, we are not immune to the dangers that appear on the horizon of this XXI Century.

World instability, the struggles of civilisations and cultures, religious fanaticism, the depletion of resources, the inequality of the classes, poverty, migrations and wars, to name but a few of the important vectors, are going to influence the historical evolution and place Spain, which is in the geographical crossroads in the social, political and strategic crossroads as well, that is if it is not already there. This will require brave decisions and decisive leadership in security matters. All of this will make it possible to anticipate events, make useful decisions and be prepared to give answers to threats, both in preventive and operational security, which is a question for everyone as in the more specific and professional which corresponds to the Security Forces and Corps.

From the perspective of the ISPS Code, we must make it quite clear that it will not mention ports, as the Code always refers to port facilities, in the understanding that they are subareas of the ports. That is the way it is and therefore inside a port there can be several port facilities: docks for cruise ships, for coal ships, containers, oil tankers, each one with their own corresponding plan and with their PFSO. This is vital if we wish to understand that the intention is that the different port facilities become security capsules within a more extensive port space but in which the security measures are not so strict. In Spain, the Ports of General Interest would be a kind of second circle of security, on a first area that represents the specific port facility. Therefore a typical Port of General Interest may have:

- One or several port facilities for cruise ships (public and managed by the Port Authority)
- A port facility for containers (usually managed by concession holders and therefore private for our purposes).
- A port facility for general cargo (public, normally if it attends and gives service to several users).

- A port facility for liquid bulks (public).
- A ro-ro terminal type port facility (private)
- Facilities that include those of anchoring and areas fro manoeuvring, etc. (public).

7.2 Port organisation. Autonomy and management efficiency

Speaking of the Ports of General Interest, the new legislation of the Spanish public port system, issued in 1997 and 2003, aims at giving a leading role to each of the ports, individually, and to all of them collectively in so far as they are entities that have to operate with business criteria, as economic units and offer surfaces and services, giving more freedom of decision both in procedures and in business systems to the Port Authorities and entities that manage the ports. Thus a Public Entity is created with independent management and with legal personality and its own budgets which has to address its duties with criteria of efficiency and good business.

It may be said that the Public Entity Ports of the State takes on the role of a large company which reports to the Ministry of Development for guidelines and objectives relating to management. In the last decade the autonomous Communities have taken on a more important role which conditions the exclusive competence of the State as established in the Spanish Constitution.

Ports of the State is a public entity in charge of the execution of the government's port policy and of the coordination and control of the efficiency of the port system.

The successive laws of ports have gradually made it possible to change from a model inherited from a historical past with other circumstances which was very interventionalist to a much more liberal one in line with our current economical, geopolitical and strategic environment. Thus, maritime companies will have more flexibility to face the challenge of competitiveness; to be able to operate with business criteria and without certain easements that gave the old ports such a rigid organisation which responded to a different economic model.

Spanish maritime activity is developed not only in the ports but also in the spaces in which Spain exercises sovereignty, sovereign rights or jurisdiction and even in other navigable waters.

There are also private ports which are taking on more important roles. These are large oil, gas, coal terminals etc., which, through concessions, have become managers of their own activity without them having public port services. This has been possible thanks to the concentration in recent decades of companies and the privatisation of important sectors of the activity that were in public hands. Now the larger volume of business and the greater business dimension make self management much more feasible.

On the other hand, the Autonomous Communities have exclusive competence on the appointed ports which are those that are not of General Interest, although many of them handle traffic which means that they are affected by the ISPS Code. As an example, of the 122 autonomous ports in Galicia, 8 of them have had to elaborate their own PFSP.

From what has been said we can deduce that there are three possibilities for organising maritime traffic in port surfaces.

- state (public entity. Ports of General Interest),
- autonomic (public entity. Autonomous Communities.).
- private (concessions).

7.2.1 Ports of General Interest

Regarding security and the implementation of the PFSP and to those who have to execute it, there has traditionally been an important infrastructure with respect to police presence:

- The Civil Guard, who is in charge of their custody in accordance with OL Law of the Security Forces and Corps.
- Harbour guards who, as agents of authority, have specific protection duties in accordance with the Regulations of Port Police and Port Ordinances. In recent times they did not exercise these duties in accordance with their possibilities and recently claimed a stronger role in security matters more in line with the times and with the needs and laws.
- Other security personnel also perform specific duties, especially security guards who, without a doubt, will have their field of action in those functions that do not require the exercise of authority or of public function and in so far as liberalisation limits their possibilities, they may watch over private cargo deposited in the docks, control the locked premises of concession holders, help the Harbour Guard and the Civil Guard in access control and points of embarkation, etc.

7.2.2 Autonomic ports

The Autonomous Communities have other ports[2] assigned to them. If they perform certain international traffic or are the destination of ships affected by the ISPS Code, they will need to have the appropriate plans, implement the corresponding security measures and designate the corresponding PFSO.

Moreover, inside each port they should mark and limit the port facility that serves this traffic and which are now affected.

Although they have harbour guards or other similar figures of a public nature, given the options that they have in their respective areas, they are not really in a position to offer private security services. Besides, the Civil Guard, who has been rendering more general services, has not traditionally deployed personnel for this purpose or has withdrawn them which means that they will be obliged to use private security personnel, at least in what will be the defined port facility and with access control to respond to the new and stricter demands. The PFSO will be autonomic civil servants.

In most cases these ports will have to make important investments and will have to raise the price of the services they offer. Tariffs will be increased in a significant manner. They are the ports which are least prepared in security matters to take on the demands of the new world and European regulations.

---

[2] Attribution is the title that makes it possible to occupy the state land maritime public domain.

The Autonomous Communities have been putting the accent of their investment on their ports in the area of leisure and fishing fleets and have paid less attention to this traffic.

7.2.3 Private terminals

They shall designate those responsible and take on the plans with their own personnel or with private security personnel at the same time as having to separate the spaces affected as a port facility from the rest of the spaces that make up the surface of the concession.

From the point of view of security they have private services and updated security systems which means that the effort required to get up to date to answer the new demands will be less. Maybe they should make an effort in the surveillance of the adjacent waters, provided that they are included in the concession. They shall have a capacity for response, with personnel and surveillance and patrolling boats, inside the waters that are included in the area of the concession and shall be the current priority from a calm and novel analysis of the potential risks.

In the same way, they shall evaluate the possibility of limiting their maritime area with luminous buoys to alert intruders that they are entering a forbidden area.

7.3 Purpose of the ISPS

The purpose of the PFSP will be to limit, within each port, certain areas which will be affected by the ISPS Code because of the traffic they have and the type of ships that will dock there.

Because of the above, they shall designate a number of people responsible for security matters who, under the management of the PFSO and other public and/or private security personnel, are going to plan security as per the prescriptions of the Code, by developing their respective PFSP, carrying them out and guaranteeing their implementation and revision if appropriate.

Besides, all of those who take on competences in matters of security, must carry out exercises and practices to verify that the personnel of the port facility dominate all the protection tasks that are assigned to them at the different levels of protection, and identify any security deficiency that must be repaired such if it has any incidence in the port activities it is corrected.

In order to guarantee the efficiency of the provisions of the PFSP they must carry out drills at least every 3 months unless the circumstances require otherwise. In these specific drills different elements of the plan such as the threats to protection must be tested.

The drills must include all the possible activities according to the main activity of the facility in question and of the traffic managed there. But they must be focused on the area of security, mainly on people. For activities related to the environment with contingencies for dangerous goods, etc., there are other more specific plans and drills that can be carried out in a coordinated manner or not.

It will be extremely important to work with real hypotheses, such as:

- bombs,
    - warning on the ship
    - in the terminal
    - at another part of the facility
- taking of hostages,
- suicide terrorists.

Although the matter is dealt with in a general manner, in practice it should be adapted to the specific needs of each port facility so certain considerations that might be common to most incidences will be made.

Calm and reasoning are basic qualities that must be instilled into those responsible for security for a better management of the crisis at its worst.

Any alarm relating to parcel bombs, car bombs, etc. must be reported immediately to the FCSE, the PFSO, the SSO of the Port Authority, the fire service, Civil Protection and Health and of course the Port Authority.

Then, when the place in which the incident that represents the threat is known, both in the ship and in the port facility, maximum attention must be paid to the possible harm to people, especially if there are large agglomerations of people such as in passenger or cruise ships. Then people must be evacuated towards neutral areas away from the focal point of the incident. People will be disembarked from the ship starting with the passengers and then the crew only in very exceptional cases and with the consent of the Captain.

If the incident so permits, the most important people should at least remain on board, in order to manoeuvre the boat if required. In so far as is possible the passengers should disembark with their hand luggage and personal belongings which will make it easier for the Security Forces and the specialist teams to search for the artefact.

Evacuation shall be coordinated with the Security Forces and Corps, who should take the initiative once they are on the scene. The ship's captain, the SSO, the PFSO and the person in charge of the Security Forces and Corps shall remain together or in contact in case they need to make any technical consultation or specific collaboration is required.

If it were necessary to move the ship and an isolation area has been designated in the port, it will be taken there, with the Captain's consent and under his command.

The isolation of the area corresponds to the Security Forces and Corps who shall secure a deserted area in the vicinity of the incident and shall establish the adequate protective measures by trying to divert vehicle and pedestrian traffic from the place and keeping curious onlookers away. The evacuated people should not be sent to areas that have not been checked or are deserted in case other artifacts have been placed there as a trap to cause further damage.
Evacuation at first responds to the needs of the emergency. Later it must be planned and approved by the Delegates or Subdelegates of the Government, especially in the case of buildings.

The Security Forces establish themselves in certain points, linked and communicated with each other, in control of the evacuated surface and maintaining contact with those responsible and with the coordinator of the team of specialists in case it becomes necessary to extend the area or evacuate new areas.

A detail that should not be forgotten when evacuating a ship or a port facility is that the person or persons who placed the bomb may be among those evacuated. Therefore it is convenient to identify all those evacuated, once the danger to their lives has been controlled.

All equipment must be inspected both manually and with dogs, always by specialists of the Security Forces and Corps. They will be given all the technical and material assistance they require from everyone.

The Area Centre or Marine Search and Rescue Centre warns those navigating in the area in case any ship comes close to the area while the police services patrol the water side of the ship and of the facility creating an area of exclusion for safety reasons.

As the port facilities subjected to the ISPS Code are restricted areas with strong security measures among which is a strict access control, the first and most important thing will be to open the accesses to avoid avalanches leading to bottleneck situations before starting to evacuate the area or to channel the crowd in a safe direction.

The fire extinguishing or health services remain alert in the surrounding areas but away from the danger areas, closed off by a fence or tape.

In the case of a bomb scare which leads to the evacuation of people, because they are in the area where the bomb has been placed, the first thing will be to cordon off a sufficiently large area which will be made larger still as more personnel arrive and time passes with the main objective of avoiding human victims and material damage.

Any evacuation of people in a situation of crisis requires that right from the start those managing the situation take into consideration a series of facts about how crowds react. Reactions are unconscious and very different and sometimes quite opposed to the way that an individual would normally behave alone. For this reason the port facility's uniformed security personnel, who will be a visual reference, in following the instructions of the SSO and of the PFSO, depending on whether the incident occurs on board or in the port facility, or the person responsible for security in charge of resolving the crisis once the Security Forces and Corps have appeared on scene, must be aware of the main characteristics and behaviours of the masses. These may be summarised as the following:

- Groups of humans obey certain unforeseeable automatisms within the situation they find themselves immersed.

- The crowd is impulsive, unstable and in the end, can believe any rumour no matter how unfounded it may be.

- The crowd is characterised by an accidental unit of thought that is determined from its being immersed in a situation that is normally unkown to it and for which it is not rationally prepared. The individual personality of each person is replaced by a momentary collectiveness which leads to a collective personality through a strong suggestive effect. Impulses, conditioned by fear, replace reasoning.

- Intelligence is minimised, the capacity for reasoning practically disappears, the masses move on impulses and credibility reaches childish proportions. Any rumour that is spread reaches the masses with an uncontrollable sense of truth.

- False news, no matter how absurd and incredible it may be, spreads through the masses with incredible speed and provokes unpredictable reactions just seconds later and may even suddenly change the course of events.

- The crowd becomes a throng and lacks the effective authority, with only the weight of its numbers, which means that this emotional unstability does not keep up its demands for very long, as it is incapable of holding a lasting desire such as a constant thought.

- The masses do not control their impulses, do not premeditate at all. For this reason, their purposes, objectives and capacity for action are aspects that must be known at all times through efficient, in depth and timely information.

- The reasaoning of the crowd is based on very simple ideas, through the association of similar cases and the generalisation of special cases. The crowd lacks a critical spirit and a capacity for analysis.

- Imagination is representative, powerful and very active.

- The agglomeration of a large number of people occasionally runs the risk of becoming a crowd and in any case, when there is no order and unexpected reactions, can provoke accidents, aggressions and injuries to people and damage to objects. A situation that produces concern or surprise in the crowd can degenerate into fear which can spreadlike wildfire to end up in a situation of panic or collective hysteria with fatal consequences which means that this cirumstance will always have to be taken into consideration. No one can forget the human avalanches that have occurred in football stadiums and which have caused numeorus victims. These circumnstances will have to be taken into account at all times so that a hasty evacuation does not lead to more victims than the original crisis situation itself.

- On the other hand, the more pacific human concentration, when moving in a certain direction, takes on a terrible force that can overcome the personnel located in a certain point, if this reaction has not been foreseen or if the stimulus that provoked it has not been avoided.

- All of this makes it necessary at all times to consider all the possibilities that could overwhelm us; these precautionary measures will be greater as the number of people congregated increases and the circumstances must always be evaluated in any case. When action is taken it must respond to criteria of a strictly professional nature and shall adopt the general approaches and appropriate strategies in virtue of it.

- The preventive approach must closely evaluate the physical variables of the context (amplitude of physical spaces, entrances and exits, direction of the voyage, presence of impediments and any other element of possible interest) in order to be able to use them. This is a prior condition that must be contemplated in the PFSP and the ordinances in each port, for their facilities.

- The presence of emotion in the masses is always a powerful element and therefore is easily impressionable and controllable. Ideas become slightly lethargic, behaviour becomes a priority. It is necessary to be correct in dealing with people and to show uniformity, composure and discipline because the first impression is very important and the Police is always an important reference for the crowds in these situations.

7.4 Situations that could cause panic

a) An observed threat

A threat can be physical, psychological or a combination of both. It will be aggravated when it occurs on a ship docked in a port because the spaces are reduced and the escape routes narrow.

The threat of a bomb or a fire, for example, on board a ship is considered as imminent when there is no time to lose and everyone tries to escape, These incidents must be foreseen, be tested and taken in by those who intervene in security. In the same way, although in different circumstances, we can speak of a port facility, although the spaces and the escape routes have greater and better possibilities when it comes to evacuating crowds of people.

b) Partial trap
There is only one escape route (or maybe a limited number) in a situation dominated by an observed threat.

c) Partial or complete elimination of the escape route

The escape route may be blocked or overlooked.

d) Failure in communication between the front and back ends of the crowd

The false assumption that the exit is open makes the back of the crowd press forward to try to get there. This pressure can lead to those at the front being suffocated, trampled on or knocked over. When trying to get out, accesses, even emergency ones must all be speedy and open.

7.5 Control of the crowd

It will be possible to control the crowd by:

- Having a final action plan, within the SSP or the PFSP, for each eventuality and inform all security personnel of their existence and their procedures.
- Having personnel adequately trained for the correct execution of the plan, and leaving a small part of the crew (or ground personnel, depending on where the incident took place) on standby to cover any contingency that might arise and not be foreseen in the evacuation plan, for immediate use if the emergency were to take a turn for the worse.
- Having all loudspeaker systems and transmissions ready and operating in good condition and perfect order, in the case of an emergency.

- Having the crew of the ship and the security personnel of the port facility in their respective posts before the crowds arrive or the evacuation commences.
- Establishing a system of communications among all those peole who have specific security duties.
- Isolating and immediately removing causes of tension from the crowd, such as hysterical individuals, drunk or disorderly people and/or those who commit antisocial acts.
- Taking care that no crew member or security personnel in the facility that is part of the operation, is isolated in the middle of a crowd because although it is pacific there could be elements in it that could make it hostile in a situation of stress.
- All those responsible for security that are available, either on board or on land, coordinated by the SSO or the PFSO until the Security Forces arrive, must contribute to avoiding panic as well as carrying out their other duties.
- A calm and serene but firm attitude must be maintained in any situation that arises.
- Special tact is required in dealing with women, children and the elderly, given their special charactristics as in these situations they may be more vulnerable.
- When the crowds are dispersed it may be easier to control them if they are grouped, though this must not lead to forgetting that the most important factor when faced with a threat is to quickly clear the area around where it may be detonated at any moment.
- Without putting the floatability and stablility of the ship in danger and with the knowledge of its Captain, people must be moved from top to bottom or viceversa depending on the emergency and where the bomb is located if evacuation is not recommenndable. A safe area must be considered beforehand.
- If a ship is to be evacuated in the dock the procedure will be as follows:
    - All of the crew will be informed and situated in their posts in line with the previously established plan. All personnel shall have means to communicate with the person responsible for the plan.
    - The passengers will be adequately informed of the situation without alarming them, telling them clearly and concisely where, how and when they have to go. The meeting point must have the required conditions of safety in light of the nature of the emergency and the number of passengers.
    - Before starting the evacuation route must be checked to make sure it is free form obstacles.
    - Crew will enter the upper decks to start evacuation from there (or the lower decks if evacuation is upwards) cabin by cabin and not leave anything behind them. The crew will occupy transit areas and shall prevent the evacuees from blocking passage ways or the evacuation routes.
    - In the cabins or lounge areas with a large number of people they shall enter if possible along the walls to the far end of the room and evacuate from their outwards towards the chosen route.
    - Another possibility is to evacuate progressively forming a kind of flowing chain.
    - Attempts must be made to avoid closing open doors and of evacuated places becoming occupied.
    - Complete evacuation or grouping will continue level by level or lineally in a previously designated area away from the crisis point or towards the ramps or disembarkment gates if possible and this way and option are considered valid.

- o Do not forget to check everywhere and block the lifts and emergency staircases so that they are not used without authorisation or by the masses beyond their technical possibilities, thus blocking them.
- o Once the evacuatiuon is completed a head count will be made and the evacuees identified.

Once the area has been evacuated it shall be isolated using the means available. At first, this will normally be a plastic tape which must be included in the contents of the official vehicles and should have some text message repeated on it along the lines of "Police. Do not pass."

At the same time as evacuation is being secured, the incident must be reported to the competent or nearest Security Forces so that they can adopt the required measures. Once they arrive they shall take over control of the management of the crisis. From this moment on, the port police shall give the assistance required of them as it will now be the Security Forces who take the inititiatives they consider appropriate through their specialist teams to control the incident and in matters related to terrorism.

The incident shall be resolved by specialists in defusing bombs and normally they will be accompanied by dogs specially trained in locating explosives.

Another matter that has to be considered is if hostages are taken on the ship. As this a place of veery difficult access if there is no collaboration from the inside, these situations are very difficult to handle and much will depend on whether the taking of hostages includes having taken control of the ship and its crew, which on the other hand, is not easy if the establsihed security measures have been taken. On other occasions it could be that a specific area of the ship is taken over and with a group of hostages. In any case these are extremely complicated situations that require crisis management by specialists accordng to the demands that are made. Any act of taking hostages involves negotiation of the demands. A reasonable period of time is usually allowed and it is important to note that it is usually the specialists who take over the situation. The port police and others responsible for security must collaborate and advise, as far as required of them and must forget that the public safety and maritime safety must be combined so as not to put the ship and the rest of the possibly unaffected crew members and passengers in danger.

7.6 Drills

Drills must be made at least once a year, but without more than 18 months elapsing between them. The PFSO will participate in them together with the Government authorities, the CSO and the SSO if they are available. Despite the generality of the Code, it is obvious that Government Authorities refers to the Security Forces and Corps deployed in the port in question. The requests for participation of the CSO and of the SSO in joint drills must be made after considering their repercussions on the security and operation of the ships. These drills must try out the communications, coordination, the availability of resources and the way of acting in the case of an event.

Drills can be:

- Made on a full scale or live
- Be a theoretical simulation or a seminar.

Security is personified in the harbour guards and in private security who are those who take on the main role of the preventive functions of private security depending on whether they are public or private terminals. In the first drills they will need to be familiar with the contents of the ISPS Code and with the port Regulations and Ordinances. This need will be all the more important in private security.

At the beginning of awareness training, given the specific nature of the matter, it is important to keep in mind that the seminars are something that are quite necessary to become acquainted and familiar with the problems that are being evidenced in this study. It would be a good idea if the Port Authorities and private companies signed protocols in this matter wth respect to training and that the local or autonomic security academies use them for these purposes.

- Combine them with other drills that for example give a response to an emergency or other drills related with the State authority managing the port.

7.7 Content of the PFSP

The preparation of the PFSP is rhe responsibility of the PFSO. Although it is not necessary for the PFSO to personnally handle all the duties that correspond to this position, in the end he will always be repsonsible for the tasks being adequately completed.

The content of each PFSP varies according to the special cirumstances of the port facility in question. This will be more complex and more effort will be required in security matters in the case of those ports that are specifically involved in the traffic of ships dedicated to the regular transport of passengers, of which we have a lot of experience in Spain and especially in the port of Algeciras where there are significant movements of people in holiday periods across the sea to the ports of Afrcia and then back as they return. In the same way special attention is required for cruise ships, especially in the ports of embarkation, such as Barcelona, but also in those used as ports of call, although to a lesser extent.

In the Port Facility Security Evaluation (PFSE) the special characteristics of the port facilities and the risks for their security will have been identified, giving special priiority to human life as is logical. When preparing the PFSP it is necessary to take these security considerations into account in order to take the measures to minimise the risk of their being a failure in security and its consequences. The states may elaborate guidelines on the preparation and the content of the security plans for port facilities.

From internal regulation, the Regulation of Exploitation and Policing and especially the Ordinances of each port, in so far as they adapt the reality of the traffic, threats and specific problems to the different existing port facilities, it will be a useful instrument to accommodate these demands with the reality of the port, which wll give those responsible for security, the most elemental criteria for carrying out their work without prejudice to the specific instructions that the Port Authorities may establish.
Apart form the fact that the contents of the PFSP should be in harmony with the stipulations of the Ordinances that are elaborated, every PFSP should:

- Give a detailed description of the organisation of the security of the port facility that should be included in the Ordinances of the port in question.

- Give a detailed description of the organisational links with other authorities and the configuration of the communications systems that are required for the efficient operation of the organisation and of its links, including those ships that are in the port. The knowledge of where the nearest police stations are and the means available in case they are required and the channels of communication must be available for all those who perform duties related to security in the facility.

- Give a detailed description of the basic security meausres, both physical and operative that have been adopted for level 1.

- Give a detaled description of the additional measures that make it possible for a facility to pass on without delay to level 2 and if required to level 3.

- Foresee periodical revisions and audits of the PFSP and their possible amendment based on experience or on a change of citrcumstances.

- Give a detailed description of the procedures for reporting to the corresponding points of contact with the Contracting Governments.

All of the PFSP must be approved by the Government under whose jurisdiction the port facility lies. They must elaborate procedures to evaluate the efficiency of each PFSP. The PFSP must contemplate measures to preserve the records of all events or threats as well as their revisions and audits, training, exercises and drills. The fact that the port directors have approved their own security plans does not seem very congruent with the stipulations of the Code, regardless of whether or not they send them to their superiors in the Public Entity, where they will be subjected to the report of the Secretary of State for Security of the Ministry of the Interior.

We must remember that the use of firearms on board ships, or nearby them and in the port facilities may imply risks for security, especially regarding certain dangerous or potentially dangerous substances and must be taken into careful consideration. Should a Government decide that it is necessary to have armed personnel in these areas, the Government must make sure that this personnel is duly authorised and has received adequate training in the use of weapons and is conscious of the specific risks for security that exist in these areas. If a Government authorises the use of firearms it must give specific security guidelines on their use. The PFSP must contain specific guidelines relating to this question, especially with respect to their application to ships that transport dangerous goods or potentially dangerous goods.

Weapons must always be used in accordance with the basic action principles included in article 5 of OL 2/86 on Security Forces and Corps, Such principles are congruency, proportionality and opportunity and always in self defense or in the defense of third parties. In any case their use is problematic and must be reserved for specialists in security.

7.8 Confidentiality

The governments shall make sure that measures are taken to avoid the unauthorised distribution of confidential material on security and may name an authority to carry out the functions of security relating to the port facilities. Appropriate measures must be taken at all times to guarantee the confidentiality of the contents of a PFSP.

The PFSP shall include common elements at all levels including, among others, the procedures and practices to safeguard the confidential information on security in either paper or electronic format.

Confidentiality is not only a requirement in the performance of a duty in a job but the Spanish Penal Code severely sanctions the lack of it in certain circumstances because it can lead to certain prejudices for third parties, or the State or the institutions.

In the private matter of relationships between citizens, article 197 sanctions the person who "in order to discover the secrets or violate the intimacy of another without their consent, takes possession of their papers, letters, electronic mail messages or any other documents or personal belongings or intercepts their telecommunications or uses artificial techniques for listening, transmitting, recording or reproducing sounds or images, or of any other communication signal" will be punished with penalties of up to four years in prison and a fine.

It also sanctions with the same penalties those who "without being authorised, takes possession of, uses or modifies, in prejudice of third parties, reserved data of another of a personal or family nature, that are recorded in computer, electronic or telematic files or archives or in any other type of public or private file or record. The same penalties will be imposed on those who, without authorisation, accesses these data by any means and who alters or uses them in prejudice of the owner of the data or a third party."

The penalties become more severe if "the data or facts revealed or the pictures captured as referred to above are distributed, revealed or leased to third parties."

They are also more severe if the facts described are carried out by people in charge of or responsible for the files, computer, electronic or telematic supports, records or archives and even more if the reserved data are distributed, leased or revealed.

More severe penalties are also applied when the facts affect data of a personal nature that reveal the ideology, religion, beliefs, health, racial origin or sexual life or if the victim is under age or disabled; in this case the higher level of penalties will be imposed. Conducting these activities for financial benefit is also punished.

Article 198 punishes in a more severe manner and with the penalty of suspension any authority or civil servant who, with the exception of the cases permitted by the Law, and in the absence of a legal case for the offence, abuses the position they hold and commits any of the acts described above.

Article 199 contemplates and punishes the cases in which a person reveals the secrets of others obtained through their job or work relations and the professional who, in non compliance with their obligation to remain silent, reveals the secrets of another person.
What we have seen up to here will be applicable to anyone who discovers, reveals or gives away private data of legal entities without the consent of their representatives.

According to article 201, in order to proceed against the crimes mentioned above it is necessary for the victim or their legal representative to report it. When the person is under age, disabled or unable to report the crime, the Public Prosecutor's Office may do so.

Article 278 refers to the person who, in order to reveal a company secret, takes possession of data, written or electronic documents, computer files or other objects referring to them by any means, or who uses any forbidden means or instruments. The penalty is more severe if these secrets are distributed, revealed or given away.

The stipulations of this article are understood to be notwithstanding the penalties that may arise from taking possession of or destroying computer files that could be considered as crimes of damage.

Article 279 has more severe sanctions for distributing, revealing or giving away a company secret if the person involved has a legal or contractual obligation to keep it.

Article 413 and the following address disloyalty in the custody of documents and the violation of secrets. Article 413 penalises the authority or public servant who knowingly removes, destroys, renders useless or hides totally or partially documents whose custody is their responsibility due to their position; they shall incur in the penalites established in the Code and in the special suspension of employment or a public office for a period of three to six years.

There are other articles that contemplate other facts and conducts outlawed by the Penal Code but those mentioned are sufficient for our purposes in order to approach the confidentiality requirements of the Code for those people who have access to specific security plans which the Code specifically aims to protect.

8. Port facility security plan (PFSP)

Urgency, immediacy and novelty quite often make us lose perspective of things and confuse the whole with the part. Spanish ports have already structured their own security system, although it has been quite weakened in recent times in which economic liberalisation has started to appear. The Civil Guard and the harbour guards were already offering this general service and were making sure that our public ports offered an acceptable level in this field: the first specifically and the second in a more general manner. All of this goes on as it is still in force.

We must not forget that the ISPS Code implements plans and designates people responsible for activating certain measures on specific port surfaces, known as *facilities*, at the moment in which a ship, of the ones that are affected by the Code, enters a port terminal. General security will continue to be equally important though attention is now focused on and is redirected towards a more dynamic and active security at certain moments in very reduced port spaces.

According to article 132,2 of Law 48/2003, "following a favourable report from the Ministry of the Interior and of the autonomous body with competences in matters regarding public safety on those matters that are of their competence, each Port Authority shall elaborate a plan for the security of ships, passengers and goods in the port areas against antisocial and terrorist acts which, once approved in accordance with the stipulations of the applicable legislation, will form part of the port ordinances."

In a reasonable interpretation, the bulk of this "plan for the security of ships, passengers and goods" can now be given two equally valid interpretations:

- it refers to a general plan for each Port of General Interest which will include the space reserved for the various port facilities plus the rest of the port surface, that is, it would continue to be a comprehensive port plan for the whole port.
- it refers to the different PFSP to which the Code now adapts as if it is literal, it deals with the "port areas against antisocial acts" which is a concept that is perfectly interchangeable with that of *"port facilities"* defined in the Code. In any case the concepts and contents change over time and are eventually finely tuned.

The impression is that the legislator expressly looks for a lack of definition so as not to enter in contradiction with the text of the Code which was already known but was not final on the date that the

Law was issued. Undoubtedly they were thinking of the Code Project and did not wish to be in contradiction with its contents.

The ISPS Code does not go into details about how port security is organised in each of the recipient countries that underwrite the SOLAS agreement which, on the other hand is logical given the huge variety of port organisations in all the coastline countries in the world Other applicable instruments in more reduced areas do it. This is the case of the EU. We insist here that the Public authorities responsible for security, the Port Authorities and the Maritime Authorities should pay more attention to the port Regulation and Directive so as to implement a legislation that makes it possible to adopt such demands within national legislation. We are speaking about the Code when these instruments are going to go further in their demands.

Defining the limits of the ports for security purposes, aside from or coinciding with the areas of commercial service is a constant requirement in the test of the Directive Project. That is how it was in the Law which defined the service areas in article 15.

Implementing the elaboration of the Projects of the Regulation of Exploitation and Policing is a requirement that cannot be delayed any further and to which important efforts must be dedicated. Besides, these instruments of internal legislation must go much further than what was done in other times in the Regulations and Port Ordinances in which neither the volume of the traffic, nor the types of traffic, nor the security demands were anything like they are today. The traditional format must be broken and we must have a detailed and accurate regulation.

Aside form the interactions that involve the SSP, the PFSP must have a nucleus of common elements whose non-compliances must be corrected immediately under the watchful eye of the Port Authority invested with the power and competence to correct small slips with the appropriate sanctions or warnings. All those non-compliances related to the organisation and exploitation, to spaces and accesses have their place in the Regulation. The Ordinances will be capable of particularising those differing elements which are irreconcilable in a single text, according to the changing circumstances represented by the constantly changing traffic.

If the development of the argument focuses on what interests us, the PFSP must also connect with the stipulations of the SSP like two communicating cells, in the supposition that it reaches its maximum expression in the moment of the ship-port interrelation. The two realities must form a single unit, a capsule in which security is the defining and integrating elements, with the objective of achieving, in the space and time in which the interface takes place, a level of security that guarantees the operation of the ship and of the port facility, depending on the specific circumstances of the ships, of the facilities, of the cargos and even of geographical places. All of this will contribute to minimising the risks of a terrorist attack without interfering excessively in the commercial functions and those of another nature represented by maritime transport and which must not be forgotten. Conjugating security with the demands of the flexibility and versatility of maritime transport must be a constant priority.

There are three basic personal responsibilities in achieving these objectives:

- The CSO who must make sure that the SSP is implemented and maintained and coordination with the PFSO and with the SSO. The obligation is reciprocal because the PFSO must be coordinated with the SSO and with the CSO. The same goes for the SSO.

- For his part the SSO must coordinate the security aspects of handling the ship's cargo and provisions with other ship personnel and with the corresponding PFSO.
- The PFSO to whom we refer in greater detail.

On the other hand there are two preventive and operational security instruments:

- The Ship Security Plan (SSP)
- The Port Facility Security Plan (PFSP)

As for coordination, the PFSO must be in perfect harmony with the SSO and must be the reference for communications and goings on in the facility given that it is the PFSO that guarantees permanence and continuity against the sporadic presences of the ship. He should be aware of certain facts that we describe below.

When a PFSO is informed that a ship is in a security level that is higher than that of the port facility, the officer must report to the competent authority and keep in contact with the SSO and coordinate the necessary measures.

On the other hand, if a PFSO is informed that a ship has difficulties in complying with the provisions established in the SSP and in the case of security level 3, in order to attend the security instructions given by the Government in whose territory the facility is located, normally through the Security Forces and Corps, the PFSO and the SSO shall keep in contact and coordinate the appropriate measures.

On the other hand among the tasks and responsibilities of the PFSO is that of coordinating the implementation of the PFSP with the SSO and the CSO.

The PFSO shall guarantee the efficient coordination and implementation of the PFSP through his participation at appropriate intervals, taking into consideration the guidelines given in part B of the Code.

From these observations we must suppose that guaranteeing, with human and material resources, the coordination of the joint security that interrelates the ship with the port within an area of security for a limited period of time is the main objective and priority of the Code. It is essential that it is understood this way because maximum efforts cannot be maintained too long due to the high cost involved.

8.1 Elaboration of the PFSP

The ISPS Code does not include the concept of port as it has been understood until now in Spain under Law 27/92, on Ports of the State and the Merchant Navy[1], as a group of organisation, spaces,

---

[1] Article 2. Maritime ports: Concept.

waters and facilities. The concept of port facility defines a specific area, in which the important thing is not so much the space it refers to but rather the function it offers, as all of its possibilities in security matters are activated and strengthened to a maximum in the moment of the ship-port interrelation. It refers more to a temporary, dynamic and flexible moment within a reduced space, than to the more general and static concept that was contemplated until now in our national legislation. However, on the other hand, it places the port facility into the function of the ship it serves, as it includes in the concept anchoring areas, standby docks and accesses from the sea which for us would be the navigating channel and entrance to the port.

It is important to highlight this new concept of facility against that of port only for the purpose of security as otherwise we run the risk of confusing the part with the whole as already explained and which must not be forgotten. Ports, in a global manner, carry out many other functions as an entity and organisation that must not be forgotten, even in matters relating to security, nut this is due to internal demands and to the national organisation that is still in force in all of its possibilities.

This is the important novelty and the Regulation of Exploitation and Policing, or the Regulation of Policing, if it is decided to elaborate separate instruments, following a modification in the Law of Ports, must be capable of addressing the responses from this new dimension of specific, active, flexible and temporary security.

For the sake of guaranteeing the security required by the international situation in a specific climate represented by international terrorism, certain traffic that is considered as a risk is subjected to special surveillance in the moment that the ship approaches the port and in a special manner when a "ship is affected directly or indirectly by activities that include the movement of people or goods or in providing port services to the ship or from the ship."

The main threat, objectively considered in accordance with current circumstances and the potential objective of a hypothetical terrorist attack is the ship. This does not mean that certain port facilities themselves might not be a target, and especially those dealing with petrol and chemicals.

But the main objective of any terrorist, form the point of view of his evil intention to cause as much damage as possible, would be to take over the ship, with hostages, which could themselves represent a sensitive target either because of the people being transported (cruise ships and passenger ships) or because of the cargo (oil, chemical products, gases) and shall do it in the way that taking possession of

---

1. For the purpose of this Law, maritime port is referred to as the group of land spaces, maritime water and facilities which, located on the sea shore or river banks, meets the physical, natural or artificial and organisational conditions, that make it possible to carry out port traffic operations, and is authorised for the development of these activities by the competent Administration.
2. In order to be considered as ports they must have the following physical and organisational conditions:
    - Surface of water, with an extension of no less than half a hectare, with either natural or artificially obtained adequate harbour and depth conditions for the type of ships that will use the port and for the operations of maritime traffic that is intended for it.
    - Anchoring areas, docks or docking facilities that facilitate the approach and docking of ships to carry out their operations or remain anchored or docked in adequate conditions of safety.
    - Spaces to deposit and store goods and merchandise.
    - Land structures and adequate accesses for their traffic that guarantee their connection to the main transport networks.
    - Means and organisation that make port traffic operations possible in adequate conditions of efficiency, speed, economy and security.

the ship allows him to use it as a lethal weapon against any strategic target such as another ship, a refinery or a military arsenal or to block a navigational canal etc., in such a way that could cause the greatest possible number of victims and damage to properties thus achieving a greater repercussion in the media.

With respect to cruise ships we must consider the reality in Spain that the two most important ports of Europe today are Barcelona, .with almost 1 million cruise passengers and Balearic Islands which is not far behind. Almost 6% of tourists who visit our country do so on board a cruise ship. The port of Barcelona hopes to become one of the top ten in the world in this type of traffic. Security and flexibility should go hand in hand with these aspirations. The Association of cruise ports of the Mediterranean, Medcruise, is very concerned about security. It also seeks to create security standards in the Mediterranean so that each port facility is not surprised with its specific measures and demands. This is a reasonable petition to give local responses when the interests involved are the same.

The port facilities aimed at this type of transport must also be in a position to give responses to ever larger ships which will be even bigger in the future. Royal Caribbean has announced the construction of the "Ultra Voyager" which will be larger than the "Queen Elizabeth 2" for 4,000 passengers and 160,00 GT. The port infrastructures must be prepared to take in these megaships.

For this reason, although it is addressed in a general manner in the elaboration of the PFSP, the port managers must realise that there will be as many realities of the PFSP as there are ships, cargos and the facilities that they use.

Thus, among the security measures for a cruise ship more attention will be given to the control of accesses, of vehicles, of unaccompanied packages and of provisions. As these ships transport very large quantities of people, the ship must be protected from the water. Not all ports are the same either: there will be ports of call which, because of their geographical location or the social and political conditions of their surroundings, potentially offer a greater risk. Nor is it the same that a given port facility be the origin of these pleasure trips or just a mere port of call for a few hours.

Besides, each state that is part of the SOLAS Agreement must be more involved in the elaboration of the PFSP, in such a way that two ports that could be considered as having an equally potential risk do not implement differing measures. This has already happened in our country in the early days of the Code. Little by little the situation has calmed down and been moderated though more through logic than because specific instructions had been given for the purpose.

In a petrol terminal the main measures will be very different because the most important thing is the risk of an attack on the ship and the goods transported in it. The danger for people is there too but to a lesser extent in that there is a low number of qualified personnel and no agglomeration of the kind involved in the movement of people on a ship and on a cruise or passenger terminal. A petrol or gas terminal is managed by large companies with private concessions. Due to its characteristics, a petrol terminal will already have strict access control, a fenced perimeter up to a significant height and the interior will be patrolled by guards, etc. Moreover, most likely it will have a large number of private security guards because in Spain, given its volume and specificity, it is managed by large private companies. These measures will be intensified when the ship interacts with the terminal and during the dangerous process of unloading.

In a petrol terminal it will be necessary to make fire fighting measures and measures to combat contamination compatible with those implemented by the Code, but given the normal level of security at this type of establishment, which is generally high, the implementation of the Code at level 1 will not require too much effort or cost. Besides, their personnel is high specialised. The private security personnel that work there is also familiarised with these procedures.

As in the case of the cruise ships the risks to be contemplated are those of placing explosive artefacts, attacks with grenades, a remote controlled ship bomb, explosives attached by divers, a car bomb or a personal suicide attack. These are places where both the terminals and the standby docking areas must be protected.

Without wishing to give endless examples of the possibilities of the port facilities and as reflected in the declaration of intention of the proposal for the community Directive "ports make up the essential link in a chain of transportation, as they connect on the one hand, the land and maritime transport of goods and on the other hand the flow of passengers. Ports are often places where dangerous cargos are delivered or are important points for chemical or petrochemical production or are very close to city centres. It is obvious that a terrorist attack on a port can seriously disturb the transport systems and generate a chain of effects on the surrounding industry, as well as causing human victims in the port itself and among the neighbouring population."

The transcribed paragraph gives a clear and precise idea of what a port in general is and a port facility in particular.

The PFSP shall include the following as common elements at all levels:

1. The function and structure of the organisation of the security of the port facility. In the case of the Ports of General Interest, which are the object of this study, the Board of Administration has the ownership, power and competence to implement the functions of special police which will be carried out through the director of the port or person responsible for security. These functions will be performed by the harbour guards and other personnel of the Port Authority, duly qualified and registered with the police service. This does not mean that at certain moments they cannot resort to private security for certain functions that do not involve the exercise of authority.

   The function will be adequate in virtue of the characteristics of the facility and of the traffic, of the threats and other circumstances. It shall consist of the passive security measures that allow the control of accesses, the surveillance of people, goods and spaces of the facility in order to guarantee security and especially when the ship and the facility interact.

   According to the levels of security these measures are increased or decreased to adapt to the circumstances. The elaboration of the Plan must evaluate which services will be strengthened and to what extent the security levels are increased.

   The structure of the security will include everyone, each one with their own level of responsibility within the global concept of preventive and operational security. Logically those in charge of the port police take on the leading role in special and specific security in accordance with their internal organisation.

2. The tasks, responsibilities and training requisites of all the port facility personnel that have security functions and the performance control measures that are necessary to evaluate the efficiency of each person.

It is obvious that the task of surveillance and security in the facility include controlling access with uniformed personnel who will have to be trained for this purpose and also in the use of those instruments that will help them in their function of control, such as closed circuit television cameras, metal detector gates, scanners, etc.

Such measures will require a minimum of technical and professional knowledge that will need courses and drills so that they can be considered efficient at the same time as the harbour guard personnel acquires the skills required for handling for what for them is a novel question.

They must know, albeit in an elementary manner, how international terrorism works and what its most common tactics, methods and procedures are.

They must know about weapons and dangerous instruments and have general notions about certain explosives, especially how they are assembled and what their basic components are so that if they were detected in the scanners they could recognise them. The use of scanners to recognise personal belongings and baggage requires practice to interpret the different silhouettes and objects that appear on the screen.

It is obvious that this knowledge will be in function of the responsibilities in matters of security and harbour guards must take on the main tasks; if the question is dealing with the control of passengers and baggage, under the direct supervision of the Civil Guard of the port, who are responsible for these specific functions just as in the airport.

3. The liaison of the port facility security organisation with other authorities that have security responsibilities.

In this study we have argued the need for the creation of the Security Boards or what would be called the Port Security Committee[2]. The proposal for a Directive by the European Parliament and the Council to improve maritime security speaks of what it calls the port security committee which would advise the responsible authority. The Directive dedicates its article 10 to this authority and it should be implemented at both a local and a national level.

---

[2] The composition of the Port Security Committee may vary according to the ports, but will always reflect both the operational functions of the port and those exercised by the public authority therein. The Committee shall act in accordance with the principle of "need to know" (article 10 of the Proposal for the Directive).

No matter what it is called, a body is required at a local level with a representation of the port director, the Civil Guard officer assigned to the port, the person in the National Police Force responsible for documentation and immigration and passport control, the security officers of the different port facilities present in the port and the Port Police Chief if this is not carried out by the Director or a PFSO.

This body should establish the appropriate links according to the location and the proximity of the different units. In recent times and as a result of improvisation, in certain ports we are witnessing the paradox that in the face of a crisis, the Security Forces and Corps had to react quickly, they would have to take an enormous detour to get to the port.

In the ports communications of any type are very useful but the reaction of the Police Forces in the face of a crisis is what is really important; therefore the best and quickest reaction should be made available to them. In the end, all preventive measures depend on the crisis, first and foremost to avoid it, but if it happens the Security Forces and Corps shall take on the leading role and this has not always been taken into account in the PFSP.

Accesses to the police stations in the vicinity of certain terminals have been closed. If security is a global and integrating concept, a special effort must be made by those responsible for policing the port and by the Security Forces and Corps, in order to be able to offer common and coordinated answers in extreme situations in which the life of people or the integrity of things is in danger.

In any situation it is undeniable that the Ports of General Interest need a control centre (some already have one) which establishes the management of the services, their coordination, a permanent surveillance shift is offered, there is a small emergency response standby service and communications are centralised and the screens in reception play images captured by the cameras that are installed. The surveillance of the port spaces must be complemented with that of the surface of the waters.

4. The communications systems available to maintain continuous and efficient communications between the security personnel of the port facility, the ships that are in the port and the authorities with security responsibilities.

Due to the demands of international legislation, emergency channels are currently being used at sea that allow permanent communication with the Control Centres and Maritime Traffic of the State Society of Maritime Rescue and Security (SASEMAR). Any communications system that expects to be useful shall take these conditions into consideration and especially with respect to ships so as to make their transmissions compatible with those in use in the port.

This communications system must allow a direct communication with the Operations Centres of the Civil Guard Services (COS 062) and with the Control Rooms of the National Police Forces (091).

Integrating maritime communications with port communications and with those of the police Coordination Centres must be a task for the Port Control Centre to which we refer above.

In Spain, the specific procedures to communicate alarms depend on who detects the alarms.

If the alarm comes from the ship, the SSO will be responsible for it reaching the CSO who in turn shall make sure it reaches the SASEMAR and the Permanent Centre of Information and Coordination (CEPIC). If the SSO could not connect with the CSO he shall make the aforementioned communications. The CEPIC communicates the alarm to the Secretary of State for Security (SES) which is the organ of the Ministry of the Interior who shall make it known to the maritime organisation, the General Directorate of the Merchant Navy and the Public Entity Ports of the State. The SES shall in turn inform the Security Forces and Corps in charge of resolving the crisis represented by the threat. At the same time the SES shall determine the level of security applicable to the ship and, if appropriate, to the port facility in which it is located or to which it is heading.

The CEPIC must then communicate with the Harbour Master affected by the event, so that he can establish the appropriate communications with the CSO and with the ship in terms of maritime security. The CEPIC shall also notify the Port Authority affected so that it can be communicated to the PFSO of the port facility that is going to be affected.

If the alarm is detected by a port facility, the PFSO shall communicate it first of all to the Port Authority who shall inform the Harbour Master so that he in turn can make it known to the CSO, who shall inform the SSO and the Captain and those responsible for security on board.

At the same time the Port Authority shall make another communication to relate the alarm and other circumstances to the CEPIC who shall transmit the threat to the SES who shall make it know to the Public Entity Ports of the State and the General Directorate of the Merchant Navy and more importantly, shall inform the Security Forces and Corps of the State who shall be responsible for resolving the crisis and everything that implies.

The SES shall be responsible for determining the levels of security that the response to the crisis determine and shall communicate it through the same channels as it received the news.

If the alarm comes from the news that the Security Forces and Corps of the State or other security forces receive or from third parties that have reported the facts that determine the threat, once it reaches the Coordination Centres of the Security Forces and Corps it will be transmitted to the SES, who shall report in the reverse order of that described above through the CEPIC to the Port Authority and to SESEMAR so that the circumstance of the threat can in turn be made known first to the PFSO and the port facility and then to the CSO and the SSO. The level of security that is to be applied and the specific instructions to address the crisis shall be given together with these notifications.

Ports of the State and the General Directorate of the Merchant Navy shall coordinate with their respective organisations, the former with the Port Authorities and the latter with the Harbour Master and SASEMAR.

At the same time, the SES shall be in contact with the Delegates or Subdelegates of the Government who are affected by the size of the crisis in order to adopt the appropriate measures that make it possible to give an adequate response to the crisis in question. These coordinate the Security Forces and Corps although at first it will be the Civil Guard who is responsible for addressing these crises as they are in charge of the surveillance of the territorial sea and of the ports. Besides in the territorial sea they have the naval means to provide security in and from the water.

5. The procedures and safeguards required for these communications to be continuous are guaranteed at all times.

   Given the current status of the techniques and science of telecommunications, the possibilities of secraphones provide different procedures to guarantee the confidentiality of these communications. Systems to encrypt written messages have also become more generalised which means that in our country at least the only problem is one of money.

   Integrating the communications that must respond to these needs into one should not offer too big a problem regarding communication or confidentiality.

6. The procedures and practices to safeguard the confidential information on security on paper or in an electronic format.

   The Code allows the PFSP or the SSP to be kept in a computer format. Each person involved in the duties and responsibilities of security shall know the part of the Plan that affects them, but the Plan as a whole and certain stipulations of it are secret and its confidentiality must be guaranteed not only with regard to the outside of the ship or the port facility, but also on the inside and with the rest of the crew. A good criterion when establishing the degrees of access and of confidentiality is to use the principle consolidated in the EU, which is that of the *need to know*. In matters of security nobody should know more than is necessary to carry out their duties and only a few people, who are involved in the decision making process, should know the whole Plan. This is one of the best ways of avoiding the unjustified diffusion of security matters.

   For this reason, anyone responsible for security will be obliged to have access to a Security Plan on computerised paper in an electronic format, but only to the level of their participation and responsibility. Therefore, in the case of electronic files, codes will be applied according to the needs and the levels of knowledge required. The maximum level of access will only be available to those responsible for making decisions.
   The plan may be kept in an electronic format and will be protected against unauthorised access or diffusion.

   But the PFSO must know that the SSP are not subject to the inspection of the officials authorised by a Contracting Government, but if they have reason to believe that the ship does not meet the requirements and the only way of verifying non-compliance is to examine the requirements corresponding to the SSP, limited access of an exceptional nature to the sections of the Plan relating to the non-compliance will be allowed, but only with the consent of the Government of the ship in question or of the Captain. It will be necessary to specify who the duly authorised officials are and how this accreditation is carried out. They should be officials from the Security Forces and the Public Entity such as the person responsible for the Port police service or the PFSO in each port facility.

7. The procedures to evaluate the efficiency of the security measures, procedures, and equipment, including the procedures to identify and correct any failure.

The measures that are put into place in each case within the contents of the Plan must be justified and efficient thus avoiding superfluous and useless ones. Their evaluation shall be constant and must be based on direct observation and on the analysis of risks which are variable in time and depend on the cargos and on the origins and destinations of the ships that access the terminal. We must not forget that the port facility depends on maritime navigation and the traffic of goods and it is to this interaction that the Code dedicates special attention.

This focus is not always clear in the Spanish ports. They usually adopt strong, often exaggerated and unjustified, security measures on land leaving the maritime part of the port facilities practically unattended. The biggest dangers for a ship in port, given the techniques and procedures of modern terrorism, are going to come from the side of the ship facing the water. There is no doubt about this. High speed boats represent a risk that has to be taken into account.

On the other hand, the port authorities must not delay in providing port police or contracting private security that is capable of maintaining some kind of surveillance on certain anchoring berths. The anchoring berth is always a likely target for certain ships because of the traffic they bring and where they are much more vulnerable than in the port which means that regardless of the security measures that the ships must implement, the port authorities have to have their own security or allow them to contract private security. This security will be an added cost which means that prudence must be applied in the demands and each case must be evaluated.

8. The procedures to present and evaluate reports relating to possible failures or worrying security aspects.

This will require permanent checks on the system to detect flaws. The passive security systems must be carried out by specialised personnel an in accordance with previously established protocols, especially those that require specialised knowledge such as metal detector gates and scanners.

9. The procedures relating to handling the cargo.

According to the type of cargo different risk analyses will be made, with special emphasis on closed cargos such as containers and movable chests. Sophisticated electronic control devices are necessary for this type of traffic that make it possible to make an initial exploration without breaking the seals to then decide whether or not to open the containers. In any case visual control of a percentage of the containers is essential. This will be increased according to the possible risks of the situation.

10. The procedures relating to the delivery of supplies.

If the supplying companies do so on a regular basis it is possible to reach an agreement and joint measures to achieve greater efficiency. The suppliers will apply agreed control procedures on the supplies from origin and make sure that they are not accessible to third parties during transport.

11. The procedures to keep an inventory of dangerous goods and potentially dangerous goods updated and where to place them in the port facility.

12. The means for alerting the maritime patrols and specialised search teams, including experts in searching for bombs and underwater searches and for obtaining their services.

    When there is an incident that involves the presence or the use of explosive devices of any kind, the Security Forces and Corps will be called in with their specialists.

    The Civil Guard has its patrols that will be useful for responding to the possible threats and to offer security in certain circumstances though we must not forget that we are speaking about preventive security that the port maritime operates must implement and that the Security Forces and Corps take on their real leading role at security level 3 where they will have to assume the management of the crisis and coordinate the response measures.

    This does not mean that they lose the initiative to carry out specific actions aside from the stipulations of the security plans within the much wider obligation of looking after people and properties that the law entrusts them.

13. The procedures to help the SSO to confirm the identity of the people who wish to go on board, when requested.

    For those in charge of these functions, for example access control, their legitimacy to identify people is based on the possibility that they have to reject any person who does not identify themselves. From this faculty to exclude those who do not meet the above conditions comes the possibility of identifying. Only the Security Forces and Corps may proceed to take a person who refuses to identify themselves to the nearest police station in accordance with the procedure established in OL 1/92 on the Protection of Public Security.

    The following pages give a detailed account of these procedures.

14. The procedures to facilitate land leave for the ship's personnel, changes of personnel and access to the ship for visitors.

    The Code wishes to guarantee the possibility of going on shore because it is essential for embarking or disembarking after the agreed period of service. These measures that are now being put into practice should not have a negative repercussion on the embarked personnel that is part of the crew when it comes to them going on shore. The International Labour Organisation (ILO) was considered n the elaboration of the Code.

    In its 283rd meeting, held in March 2002, the Board of Administrators of the ILO included the question of greater security in the identification of seafarers with a view to adopting a protocol for an Agreement on the identity documents for seagoing people of 1958, as an urgent matter on the agenda of the 91st meeting of the International Labour Conference.

    As for access for visitors to the ship, there are no problems at security level 1. At security level 2 they should be restricted to accompanied visits and at level 3 they should not be allowed.

The measures that may be adopted for each level of security with relation to the following aspects are detailed below:

- Access to the port facility.
- Restricted areas of the port facility.
- Handling cargo.
- Delivery of the ship's supplies.
- Unaccompanied baggage.
- Surveillance of port facility security.

8.2 Access to the port facility

The purpose of access control is to prevent the unauthorised access to ships and port facilities and to their restricted areas. There may be three types of important controls and each one of them is more demanding than the previous one; access to the port, access to the port facility and access to the ship. Once inside the ship a system must be perfectly defined in which the areas to which access must be restricted is specified; the bridge, the machine areas and other positions of control.

A weak point that is often forgotten is the control of accesses from the water, both to the ship and to the port facility. It is essential that the Port Authorities, port facility concession holders and those responsible for the ports in the Autonomous Communities have a system for this purpose; preventive and operational security in normal situations is their responsibility and security in the water is no less important than that on land. The Code does not distinguish and should not distinguish. Besides, these controls avoid the presence or escape of stowaways.

The anchor berths are another weak point because of their vulnerability to suicide ships. Sensitive traffic cannot be anchored for long periods of time and systems must be implemented to avoid prolonged stays in anchorage areas without discriminating against the established shifts. Stays in anchorage berths must be kept to a minimum if security is not guaranteed.

The correct identification of people, of their personal belongings and of the vehicles they drive is vital in any access control. This is something that must be clearly defined in any security plan and therefore in the Regulations and Port Ordinances.

It is important because it means interfering in the personal affairs of citizens and must not be done in an arbitrary manner, but rather in accordance with the formalities required by the laws and with maximum respect for people and their rights.

This should not be a hindrance for those who carry out these controls to have the knowledge, without it being of a discriminatory nature, of the characteristics and behaviour patterns of those people who might be a threat to security and who intend to infiltrate these controls. The main purpose of any access control is to prevent people who intend to cause damage and the instruments they use for that purpose from getting on board a ship or inside a port facility.

Those responsible for access controls must have some knowledge of the techniques used to avoid security measures.

Given the organisation of the Spanish ports and in particular, the organisation of the ports of the State or Ports of General Interest, to a certain extent the port facilities to which the Code refers, the control of access to the facility will be like a second filter following the first one at the entrance to the port. All State ports have access control that have been updated with electronic measures and at the same time have provided access cards to the different areas entitling people and vehicles for those people who are related with the port in any way.

Throughout this text whenever a reference is made to cards the expression must be understood in the ample sense and as relating to any similar procedure that is implemented for the same purpose such as supports, pieces of card, identity ovals, etc.

As inside each port there will now be different port facilities with their corresponding plans and their respective people responsible for security, it will be in these more restricted areas, even those that are fenced off, in which access control is more specific and more related to the facility in question.

The PFSP must contain the security measures that are applicable to all the means of access to the port facility.

For each one of them, the PFSP must indicate the places in which access is restricted or forbidden at each level of security. For each level of security, the PFSP must specify the type of restriction or prohibition that will be imposed and the means to guarantee that they are observed.

For each level, the PFSP must indicate the means of identification that are required to gain access to and remain inside the facility, which might require the establishment of an adequate system of permanent or temporary identification for the personnel of the port facility and visitors, respectively. Any identification system that is implemented must be coordinated in as far as possible with the one that is applied in the ships that normally use the facility. Passengers shall prove their identity through their boarding card, ticket, etc., but generally they will not be given access to restricted areas. The PFSP must include provisions for the identification systems to be updated and so that any abuse is duly sanctioned.

Access will be denied to the port facility to any person who does not wish to or who cannot prove their identity or confirm the purpose of their visit when asked and the PFSO and the national or local authorities with responsibilities in the area of security will be notified that these people have tried to gain access. This means that the power of exclusion to the area of the facility is activated for not meeting the requisites for entry or for not identifying themselves.

This control will normally be made by the harbour guards who will not give access to those people who are not entitled to enter the area, who do not meet the specified conditions or who refuse to identify themselves. The fact that people identify themselves does not necessarily give them the right to enter if there is not a legitimate and specific reason such as boarding, taking supplies, civil servants, etc.

We could ask what the harbour guard can do when a person is denied access because they refuse to identify themselves. This will depend on the circumstances and on the person. If access is not given to someone who is merely curious there is no problem. But if someone is rejected because they raise suspicion in virtue of a previous act or other evidence and does not identify himself when asked, the

Security Forces and Corps must be notified, unless the person has been detained to hand him over to them.

The possibility of identifying a person in a general manner and outside of the access controls has been reserved by the Law of Security Forces and Corps unless someone is in an area where they are obliged to identify themselves. For example, a certain person is inside the port which means that they should have identification or be identified by a harbour guard. Moreover, if this person wishes to enter the port facility and refuses to be identified although they are not given permission to enter the facility they must identify themselves because they are inside the port where it is also mandatory to be identified and the harbour guard can do it because it falls within the scope of his obligations and competences and is within his area of responsibility.

Another case is that of the person who is rejected at access control by a harbour guard for not identifying himself, whether they are in a public space or stay there, such as the entrance to the port. Here the harbour guard cannot identify them. If he has suspicions to do so he will call the Security Forces who will identify him if they have the appropriate budgets.

The budgets for the identification of a person are established in OL 1/92 on the Protection of Public Security. Article 20 is dedicated to it.

1. The agents of the Security Forces and Corps may, in exercising their functions of investigation or prevention, require the identification of people and make the corresponding checks in public places or in the place where they make the requirement, provided that the knowledge of the identity of the person is necessary for the security functions entrusted to the agents by this Law and the Organic Law on Security Forces and Corps.

2. When identification is not achieved through any means and when it is necessary for the same purpose of the previous paragraph, the agents may, in order to prevent a crime or offence form being committed, or in order to sanction a breach, require those who cannot be identified to accompany them to nearby premises and that they have the necessary means to carry out the process of identification, only for this purpose and only for the necessary time.

3. A log book will be kept in the premises referred to above in which the processes of identification carried out are recorded as well as the reasons for them and their duration. This will be available at all times to the Competent Legal Authority and to the Public Prosecutor's Office. Notwithstanding the above, the Ministry of the Interior shall periodically send an extract of the identification proceedings to the Public Prosecutor's Office.

4. In the cases of resistance or of an unfounded refusal to be identified or to voluntarily carry out the identification checks or practices, the Penal Code and the Law of Criminal Prosecution will be applicable.

Without wishing to go on with more arguments, it must be left clear that not even the Security Forces and Corps are entitled to proceed with the identification of people in any circumstances. There must be certain prior requisites such as a report or a situation of well-founded suspicion, etc.

In this case mere identification will not be sufficient when dealing with certain port facilities that are used for passenger ships or cruise ships but there will also be a control of personal belongings of those who wish to enter them or who at least intend to board the ship.

The control of personal belongings is normally carried out in an automatic fashion with metal detectors such as scanners for personal belongings, packages and postal items.

The equipment and systems that are installed in the access controls of the ports, of the port facilities or on the ships that sail under the Spanish flag must be standardised. We are not going to go into details in the description of conventional maritime security equipment such as boats, life jackets, flares and alarms, fire pumps and circuits, security and rescue communications all of which are mandatory on ships.

8.2.1 Walk through detectors

The equipment that is used for detecting metals is very important and it must be calibrated to work at certain levels. Its use should always be in accordance with the recommendations of the manufacturer and with the instruction manuals.

In certain port facilities the convenience of installing a walk through detector in the main access for passengers should be analysed. The ideal thing would be to place the detector in the port facility and if further controls are to be made on board the ships to use manual detection equipment. But on ships the manual equipment would be of use on occasional stops and not so to control passengers as a complement of other procedures. Their use, although in a random fashion, always provides a positive preventive result.

The equipment must detect the largest possible range of metals and have special sensitivity for ferric metals. This detection must be in any situation and in any direction. Its operation shall not be influenced by its surroundings. Ferric metals are present in most short and long weapons and in most sharp and cutting instruments.

The detection of metal shall be translated into an automatic alarm without leaving anything to the free election of the operator, except for its volume. The controls for the levels of detection shall be pre-selected to avoid access to them without authorisation.

8.2.2 Portable equipment

They must be capable, in any circumstances, of detecting, small quantities of metals without being in contact with the object. Their range of detection shall include both metals with iron and those without. They are capable of locating small objects on the body of the people being controlled when the alarms go off in the walk through detectors.

They shall have both sound and visual alarms, or at least one of them.

8.2.3 X ray equipment

The requisites and guidelines for X ray security equipment are also applicable to all objects that are controlled, whatever their nature and size. Whenever the intention is to take an object on board a ship, if there is a control, it should be made using certain criteria.

- The X ray equipment must have sufficient resolution and discrimination to prohibit taking on board the ship any dangerous, illicit or forbidden product.
- The equipment shall offer a complete picture of all the objects introduced into the tunnel and without blind spots or shaded areas, and without distorting the object.
- The belt shall limit the optimum area for depositing the equipment.
- Each part of the controlled object must remain on screen for the correct amount of time for the controller to observe it clearly, with the possibility of going back to make sure of details if there is the slightest suspicion.
- The monitor screen shall combine efficiency and resolution with the comfort of the operator. 14 inches or more are sufficient.
- The images shall be presented without flashes which means that high resolution monitors shall be used (1024 x 1024 pixels).
- It shall discriminate so as to separate organic and inorganic materials.

8.3 Operational limits of the equipment and the security systems

Apart from the automatic security systems, which we analyse here, it is obvious that the equipment is limited and that in specific situations other manual and personal procedures will be necessary to check the objects that a certain person might be carrying. Very often it will be necessary to adopt personal measures, even outside of the place where the detectors and other systems are installed.

All security equipment must be kept under control and in operation to give response to the needs of its implementation on board. It shall be standardised. A special monitoring of the calibration of the inspection equipment shall be carried out before embarking and especially in the case of the metal detection equipment. It is necessary to check that each unit of the security equipment in operation, regardless of where it is located, is calibrated so that it operates at identical predetermined levels.

The supply contracts shall establish the requisite that the company that is awarded the supply is responsible for the maintenance of the security equipment and its calibration. At the same time, it shall make periodical checks and after any incident or movement of the equipment, that its operation responds to the previously determined level and that its parameters are calibrated in an identical manner.

There shall be a copy of the certification of calibration on each ship that has this security equipment.

The security equipment shall be used in accordance with the recommendations of the manufacturer, and in accordance with the corresponding procedures for use that appear in the instructions manuals.

It will be convenient to establish a calendar of preventive maintenance in order to guarantee that the security equipment operates efficiently and the possibility of it being revised in port.

At the same time, a continuity of the maintenance of the equipment shall be established to cover any failure or flaw once the manufacturer's period of warranty has elapsed.

No unauthorised modification, or maintenance or repair shall be carried out on the X ray equipment. No changes shall be made to the physical or logical support without checking that it does negatively not affect the quality of the picture.

The composition of the belt will not be changed without checking whether it affects the quality of the picture.

If there is access by modem for maintenance or updating purposes, this access shall be controlled and monitored.

Another very important control measure are the random body checks that the Security Forces and Corps may carry out in the area. The use of a body check does not necessarily mean a violation of the basic rights provided that the police action:

- has legal support,
- is rationally justified and
- is maintained within the limits of proportionality.

a) Legal support is found in article 19.2 of OL 1/1992, of 21st February[3], which authorises the Judicial Police to perform it in their function of investigating and discovering crimes.
b) Proportionality as a defining factor of what is permissible requires a fair balance between what needs to be investigated and the prejudice or harm it could cause to the person.

c) Rational justification for its part, assumes the proscription of arbitrary action in carrying out the measure which must be supported by well founded suspicions or rational and sufficient indications that justify its adoption.

This personal intervention is not therefore allowed for harbour guards and the members of private security. However, exceptionally, they may use this practice if arresting a person with a weapon, in the course of duty to avoid further aggressions. This is a question of proportionality and control.

A body search does not violate the right to freedom or to circulate freely, because the momentary immobilisation of the citizen during the time required to complete it is a legitimate practice from the constitutional perspective of police rules, if it meets the requirements of rationality and proportionality as seen above.

The body search is not equivalent to an arrest and therefore the demands established in the Law relating to an arrest cannot be extended to this action.

Jurisprudence clearly distinguishes between an arrest as contemplated in article 17.2 and 3 of the Constitution and mere retentions or provisional restrictions of freedom that are included in certain

---

[3] "Article 19.1. The agents of the Security Forces and Corps may limit or restrict, for the necessary time, the circulation or stay on public thoroughfares in the case of an alteration of the order, public safety or peaceful coexistence, whenever it is necessary to reestablish them. At the same time they may take preventive possession of effects or instruments that are susceptible to being used for illicit actions and use them as legally appropriate.
2. In order to discover and detain the participants in a criminal act that causes serious social alarm and in order to assemble the instruments or effects or evidence of the facts, they may establish controls on public roads, places or establishments to the extent necessary for the purpose of this paragraph, in order to proceed with the identification of the people who are there or who are passing by, to register the vehicles and the superficial control of their personal belongings in order to check that they are not carrying forbidden or dangerous substances or instruments. The result of the action will be made known to the Public Prosecutor's Office immediately."

inevitable practices which are not directed at limiting freedom (breathalyser tests, identifications and body searches) in which the important thing is:

- legal cover,
- respect for the principle of proportionality and
- avoiding arbitrary actions.

The right to physical integrity is not affected by the body search. The minimum intervention on the body represented by the body search excludes any idea of risk for the physical integrity of the individual. As for the right to intimacy, this is maintained if three conditions are met:

- the body search is not made by a person of the same sex,
- according to the intensity and scope of the search it is done in a reserved place, and
- degrading and humiliating postures and situations are avoided.

Jurisprudence has repeatedly stated that the problem of body searches, identifications, retentions and temporary imprisonment has always been controversial, because it opposes:

- the fundamental right to freedom on the one hand and
- the right to security against
    - criminal investigation and
    - the arrest of the alleged perpetrators of criminal acts on the other.

Perhaps it should be the fairness of proportionality that clarifies the exact measure in each specific case, in order to avoid barefaced impunity and ill treatment of the human being. The Constitutional Court has indicated that the rights to freedom and to free circulation in Spanish territory are not affected by the actions of body searching and identification because although they are inevitably a nuisance, their performance and consequent immobilisation of the citizen for the time required for completing them, makes them a legitimate police action. Members of the Security Forces and Corps have:

- the right and
- the obligation to defend security and order, persecuting crime in all its facets. It is their mission to go wherever the existence of crime is detected and shall proceed at all times, under their own responsibility in the case of inadmissible excesses, with rational precaution and also with a rational investigational spirit which leads them to act on mere suspicions, provided that these are not illogical or irrational.

With respect to motor vehicles, they are merely proprietary owned and a means of transport and therefore do not have the protection given to the intimacy of the residence by article 18.2 of the CE and as a simple object of investigation, without the guarantees and demands derived from the mentioned precept, except in exceptional circumstances in which they are used as mobile residences, such as the case of motor caravans.

The PFSP must indicate the places where people, personal belongings and vehicles are to be registered. These places will be covered so that they can operate continuously, regardless of the weather conditions, with the frequency specified in the PFSP. Once they have gone through this process, the people, their personal belongings and vehicles shall go directly to the restricted waiting, embarkation or vehicle loading areas.

The PFSP shall establish separate areas for those people that have already passed a control with their personal belongings and those that have yet to do it, and if possible, separate areas for embarking and disembarking passengers, ship personnel and their belongings so that those people that have not been registered cannot come into contact with those that have.

The PFSP must indicate the frequency with which access controls will be applied and especially whether they will be applied randomly from time to time.

At security level 1, the PFSP must establish the control points in which the following measures may be applied:

- Defining the restricted areas with fences or other barriers that the Government must approve. The fencing must be barriers that cannot be climbed over. The area must be monitored to avoid intruders. The water area must be lit up and monitored with closed circuit cameras and depending on the circumstances and the threats, with patrol ships. Docked ships shall also be lit up on this side and all ladders and any other element that might help gain access to the ship removed.

- Checking the identity of those people who wish to enter the port facility in order to access a ship, including passengers, ship personnel and visitors and confirm the reasons that they have for doing so, by checking for example passenger tickets, boarding cards, work orders, etc.

- Controlling the vehicles used by those who wish to enter in the port facility to access a ship. Dogs trained in explosive materials may be required for the control of vehicles when at a given moment an unidentified substance or suspicious package lead to believe an attack may be possible. Otherwise, lists of authorised vehicles may be drawn up and they may be given their corresponding passes which does not free them form being subjected to random searches when considered appropriate or in the case of suspicion. In order to access dark areas and hidden places the control points may be provided with mirrors and manual torches that can be fixed to them. The areas in which vehicles are registered should be adequately lit. The drivers and passengers of the vehicles being registered will also be monitored during the inspection in case an anomalous object is detected.

Barriers and efficient controls must be provided for those vehicles which may try to force their way through the established controls.

An incident that must be foreseen is the hasty abandoning of a vehicle in the vicinity of the check and control points. This action may indicate the presence of a car bomb with timing devices that can be activated by remote control. In certain places it would be interesting to have frequency inhibitors. The control of vehicles that intend to penetrate highly protected areas, due to their high sensitivity, should be separated from the objectives to be protected. Once in the control lane the driver of the vehicle should not have the chance of turning back voluntarily but only if he is not given permission to enter the area.

The data required to identify the vehicle and the driver shall be recorded on a computer file if the area is highly sensitive. The procedures contemplated in OL 15/99 on the Protection of Data of a Personal Nature must be respected as must other regulations.

- Verifying the identity of the port facility personnel and of the people who work therein, as well as that of vehicles. The fact that they have external indications such as uniforms, passes, etc., to prove their condition, or the vehicles have luminous indications or signs does not prevent them from being controlled if they show a suspicious attitude. Normally in the Ports of General Interest on most occasions these services are provided by the port authority personnel themselves and as they are such small spaces they all know each other and there will be no problem.

  If any kind of relevant and frequent port service is provided by private individuals inside the port or the port facility, those responsible shall nominate a person to act as spokesperson with the Port Authority, or with the PFSO if only one facility is affected for matters relating to security. This will be useful in so far as it will help with the security controls if the employees are given passes for access to certain areas to which the necessarily have to go; it will indicate their name and number of people who are going to enter each area; if they are given passes they will be told of the obligations they entail and it will be responsible for them and for the trustworthiness of these people and will instruct them on the confidentiality of their work.

- Limiting access to exclude people who do not work in or for the port facility if they cannot identify themselves correctly.
  Although the activity is forbidden by the legislation on maritime fishing matters of the Autonomous Communities and by the Port Regulations, fishing is practiced in many ports both day and night. This has got out of hand and permissiveness in several ports is total. The implementation of the provisions of the Code, in the first place, and of the community regulations afterwards, is going to necessarily influence on this activity, at least during the ship's stay in port as it activates the security measures in the facility.

  Although the ports had opened quite a lot to the public, the new measures will often mean limitations and discomfort.

- Registering people, their personal belongings, vehicles, etc.

  We have already spoken about this matter. According to the current levels of security, they will be more or less rigid and thorough.

- Identifying any point of access that is not used regularly and which should be closed permanently.

At level 1, any person who wishes to enter the port facility may be subjected to a check. The frequency, even of those done randomly, will be specified in the PFSP and the Government must approve it. Unless there are well founded reasons to do so, ship personnel will not be asked to register their companions or their personal belongings.

According to the potential danger represented by the traffic to which the port facility is subjected the Port Ordinances must specify how these controls are to be carried out how the normal users are given access passes or another system of access, taking into account the provisions of the PFSP.

On occasions, and depending on the traffic to which the port facility is dedicated, an updated list of authorised people and visits should be carried.

At security level 2, the PFSP specifies the additional security measures that will have to be taken and which, among others can be:

- Dedicate more personnel to the surveillance of the points of access and to patrolling the barriers of the perimeter of the facility according to the threat that has determined the elevation of the security level by the governing authorities.
- Limit the number of points of access to the facility and identify those that are closed, providing means to protect them.
- Provide means to hinder movement through the other access points, by installing safety barriers for example.
- Increase the frequency and intensity of the searches of people, personal belongings and vehicles.
- Refuse access to those visitors who cannot justify the reason why they wish to access the port facility and, if appropriate or if there are suspicions about their activities, report to the Security Forces.
- Use patrol ships to increase security in the waters of the port.

Security continues to be preventive but the Security Forces and Corps will certainly be involved according to their information and initiatives. None of this will replace the measures implemented by those responsible for the security of the facility in accordance with the corresponding plans and the specifications that appear in them as required by the SES.

Security level 2 will be applied, in general terms, when the threat is general in the sense of one of the following cases:

- Indeterminate threat against ships with a Spanish flag.
- Indeterminate threat against Spanish port facilities.
- Indeterminate threat against a specific ship.
- Indeterminate threat against a specific port facility.
- Determined threat against indeterminate ships or port facilities.

In reality this level of security represents an intermediate, unstable, transitional and indeterminate situation which means that it will have to be maintained for a limited time. It will most likely affect strategic, logistical or sensitive targets, both ships and facilities that require special measures; cruise and passenger terminals and ships, oil, chemical, gas terminals, etc.

At security level 3, the facility will attend the instructions of those in charge of addressing the event that affects maritime security or the threat to it.

Throughout this study there is a certain polarisation between the port maritime administration, within the competences of the Ministry of Development, and public safety in the framework of the responsibilities of the Ministry of the Interior. While security is activated in security levels 1 and even 2, the leading role corresponds to those responsible for security in the port facilities and ships.

At security level 3, the whole port maritime organisation, the ships and the facilities, while activating to a maximum their security measures as laid down in the respective plans, will be awaiting any instructions form the Governing Authority. In light of the imminent risk, the Security Forces and Corps, coordinated by the Governing Authorities, take on the management of the crisis. The port maritime organisation provides the necessary advice and collaboration on port maritime security.

In accordance with the established protocols and under the orders of the SES, security level 3 will generally be applied when the threat is specific. This type of level will only be established as an exceptional measure if there is credible information that an event is probable or imminent that might affect security in any of the following cases:

- Specific threat against a Spanish ship.
- Specific threat against a determined port facility.
- Threat against national ships in a specific port or conflictive area.

In the application of a certain security level, the circumstances of national or international risk of the place and time, as well as the details of the accuracy or plausibility of the threat shall also be taken into account.

Security level 3 will only be maintained for the time that the identified threat or the real event that affects maritime security lasts.

Although the security level can pass from level 1 to level 2 and from there to 3, there is also the possibility of the security level going directly from 1 to 3.

There may be circumstances in which a ship operates at a higher security level than that of the port facility that it is using but the case should never occur in which a ship has a security level below that of the port facility it is using.

The PFSP must specify the measures that the facility can adopt in close collaboration with those in charge of addressing the event and with the ships that are there: These measures could be:

- Suspend access to the port facility or to parts of it.
- Only authorise access to those in charge of addressing the event that affects security or the threat to it. Security will be dealt with by those responsible for and members of the State Security Forces and Corps.
- Suspend the movements of people or vehicles in the port facility or in parts of it.
- Increase the security patrols in the port facility.
- Suspend port operations in all or part of the facility.
- Direct the movements of the ships in the whole port facility or in any of its parts.
- Evacuate the port facility totally or partially.

8.4 Restricted areas within the port facility

A system to request and issue identity cards must be provided for port workers, those responsible for security, members of the Security Forces and Corps and official bodies. There would be another type for suppliers of provisions, concession holders and those who provide normal services in general. The same would apply to the vehicles that are normally used for this purpose.

The method of identification that is being used, due to its similarity with that of the airports which have a certain advantage in security matters, is that of identification cards to which certain permits can be associated that allow access through automatic readers by opening doors to enter certain areas. This added control, which is included in the card, automatically selects people and makes it possible to establish different degrees and levels of access. It has many uses as it can also be associated to colours, etc.

The Proposal for the Community Directive which needs to be integrated into national legislation requires that the following specifications be considered for the cards:

- Access requisites. In some areas the requisites will only come into force when the security levels exceed a certain threshold. All the requisites and thresholds shall be detailed in the Port Security Plan (PSP).

- Prescriptions of identification, equipment and cargo control. These prescriptions may or may not be applied to the subareas: at the same time they may be applied totally or partially to the subareas. The people who have access to or move about a subarea may be subjected to control. The PSP shall be adequately adjusted to the conclusions of the evaluation of port security. When special identity documents are elaborated for the purpose of port protection, clear procedures should be established for their issue, control of use and return. Such procedures shall take into account the peculiarities of certain groups of port users, so that special measures are possible to limit the negative effects of the access control requisites. The following categories shall exist as a minimum:

    o people of the sea,
    o civil servants from the authority
    o people who work permanently in the port
    o people who work in or visit the port periodically
    o residents and people who work in the port or visit it occasionally.

Automatisms allow certain flexibility at the same time as objective security for those who work in the port or who visit it frequently for work purposes. Magnetic permits can be incorporated into the port access cards to enable access to certain restricted areas, though always in accordance with the principle of need. The people with maximum levels of access must have no criminal record related with security. The passes must be worn at chest height on the body and be clearly visible while the person is in the area that requires its use. Besides, random controls will be carried out on those carrying them and also at frequent intervals to certify that they correspond with the identity of the people for whom they were issued. It is essential to keep a control that makes it possible to remove the passes when the people no longer carry out the duties for which the pass was issued as they must be personal and non-transferable. They are no use for identification if they are not accompanied by a national identity card.

Those responsible for port security and the Security Forces and Corps may require these accreditations and identifications.

Any person who does not present a valid pass will be brought before those responsible for security and if anything anomalous is observed, before the responsible Security Forces and Corps. This is the same with respect to vehicles that do not have their corresponding passes which must be in a visible place whenever the vehicle circulates inside the restricted areas. The drivers of the vehicles must carry all their corresponding identifications.

These controls do not exempt the ship crews that are docked in the facility although the controls may be linked with those of access to the ship which will require agreements or procedures between the SSO and the PFSP.

Automatic controls must be strengthened with patrols or personal presence according to the levels of security and subjected to surveillance with video cameras in case their are failures or they are easily passed in which case they are good for nothing. In very sensitive restricted areas and with a security level of 2 or 3, it would even be recommendable to have a car in waiting to track down those who try to beat the controls or who are caught doing so. More so if they make it.

No one will be given access to areas that are not equipped.

The PFSP must indicate the restricted areas, specifying their extension, the periods in which the restriction will be valid, and the measures that will have to be adopted to control, on the one hand, access to these areas, and on the other hand, the activities carried out therein.

The Plan must include measures to guarantee that temporarily restricted areas are subjected to a security inspection before and after they are established. The purpose of restricted areas is to:

- Protect passengers, personnel on the ship and in the port facility, visitors, including those related to a ship.
- Protect the port facility.
- Protect the ships that use the facility or provide services in it
- Protect the vulnerable places and parts of the port facility.
- Protect the security and surveillance systems equipment.
- Avoid undue handling of the cargo and provisions.

The PFSP must guarantee that clearly defined measures are applied in restricted areas to control:

- Access of people.
- The entrance, parking, loading and unloading of vehicles.
- The movement and storage of the cargo and provisions.
- Unaccompanied baggage or personal belongings.

The PFSP must establish that all the restricted areas are clearly marked, that access to the area is restricted and that unauthorised presence in the area violates the security rules.

If automatic devices are used for detecting intruders, they shall alert a control centre capable of responding if an alarm is activated.

Among others, restricted areas may be:

- Areas of land and water next to the ship.
- Areas for embarking, disembarking, standby and transition for passengers and ship personnel, including registration points.
- Areas for embarking, disembarking and storing cargo and ship supplies.
- The places in which important information from the point of view of security relating to the cargo is kept.
- The areas in which dangerous or potentially dangerous goods are kept.
- The control rooms for ordering maritime traffic, help for navigation and the port control buildings, including control rooms for the security and surveillance systems.
- The areas in which the security and surveillance equipment is located or stored.
- The essential radio-electrical, telecommunications, electricity, water and other public service facilities.

The security measures could be extended, with the consent of the authorities, to restrict unauthorised access to structures from which the port facility can be observed.

At security level 1, the PFSP shall establish the security measures applicable to the restricted areas, which may consist of:
- Installing permanent or temporary barriers that surround the restricted area.
- Establishing access points that may be controlled by security guards when used, and which can be efficiently closed or blocked when not.
- Issuing passes that must be visible on those people who have a right to be inside the restricted area.
- Clearly marking vehicles that are authorised to enter the restricted areas.
- Organising patrols and guards.
- Installing automatic systems to detect intruders, or surveillance equipment or system to control unauthorised access to the restricted areas and movements within them.
- Controlling the movement of ships in the vicinity of the ships that use the port facility. In another part we have discussed the need to address security on the water side of the ship. The Port Authorities, the concession holders of port spaces that are subject to the Code because of the traffic they manage and the Authorities responsible for port matters of the Autonomous Communities have to give a response to this security demand according to the potential risks that the more sensitive ships and traffic represent. The public port facility already has these possibilities with its staff of harbour guards which they will have to give an incentive so that they are capable of monitoring not only the land spaces but the part of the port that includes the port waters, at least annex 1 of them. At first glance there are no legal obstacles for them to provide these services with private security, trained for the purpose. The concession holders of the port facilities should contract surveillance personnel to meet these demands. The port facilities managed by the Autonomous Communities with private or public surveillance should at the same time perform these duties.

For security level 2, the PFSP must indicate how the frequency and intensity of the surveillance and control of access to restricted areas is to be increased. The Plan must specify the additional security measures that will have to be taken and which may include, among others:

- Reinforcing the efficiency of the barriers or fences that define the restricted areas, using for example, automatic systems to detect intruders or patrols.
- Reducing the number of points of access to the restricted areas and reinforcing the controls applicable to the other accesses.
- Restricting parking in the areas near to docked ships.
- Further limiting access to the restricted areas, as well as movements and storage in these areas.
- Using supervised surveillance equipment and recording continuously.
- Reinforcing the number and frequency of the patrols, including maritime patrols in the limits of the restricted areas and inside the other areas.
- Controlling and restricting access to the areas next to the restricted areas.
- Preventing the access of unauthorised ships to the waters next to the ships that are in the port facility. At this level some collaboration may come from the Maritime Services of the Civil Guard through the Governing Authorities, but the purpose of these will be to sporadically reinforce the permanent group as established in the PFSP for these nearby waters.

At security level 3, the port facility must comply with the instructions of those in charge of addressing the event that affects maritime security or the threat to it, which will come from the Ministry of the Interior, in the first instance from the Security Forces and Corps, and in some situations it may even require the intervention of the defence forces and especially the Navy. Leading the event will be the Board of Security or a similar body that may be constituted to act as a crisis support group and in which all the affected public and private interests will be represented.

The PFSP must specify the security measures that the port facility may, in close collaboration with those in charge of addressing the event and with the ships that are in its, adopt measures which may, among others, include:

- Establishing additional restricted areas, within the facility, in the vicinity of the event that affects maritime security or the place in which it is suspected that the threat to security may be, and access to them will be prohibited.
- Preparing the control of the restricted areas as part of the total or partial control of the port facility.

8.5 Handling cargo

As they are considered as goods, cargos are subjected to the control of several authorities and public organisms according to their characteristics. In so far as they affect exportations and importations they may be subjected to encumbrances and controls of all kinds according to each type of cargo and their destinations and origins. This is a matter in which the Security Forces and Corps are especially alert for this and other reasons. The customs services are alert to specific traffic. Other controls are health controls or those relating to dangerous goods.

Any cargo handling system that wishes to be subjected to surveillance, given the complex port organisation and structure of the General Ports of Interest in Spain, must be done in accordance with the established protocols and with the agreement of all those who have any public responsibility over their control.

Some cargos are subjected to international protocols in virtue of international agreements. An example can be containers, which are rarely opened and when they are opened a prior study is carried out with the evaluation of risks which takes into consideration the different parameters. Closed cargos such as containers and movable chests are a potential danger because of their difficult control but for this reason the Security Forces and Corps, especially the Civil Guard and the Department of Customs Surveillance take on the responsibilities established by the Law in these matters. They must be aware of controls and direct them.

These closed cargos may be sealed and are accepted on board under different formulas which exempt the carrier from the analysis of their contents which means that they must be guaranteed from origin, at the moment the seal is put into place. Any violation of the seal will mean the container will have to be opened and investigated.

The traffic of containers is potentially difficult to control. It is growing at a high rate. It represents a threat and requires the management of both full ones and empty ones. Its enormous volume requires a big effort to control it though state of the art technology and complex risk analysis, given the low percentage of containers that are actually controlled.

They represent another problem from the international point of view as they are used by the international drug trafficking and smuggling networks to cheat the controls. These channels may be used by terrorists to introduce weapons of mass destruction or sophisticated weapons such as missiles, etc. In short, they are a challenge for security.

Controls are easier on more apparent cargos. In any case the control of cargos must be made in accordance with the action protocols agreed with and accepted by the Port Authorities, by those responsible for the port facility affected, whether it is public or managed by concession holders, by the Security Forces and Corps and Customs. Some cargos may justify the presence of other entities in their control (External Health, CITES).

The security measures relating to the handling of cargos must seek to avoid:

- Incorrect handling.
- Cargos being received or stored in the port facility that are not destined for transport.

The security measures must include procedures to control the access points to the port facility. Once inside the port facility, the cargo must be able to be identified as controlled and accepted for embarkation on a ship or for temporary storage in a restricted area before being embarked. It might be convenient to restrict the entrance to the port facility of any cargo that does not have a confirmed date of embarkation.

At security level 1, the PFSP shall establish the security measures that are applicable to the handling of cargos, which may be.

- Inspecting the cargo, the units of transport and the areas for storing the cargo within the port facility before and after the handling operation.
- Making checks to guarantee that the cargo that is embarked coincides with that which appears on the delivery note.
- Registering vehicles.

- Checking the status of the seals or other means used to avoid the incorrect handling of the cargo at the entrance to the port facility, and at the moment of proceeding to its storage in the facility.

The inspections of the cargo may be carried out by:

- Visual and physical examination.
- Detection equipment, mechanical devices or dogs.

Dogs are a great help in detecting hidden explosives. If the Security Forces and Corps do not carry out these controls they should be required for the purpose when considered appropriate. On other occasions they will do it within their own competences at their own initiative.

When there is a movement of regular or repeated cargo, after consulting with the port facility the CSO or the SSO may reach an agreement with the issuer or with those responsible for it regarding its inspection outside the facility of the sealed container, of the programming of movements, of the checks, etc. These agreements shall be reported to the PFSO in order to obtain his conformity.

At security level 2, the PFSP shall establish the additional security measures applicable to the handling of the cargo, which may be:

- Carrying out detailed inspections of the cargo, units of transport and areas to store the cargo within the port facility.
- Intensifying the checks to guarantee that only documented cargo enters the port facility for temporary storage followed by its embarkation on a ship.
- Intensifying the controls of vehicles.
- Increasing the frequency and detail of the checks on the seals and other means used to avoid incorrect handling.

A detailed inspection of the cargo may be achieved using the following means:

- Increasing the frequency and detail of the inspections of the cargo, the units of transport and the areas for storing the cargo within the port facility (visual and physical examinations).
- More frequent use of detection equipment, mechanical devices and dogs.
- Coordinating reinforced security measures with the issuer or other responsible parties, as well as the already agreed procedures.

The measures that are to be implemented from the European Directive are along these lines.

At security level 3, the port facility must comply with the instructions of those in charge of addressing the event that affects maritime security or the threat to it.

The PFSP shall specify the security measures that may be adopted in the port facility, in close collaboration with those in charge of addressing the event and with the ships that are inside it. These measures may be:

- Limiting or suspending the movements or operations of cargo in all the port facility or in parts of it, or on certain ships.

- Verifying the inventory of the dangerous goods and potentially dangerous substances that are in the port facility and checking their location.

8.6 Delivering supplies to the ship

Supplies will be provided by the companies that are in a position to guarantee the required security. The consignees, in so far as they influence in this process, must guarantee their quality and reliability. The personnel of these companies must be identified and if the supply is frequent, must have an identification card. The supply vehicles and supplies must access from the port area which means that they will be subjected to a prior general access control at the entrance to the port and to another more thorough one when they enter the port facility.

Those responsible for the vehicles must guarantee that their route from their origin does not include any stops in uncontrolled areas. Moreover, these people will be randomly controlled for the objects they are carrying when entering the facility.

The security measures relating to the delivery of supplies to the ship shall be aimed at:

- Guaranteeing that the integrity of the package and of the supplies to the ship are checked.
- Avoiding the acceptance of supplies to ships without a prior inspection or if they have not been requested.
- Avoiding incorrect handling.
- Guaranteeing that the vehicle used for the delivery is registered and that it is accompanied inside the port facility.

In the case of ships that use the port facility regularly, it will be a good idea to agree procedures for the ship, its suppliers, and the port facility with regard to the notification of the moment of delivery of the supplies and the documentation. It must always be possible to confirm that the supplies that are delivered are accompanied by some proof that they have been requested by the ship. In the case of frequent suppliers requisites can be agreed that are protected by the confidentiality of the parties for the purpose apart from the controls that are considered in each case such as confirmation by telephone, etc.

At security level 1, the PFSP shall establish the security measures applicable to the delivery of supplies to the ship, which may be:

- Inspecting the supplies.
- Notifying in advance of the delivery, the driver's details and the registration number of the vehicle.
- Registering the vehicle used for the delivery.

The inspection of the supplies may be carried out with

- Visual and physical examination.
- Detection equipment, mechanical devices or dogs.

At security level 2, the PFSP establishes the additional security measures applicable to the delivery of the supplies to the ships, which may be:

- Carrying out detailed inspections of the supplies and of the vehicles used for the deliveries.
- Coordinating with the personnel of the ships to check that the delivery coincides with the delivery note before authorising its entrance into the port facility.
- Accompanying the vehicle used for the delivery inside the port facility.

A detailed inspection of the supplies to the ships can be achieved with the following means:

- By increasing the frequency and detail of the controls of the vehicles used for the deliveries.
- More frequent use of the detection equipment, mechanical devices or dogs.
- Restricting or prohibiting the entrance of supplies that are not going to leave the port facility in a certain period of time.

At security level 3, the port facility shall comply with the instruction of those in charge of addressing the event that affects maritime security or the threat to it.

The PFSP must specify the security measures that the port facility may, in close collaboration with those in charge of addressing the event and with the ships that are in its, adopt measures which may include preparing the restriction or suspension of the delivery of the supplies to the ships in all the port facility or in parts of it.

8.7 Unaccompanied baggage

The PFSP shall establish the applicable security measures to guarantee that unaccompanied baggage is identified and subjected to an examination, which may include a control before authorising its entrance into the port facility and depending on how storage is organised, before transferring it from the facility to the ship. It is not expected that both the port facility and the ship have to examine this baggage, in the cases in which both have the adequate equipment the port facility shall be responsible for examining it. It is essential to closely collaborate with the ship and to take the necessary measures to guarantee the security of the baggage after it is examined.

Here these controls shall be carried out by the Civil Guard with the collaboration of the harbour guards or private security as is done in the airports. Dogs are essential in the process used to detect explosives.

The control may be made, in accordance with the circumstances and threats, manually or with conventional X ray equipment.

The unaccompanied baggage shall be subjected to very specific controls on the ship. An effort must be made, because it increases collective security, to transport baggage on the same ship as the people it belongs to. The link between the baggage with the passengers or crew is essential.

At security level 1 the PFSP shall establish the security measures applicable to unaccompanied baggage to guarantee that up to 100% of the baggage is subjected to an examination or control which may include the use of X ray equipment.

At security level 2 the PFSP shall establish the additional security measures applicable to unaccompanied baggage. It is expected that an examination with X ray equipment will be carried out on 100% of the baggage.

At security level 3 the port facility must comply with the instructions of those in charge of addressing the event that affects maritime security or the threat to it.

The PFSP must specify the security means that the port facility may adopt, in close collaboration with those in charge of addressing the event and with the ships that are there. These measures may include the following among others:

- Subjecting the baggage to a more extensive examination, for example with X rays from at least two different angles.
- Preparing the restriction or suspension of dealing with unaccompanied baggage.
- Refusing to accept the entrance of unaccompanied baggage into the port facility.

8.8 Monitoring port facility security

It must be possible to monitor the whole port facility, the accesses by sea and land, the restricted areas of the facility, the ships that are there and the surroundings of the ships at all moments, even with limited visibility. The following could be used for this:

- Lighting.
- Guards, including patrols on foot, in vehicles or in boats.
- Automatic devices to detect intruders and surveillance equipment.

When automatic devices for detecting intruders are used, these shall give a visual and/or audio alarm in a space with permanent surveillance.

The PFSP must specify the procedures and the necessary equipment for each level of security, as well as the means to guarantee that said surveillance equipment operates correctly taking into account the possible effects of the weather conditions or of the interruptions of the power supply.

Considering that this study is mainly focused on the Ports of General Interest, at level 1, the PFSP must establish the applicable security measures which may include a combination of lighting, harbour guard watches and security guards (if appropriate) and surveillance equipment that operates continuously and allows the personnel in charge of security at the port facility to:

- Observe the area of the port facility in general including accesses by sea and land.
- Observe the points of access, barriers and restricted areas.
- Monitor the areas and movements near the ships that are in the port facility which could require the intensification of the lighting of the ships themselves.

At security level 2, the PFSP must establish the additional security measures that are required to increase the capacity of observation and surveillance which may, among others, include the following:

- Increasing the intensity of the lighting and the cover of the surveillance equipment, including the installation of the lighting and the additional surveillance equipment.
- Increasing the frequency of the patrols on foots, in vehicles or in boats.
- Dedicating more security personnel to the tasks of observation and patrolling.

At level 3, the port facility must comply with the instructions of those in charge of addressing the event that affects maritime security or the threat to it.

The PFSP shall specify the security measures that the port facility may adopt, in close collaboration with those in charge of addressing the event and with the ships that are in it. These measures may include the following among others:

- Switching on all the lights in the port facility and illuminating all the surrounding area.
- Switching on all the surveillance equipment of the port facility and recording the activities in the facility and its surroundings.
- Extending to the maximum the period of time that the surveillance equipment can record.

8.9 Different security levels

The PFSP must establish the procedures and the security measures that the port facility may apply if its level of security is lower than that of a ship.

8.10 Activities not regulated by the Code

The PFSP must establish the procedures and the security measures that the port facility must apply when it carries out:

- An interface operation with a ship that has made a call in a port of a State that is not a contracting government.
- An interface operation with a ship to which the Code does not apply.

8.11 Approval of the port facility security plan

The PFSP must be approved by the Government in whose territory the port facility is located and shall cover the following as a minimum:

- Measures to prevent weapons, dangerous substances and devices aimed at being used against people, ships or ports from being introduced on board a ship.
- Measures to prevent unauthorised access to the port facility, to docked ships and to restricted areas.
- Procedures for addressing threats or failures in the security measures.

- Procedures for responding to any instruction on security given by the Government at level 3.
- Procedures for evacuation in case of a threat to security or the failure of the security measures.
- Tasks of port facility personnel to which security responsibilities are assigned and of the rest of the port facility personnel relating to security.
- Procedures for the interface with the security activities of the ship.
- Procedures for the periodical revision of the Plan and its updating.
- Procedures to report the events that affect maritime security.
- Identification of the PFSP and access to its contact data 24 hours a day.
- Measures for protecting the information contained in the Plan.
- Measures for guaranteeing the efficient protection of the cargo and of the equipment for handling the cargo in the port facility.
- Procedures for verifying the PFSP.
- Procedures for a response in the case of the activation of a ship security alert system in the port facility.
- Procedures for facilitating land leave of the ship personnel, changes of personnel, access of visitors to the ship.

The PFSP may combine with the port security Plan or any other plan for emergency situations, or form a part of them.

The Plan may be kept in an electronic format with procedures to avoid it being wiped out, destroyed or altered and will be protected against unauthorised distribution.

8.12 Implementation of the port facility security plan

The PFSO is the person designated to respond to the elaboration, implementation, revision and updating of the PFSP and for coordination with the SSO and with the CSO.

In order to guarantee the efficient implementation of the port facility security plan, drills will be carried out at adequate intervals.

The PFSP shall guarantee the coordination and efficient implementation of the port PFSP through its participation in drills at adequate intervals, taking into consideration the guidelines offered in part B of the Code.

Given the peculiarity of the Spanish port and maritime organisation with the multiplicity of entities, competences, powers and responsibilities, we will understand that the necessary emphasis has not yet been put on the importance of the stipulations of the Code. Here there is a cleat example that the private sector, terminals, ships and shipowners have made a greater effort that the public sector to adapt to the new demands. We will have to see how the Security Forces and Corps take charge of an event within level 3 and how in they are in a position to combine the competences of public safety with maritime security.

A standard should be issued to develop the competences and responsibilities of public safety from the understanding of security contemplated on the one hand by OL 2/86 on the Security Forces and Corps, which entrusts the Civil Guard with the custody of the Ports although it reflects other material competences of the responsibilities of the National Police Force, such as stowaways, immigration and entering and leaving national territory.

Besides the ports continue to be points of entrance and national customs which means that the demands will have to be combined with public safety, maritime security, etc.

8.13 Maintenance and modification of the port facility security plan

The tasks and responsibilities of the PFSP will include but shall not be limited to, the following:

- Carrying out an initial evaluation of the port facility, considering the port facility security evaluation.
- Guaranteeing the evaluation and maintenance of the PFSP.
- Implementing the PFSP and carrying out drills with it.
- Carrying out periodical inspections on the port facility that guarantee that the security measures are adequate.
- Recommending and including, as appropriate, modifications in the PFSP in order to correct deficiencies and update the Plan.
- Increasing the awareness of port facility personnel regarding security and surveillance.
- Guaranteeing that adequate training has been given to the people responsible for port facility security.
- Reporting events that involve a threat to the port facility to the authorities and keeping a record of them.
- Coordinating the implementation of the PFSP with the SSO and the CSO.
- Coordinating with the necessary security services.
- Guaranteeing that rules relating to the personnel responsible for port facility security are complied with.
- Guaranteeing the adequate operation, testing, calibration and maintenance of the security equipment, if it exists.
- Helping the SSO to confirm the identity of the people who wish to go on board, when requested.

8.14 The control of weapons and explosives in the port facility

Weapons, as instruments of aggression or defence have a huge importance from the moment that their use can produce irreparable effects on people. The Weapons Regulation was approved by RD 137/93, on 29th January, and indicates that the State Administration establishes the requisites and conditions relating to them. The exercising of the competences in this matter is attributed to the Ministry of the Interior.

The regulation, modified by RD 316/2000, on 3rd March, regulates certain requisites and conditions.

We must not forget that the illegal possession of weapons and explosives, just like any other activity carried out without authorisation, is a crime which is contemplated and sanctioned in the Penal Code. Thus, in relation to this matter, some of the articles of greater interest are transcribed. Article 563 punishes the possession of forbidden weapons as well as those that are the result of a substantial modification of the manufacturing characteristics of regulation weapons. The possession of regulation weapons without a license or the necessary permits will be punished whether they are long weapons or short ones.

Licenses and permits are titles that legitimise the legal possession of original weapons.

The manufacturing, commercialisation or the establishment of weapons or ammunition arsenals will be punished in those cases that refer to weapons or ammunition of war or chemical weapons, of regulation firearms or ammunition for them and of weapons and ammunition of war or defence, or of chemical weapons (article 566).

Article 567 considers the arsenal of weapons of war as "the manufacturing, commercialisation or possession of any of these weapons, regardless of their model or type, even when not assembled". The arsenal of chemical weapons is considered as the manufacturing, commercialisation or possession of them.

Weapons of war are those determined in the regulatory provisions of National Defence. Chemical weapons are those determined as such in Treaties and Agreements.

The arsenal of firearms is considered as the "manufacturing, commercialisation or grouping of five or more of these weapons, even when not assembled." With respect to ammunition, the Judges and Courts "will declare whether they constitute an arsenal for the purpose of this Chapter, taking into consideration their quantity and type."

The possession or arsenal of explosive, inflammable, incendiary or asphyxiating substances or devices or their components, as well as their manufacturing, trafficking or transportation or supply in any form that is not authorised by the Laws or the competent authority is also punished by the Penal Code (article 568).

The legitimate use of weapons shall be adapted to the basic principles of action that are contemplated in article 5 of OL 7/86, of 13th March, on the Security Forces and Corps, taking into account the principles of congruency, opportunity and proportionality and always with the objective of avoiding very serious dangers to people or to public safety.

On other occasions legitimate self defence or the defence of others will justify their use.

8.14.1 Types

They are defined in article 2 of the Weapons Regulation. Thus, in relation with firearms and with the ammunition for firearms, we can understand:

a) Short firearm: The firearm whose barrel does not exceed 30 centimetres or whose total length does not exceed 60 centimetres.

b) Long firearm: Any firearm that is not a short firearm.

It defines more types of weapons that are not reproduced here for lack of space.

The other weapons are regulated in the Regulation by categories or types. We reproduce only those of most interest:

First Category: includes short firearms, which in general we know as pistols and revolvers.
Second category: they are classified in

- Long firearms for surveillance and protection
- Long and scratched firearms for game hunting. These are long weapons that may be used due to their characteristics, together with those of war, by terrorist elements to commit their actions.

These first two categories include the most habitual weapons and the most accessible to the population in general, as they are used not only as weapons for personal defence but also have a large presence in some competitive sports.

Third category: They are classified as

- Long scratched firearms for sporting type, with a 5.6 millimetre calibre (22 American) with annular percussion.
- Shotguns and other long flat bore firearms
- Air or gas compressed weapons, flat or scratched.

It is hardly strange that many dangerous delinquents use hunting shotguns as a highly dangerous weapon by sawing off the barrel. These are known as *sawn off shotguns* that frequently appear in bank raids and attacks on other establishments such as jeweller's shops and petrol stations.

Fifth category, classified as:

- Cold steel weapons and cutting blades that are not forbidden.
- Knives, machetes or imitations used by military units.

Sixth category, classified as:

- Old or historic firearms, their reproductions or similar, preserved in authorised museums.
- Firearms whose model or year of manufacture is prior to 01.01.1870 and their reproductions. (Unless they can fire ammunition used as weapons of war or prohibited weapons).
- The rest of firearms that are preserved for their historical or artistic nature.
- In general, any muzzle loader.

We can see that these weapons have a lot to do with marine use. This is the case of revolvers and detonating pistols and flares as well as those firework devices that are obligatory on ships.

Forbidden weapons:

a) The manufacture, importation, circulation, publicity, sale, possession and use of the following weapons or of their imitations is forbidden:

- Firearms that are the result of substantially modifying the characteristics of manufacture or origin of other weapons, without the regulatory authorisation of the model or prototype.
- Long firearms that contain special devices, in their barrel or mechanisms, to hold pistols or other weapons.
- Pistols or revolvers that have an adapted shank.
- Firearms for holding or that are contained inside sticks or other objects.
- Firearms disguised in the appearance of another object.
- Sword-sticks, daggers of any type and flick knives. (Daggers are considered as those with a blade of less than 11 centimetres, double edged and pointed).
- Compressed air or gas firearms, real or simulated, combined with cold steel weapons.
- Wire or lead defences; cudgels, brass knuckles, with or without sharp points; catapults and perfected blowpipes; shurikens and nunchucks.
- And any other especially dangerous instrument for the physical integrity of people.

b) The publicity, sale, possession and use of the following is forbidden, except by specially authorised public servants, and in accordance with the corresponding regulations:

- Semi-automatic weapons of categories 2.2 and 3.2 whose load capacity is higher than five cartridges, including the one that is in the chamber, or whose barrel is foldable or removable.
- Self defence sprays and all those weapons that use gases or aerosols as well as any device that includes mechanisms capable of projecting stupefying, toxic or corrosive substances.

From the above the exception are self defence aerosols which are considered permissible, in which case they can be sold at a gunsmith's to people who prove that they are of legal age by presenting ID, passport, authorisation or residence permit.

- Electrical, rubber defences, tongfas or similar.
- Silencers applicable to firearms.
- Cartridges with perforating, explosive and incendiary bullets as well as the corresponding projectiles.
- Ammunition for pistols and revolvers with dum-dum or hollow bullets, as well as the bullets themselves.
- Long sawn-off shotguns

c) The possession of imitation firearms that may lead to confusion about their nature is forbidden, even though they cannot be turned into firearms, except at home as a decorative object or collector item.

d) The use by individuals of knives, machetes and other cold steel weapons that are part of duly approved armaments is forbidden

8.14.2 Transportation of weapons

The SSO and the PFSP shall coordinate everything relating to weapons with the Intervention of Weapons of the Civil Guard. The weapons and objects indicated in article 3, section 3, of the Regulation of Weapons to which we have already referred must be transported in a safe place in the ship. The same can be said for any potentially dangerous or offensive substance. In any case they will be kept in a safe place so that no one can get hold of them.

The Captain of the ship and the SSO shall have the places, security means and procedures for the storage, collection and delivery to their owners of the weapons that have the corresponding license and guide.

It is essential that firearms are not loaded. If they are for personal use, hunting or sport, they may travel with their corresponding ammunition in place. All of this under the stipulations of the Regulation of Weapons.

The forbidden weapons, to which we have already referred, will not be admitted on the ship for transportation. Moreover, those responsible for security shall require the presence of the port Civil Guard so that they can confiscate them.

Weapons and other instruments susceptible to causing harm cannot be transported as hand luggage which means they must be checked in, in order to avoid them being on hand during the voyage. The Intervention of Weapons of the Civil Guard shall control and authorise the process.

As for other weapons or objects that might be used as offensive elements and which do not require the authorisation of Intervention of Weapons, the Captain or the SSO if delegated for the purpose shall have the final word.

In Spain anything related to weapons is the competence of the Ministry of the Interior and it is the Civil Guard of the Security Force that is in charge of this competence. Therefore, any incident regarding this matter shall be reported to this Body.

The armed Forces and the Security Forces and Corps who are on duty may travel with their own weapons once they have been identified as such in the access controls and by the ship's Captain.

It is very important that no weapon or dangerous instrument likely to cause damage or harm or to be used as weapons of any kind may be transported as hand luggage, with the exception of the provisions for the Armed Forces and the Security Forces.

8.15 Explosives

Chapter V of the Regulation of Explosives, published by RD 230/98, on 16th February, contemplates the maritime transport of explosives. We highlight its basic regulation. This regulation must be known by all maritime operators, especially by those who take on responsibilities in security matters related to the ISPS Code.

Some articles of interest are transcribed.

Article 264 requires that, in general, the maritime transport of regulated materials abides by the stipulations of the International Agreement for the Safety of Human Life at Sea, of the International Maritime Code on Dangerous Goods (IMDG), of the Admission, Handling and Storage of Dangerous Goods in the Ports, approved by RD 145/1989 of 20th January, and in RD 1253/1997, of 24th July, on the minimum conditions required of ships that transport dangerous or contaminating goods, with their origin or destination in national maritime ports

This regulation is extended to the stipulations in the Law and the regulation of Private Security and similar provisions and to the stipulations of this chapter and in the technical instructions that affect it. According to article 265.
"The competence of the matters regulated by this Chapter shall correspond to the following Departments:
a) The Ministry of the Interior regarding the regime of surveillance in the loading and unloading operations in the port.
b) The Ministry of Development in those aspects that are specifically attributed to it, and specifically, in the regulation of admission, handling and storage in the service area of the ports.
c) The Ministry of Industry and Energy regarding authorised packaging and the classification and compatibility of the regulated materials."

Article 267 states that the competent authority, the Ministry of the Interior through the Civil Guard, shall exercise the supervision of the custody of said materials and of the activities related to them whenever they are in the port area and makes the Captain or skipper of the ship responsible from the moment they have been embarked. In the future and once the Regulation and European Directive to implement the ISPS Code have been approved, the security officers will have a lot to do with this type of responsibilities.

According to article 268 "any ship that transports regulated materials will have to observe the prescriptions indicated in this Chapter in any of the water and air space in which Spain exercises sovereignty, sovereign rights or jurisdiction."

On the other hand no ship may run aside any other with a cargo of regulated materials without the prior written authorisation of the maritime captain and the conformity of both captains (article 269).

During their stay in the port, these ships must remain in the place assigned to them. They may only move when they have obtained the corresponding permission.

The ship shall have personnel on board to cover the port guard on deck and in the machine room as well as those that may be necessary to carry out an emergency manoeuvre and even to manoeuvre at any moment. The port guards shall always be organised in accordance with the International Agreement o Training Rules, Titles and Guards for Seafarers and the resolutions of the IMO on the matter.

At the same time, during its stay in the port with regulated materials, the ship must keep its engines running and ready to leave at any moment. Therefore no repair may be made to prevent or delay its departure without the specific authorization of the maritime Captain, after consulting the dock or terminal operator if the ship is docked in specialised terminals.

The vehicles that bring or take regulated materials to and/or from the port area will have to comply with the requisites of the traffic guide that this Regulation sets forth and shall exhibit the corresponding plates and labels (article 270).

The Port Authority shall grant priority to the activities and manoeuvres that the mentioned ships will have to carry out to make their stay in the port as short as possible, and in the case of force majeure or another exceptional circumstance that prevents the immediate departure of the ship, the General Directorate of the Civil Guard shall dictate the corresponding orders to reinforce the conditions of public safety and shall maintain special surveillance both on board and in the vicinity of the ship (article 271).

Due to their clarity we literally transcribe other articles of interest:

"Article 272.
At the entrance to the port area, the person in charge of the transportation shall present the traffic guide and the embarkation permit for the goods to the corresponding port authority. The port authority shall communicate the arrival of the goods in the port to the competent authority, which following the appropriate checks shall confirm the authorisation, establishing if appropriate the additional prescriptions that are necessary."

"Article 273.
1. Access will not be allowed to the dock or terminal by land of any type of regulated material until the ship that has to receive them is duly docked and ready to start loading and all of the corresponding general provisions have been met or until the vehicles that have to receive them are in the dock area ready to start the transport.
2. Both the ships that have loaded regulated materials and the vehicles from which they were unloaded shall leave the port as soon as the loading operation is completed. The operations will follow the instructions of the maritime captain and of the Director of the port, respectively."

"Article 274.
1. The regulated materials shall be loaded or unloaded directly from the ship to the vehicle or vice versa. Under no circumstances shall they be stored on the dock, in sheds or in warehouses. This rule may be excepted when dealing with non metallic cartridges or other security ammunition.
2. During the operations of loading or unloading of explosives, the loaded vehicles that are on standby shall wait at a prudent distance from the ship with which these operations are carried out, a distance of no less than one hundred metres."

9. Functions carried out by the ports

The implementation of the security measures which we have been talking about; the terrorist threat that is so topical and so fanatical and which does not hesitate to cause unpredictable massacres against any human concentration, regardless of their sign or condition, provided they do not coincide with the ideological or religious beliefs; religious fanaticism that leads to suicide as in the cases of the human bombs which have recently become so sadly fashionable in attacks and conflicts, make all sensitivities and efforts focus in certain directions.

This brings us to the collation that it is in the port facilities where international traffic takes place and where, apart from security, the State is present with other control activities, both on the trade and on the duties. The concept of the customs port must be present, although in the EU these controls have been reduced drastically due to the freedom of movement of goods and people, though they are still used for other traffic which originates from other parts of the world or which are their destination.

On the other hand, drug trafficking makes the ports a priority target to place their illicit goods in Europe and we have plenty of experience in this matter in Spain. Large quantities of cocaine or hashish camouflaged under the appearance of other objects or inside them are frequently found on board ships of all descriptions and especially on board merchant ships. They are also found in kit bags, ventilation ducts, food tins, etc. The imagination of these very dangerous delinquents makes it impossible to predict what the chosen method will be in each case for the fraudulent introduction of these goods which are so harmful for the health.

A certain selective immigration, through the process of what is known as stowaways, is also trying to enter our country on board merchant ships. On other occasions the crew members themselves, normally those of a lower professional category, take advantage of any slip, abandon the ship and disappear from it and do not return at the time the ship is due to leave.

On other occasions, it happened with scrap after disembarking in the USSR. The products deposited in the ports may be dangerous for health because, for example they contain certain levels of radioactivity. Other products can also be camouflaged and be smuggled into our country to prejudice local trade. It is not so long ago that ships full of tobacco would linger near our coasts waiting for the dark and then clandestinely unload huge amounts of "American cigarettes" without paying the corresponding taxes.

Irregular immigration by sea has bombarded our coasts in an uncontrolled and ever growing manner. Migratory flows have come to affect certain ports in the south of Spain and its islands. The phenomenon is growing and we have so often seen ships loaded with immigrants drifting around the Mediterranean Sea, some of which have disembarked in Italy. The same has occurred in the ports of the Canary Islands on more than one occasion.

The intention here is not to make a list of the incidents that may arise in the ports but the impression is that security in the ports has led some Port Authorities to taking unilateral decisions, based only on this consideration, with the best of intentions but without contemplating these reasonable hypotheses and almost forgetting other regulatory texts and their demands in these and other matters, such as external health, CITES, etc.

9.1 The port as a frontier

Aside form other consideration, Spanish ports, in general, are not only the destination of large ships but also of a numerous sporting fleet that comes to our coasts and docks in our marina or anchor in certain sheltered places around the coastline with very little control.

Sports boats from any part of the world can remain around the Spanish coastline with hardly any control. First of all because the Spanish maritime organisation, especially the Harbour Masters reporting to the General Directorate of the Merchant Navy has not got round to efficiently organising this sector of activity. Even today there is not a computerised file of the Spanish sporting fleet through the terminal to the Security Forces and Corps.

Other boats, especially high speed boats, sail around our coasts with hardly any administrative difficulties and even the General Directorate publishes articles to suppress the legislation that affects them without contemplating any alternatives, unaware of the fact that this legislation could not be repealed because it would leave Organic Law 1/92 of 21st February on the Protection of Public Safety, without content, given the repercussions that RD 1189/89 of 15th September has on it, wherein it regulates the traffic of special high speed boats in Spanish maritime waters.

OL 1/92 supposes that high speed boats (HSB) are regulated and sanctions non compliance with this regulation. If all the legislation were suppressed as recommended now, the OL would operate a blank in this sector.

Boats in general and HSB more specifically are an important element of illicit traffic and the final step for its introduction on land.

The matter is complex given that the sea is an element of internationality itself which means that we cannot overlook the international legislation that affects us. On the other hand, the OL on the Protection of Public Safety of 1992 considered the navigation of the HSB as a vital activity for public safety which means it has attracted certain breaches that could be found in the Law of Ports and Merchant Navy and to which however the legislator has opted for giving them this treatment.

Today there are countless boats on our coasts known as semi rigid boats with several motors or outboard motors whose almost exclusive dedication is to introducing drugs and illegal immigration to our country.

Because of their high speeds and high capacity for transport, these boats should be better controlled because their use in illicit activities makes them equally accessible to terrorists who could use them for illicit purposes to perpetrate an attack on some ship in some port.

9.2 The port as customs

Apart form other considerations, OL 12/1995 of 12th December, regulates the Repression of Smuggling.

According to its "statements of reason" in recent years, the Spanish customs has gone through a period of unprecedented changes. The configuration of the EU as an internal market, established in the Single European Act has bough about the freedom of circulation of goods that are not subjected to controls as a consequence of crossing internal frontiers. This new situation makes it necessary to modify the existing legislation referring to the intra-community circulation of goods which responded to a model based precisely on the imposition of a frontier control which in turn leads to the recommendation of a legislation that helps to repress the illicit introduction of good in customs territory.

With the admission of the single market, the Spanish customs is no longer a fiscal frontier for the traffic with other member States of the EU. The basic challenge of the single market in this field consists of making the facilities given to the free movement of goods compatible with the need to maintain the efficiency of the effort to repress smuggling.

The Law itself defines some concepts of interest which we transcribe:

"1. *Importation*: the entrance of non community goods into Spanish territory within the customs territory of the European Union, as well as the entrance of goods, no matter where they are from, in the territorial area of Ceuta and Melilla. This includes the entrance of goods from exempt areas.

2. *Exportation*: the departure of goods from Spanish territory. The departure of community goods from Spanish territory inside the customs territory of the European Union, to the rest of said territory is not considered as exportation.

3. *Exempt areas*: the areas and free warehouse s and customs warehouses defined in articles 166 and 98, section 2 of Regulation (EEC) number 2913/92, of the Council, of 12th October, 1992 in which the Community Customs Code is approved.

4. *Community goods*: the goods defined as such in section 7 of article 4 of Regulation (EEC) number 2913/92, of the Council, of 12th October, 1992 in which the Community Customs Code is approved.

5. *Non-community goods*: the goods defined as such in section 8 of article 4 of Regulation (EEC) number 2913/92, of the Council, of 12th October, 1992 in which the Community Customs Code is approved.

6. *Restricted goods or items*: the articles, products or substances whose production, acquisition, distribution or any other activity related to them is considered by the Law lf the State as a monopoly, as well as those relating to tobacco and all those that the Law grants the same condition.

7. *Forbidden items*: all those whose importation, exportation, circulation, possession, commerce or

production is expressly forbidden by a provision that has the category of Law or by a regulation of the European Union The prohibition will be limited for each item to the performance of the activity or activities that are specifically determined in the regulation and for the time indicated by it.

8. *Defence material*: armament and all products and technologies specifically conceived or modified for military use such as instruments of force, information or protection in armed conflicts, as well as those destined to the production, testing or use of them and which are included in Royal Decree 824/1993 of 28th May, or provisions that replace it.

9. *Double purpose material*: the products and technologies of normal civil use that can be applied to any of the uses listed in the previous paragraph and which are included in Royal Decree 824/1993 of 28th May, or provisions that replace it.

10. *Precursors*: the substances and products susceptible to being used in the cultivation, production or manufacturing of toxic drugs, narcotics or psychotropic substances listed in tables I and II of the United Nations Convention of 20th December 1988, on the illicit traffic of narcotics and psychotropic substances and any other products in the same Agreement or in future agreements ratified by Spain.

11. *Customs debt*: the obligation defined as such in paragraph 9 of article 4 of Regulation (CEE) number 2913/92 of the Council, of 12th October 1992 in which the Community Customs Code was approved."

On the other hand in Spain smuggling is considered as a crime if it has an economic effect or for the items it may generate.

According to article 2.1 "A crime of smuggling is committed whenever the value of the assets, goods, items or effects are equal to or above 3,000,000 pesetas, those who:

Import or export licit goods without presenting them to be dispatched in the customs offices or in the places provided by the customs Administration.

Hiding or criminally removing any type of goods from the customs Administration within the places provided will be equivalent to not presenting them.

Carry out trade operations or possess or circulate licit non-community goods without complying with the legally established requisites to accredit its licit importation.

Use the goods in transit for consumption in non-compliance with the regulation of this customs regime, established in articles 91 to 97 and 163 to 165 of Regulation (EEC) number 2913/92, of the Council, of 12th October, and its applicable provisions and in the TIR Agreement of 14th December 1975.

Carry out operations of importation, exportation, production, commerce, possession, circulation or rehabilitation of restricted or forbidden items without complying with the requisites established by the laws.

Remove goods from Spanish territory that form part of the Spanish Historical Heritage without the authorisation of the State Administration when this is required.

Without complying with the legally established requisites, carry out operations of importation, exportation, production, commerce, possession, circulation of species of wild fauna and flora and its parts and products, of species included in the Washington Agreement of 3rd March 1973 and in Regulation (EEC) number 3626/82 of the Council, of 3rd December 1982.

Obtain through false means or any other illicit manner the customs dispatch of restricted or forbidden items or licit goods or the authorisation of any of the acts referred to above.

Transport non-community goods or restricted or forbidden goods on a ship of a lower standing than that permitted by the regulations, unless authorised to do so, in any port or coastal area not prepared for customs duties or in any part of Spanish internal waters or territorial seas."

In conclusion, we wish to make it clear that the ports are something more than a commercial area, where, through the Port Authority, the State provides a series of services and surfaces for the intermodality in the large scale commercialisation of goods. That given their strategic, logistical and commercial importance which no one doubts, the ports must be safe, but that they also perform other functions that must not be forgotten when it comes to taking important decisions.

Any variation of the port strategy must achieve the necessary consensus of all those involved, both public and private.

9.3 Customs and frontier

The Adhesion of the Kingdom of Spain to the Agreement of the application of the Agreement of Schengen of 14-6-1985, reminds us and obliges us to accept the port in its double function of internal and external frontier. For the purpose of the Agreement, Article 1 states:

"Internal frontiers: Common frontiers of the contracting parties, as well as their airports with respect to national flights and their maritime ports with respect to the regular ferry links exclusively to and from other ports in the territories of the contracting Parties and in which there are no ports of call outside those territories.

External frontiers: Land and maritime frontiers, as well as the airports and maritime ports of the contracting Parties, provided that they are not internal frontiers."

On the other hand, article 3.1 determine that the "external frontiers can only be crossed through frontier passes and during the established opening hours. The executive Committee shall adopt more detailed provisions as well as the exceptions and types of frontier traffic and the rules applicable to the special categories of maritime traffic, such as pleasure sailing or coast fishing."

In the following pages we shall summarise the most relevant national and international regulations which, in some way, impact on the need for public safety in ports in the light the various forms of exteriorisation of the threats of organised international delinquency. A delinquency that has basically affected immigration, drug trafficking and smuggling and which has now spread to international terrorism.

9.4 International regulations

On the basis of the stipulations of article 18 of the Convention against the illicit traffic of narcotics and psychotropic substance of 20.12.1988[1], in free trade areas and ports:

"1. In order to eliminate the illicit traffic of narcotics, psychotropic substances and substances which appear in table I and II from the free trade areas and ports, the Parties shall adopt measures which are no more lenient than those that they apply in other parts of their territory.

2. The Parties shall try to:

a) Monitor the movement of assets and people in the free trade areas and ports for which they shall empower the competent authorities to inspect the cargos and ships upon arrival and departure, including pleasure boats and fishing boats, as well as airships and vehicles, and when appropriate, to register the members of the crew and passengers as well as the corresponding baggage;

b) Establish and maintain a system to discover deliveries that are suspected of containing narcotics, psychotropic substances and substances that appear in tables I and II, which enter or leave said areas;

c) Establish and maintain surveillance systems in the areas of the port and the docks, in the airports and in the frontier control points of the free trade areas and ports."

The possibilities for action that the transcribed article offers are ample and require measures to be implemented both in the methods and in the development of the regulation, including adapting police services with competences in the ports to the new demands that the growing threats present.

9.4.1 Agreement for the representation of illicit acts against the safety of maritime navigation

Within the context that we are analysing, in order to achieve a broader perspective although not directly related with the object of this study, the existence of other agreements related with maritime security take in a huge importance and are part of a whole: security which should be interpreted as a whole and not as unconnected parts.

A study is being carried out on the reform of all the maritime legislation related with security. It is advanced, using article 20.1 and 2 of the Agreement for the repression of illicit acts against the security of maritime navigation, adopted in Rome, on 10th March 1988.

It will be carried out in accordance with the provisions which grant the United Nations (UN) the power to convene a conference of the participating States in order to review or amend it. As an essential requisite it must be at the request of a third of the participating States or of 10 participating States if this number is higher.

These mechanisms have been implemented.

---

[1] BOE number. 270 of 10-11-1990

We can see that the modification of the Agreement and of the Protocol, proposed by the US, is a measure that is complementary to those mentioned and to others in use to make international maritime transport safer and to minimise, as far as possible, the risk of the threat of international terrorism from traditionalist Islamic sources. It must be put into this context.

One of the potential instruments of the threat is weapons of mass destruction, with very low costs and with enormous consequences if they fall into terrorist hands. If these people are in a position to use them they will do so. This is not an extravagant hypothesis but something that is feasible and even predictable. Spain wakens each day to the proof that it is among its targets as has already been shown.

Spain is well aware of the devastating consequences of terrorism and has recently been dealt another brutal blow so should not be foreign to the initiatives that seek to make our world a safer and freer place and in consonance with the international environment in which we are immersed should be totally committed. Our safety and stability rides on it.

Article 3 of the Agreement includes a measure of commitment to typify certain conducts as criminal in national legislation which is undoubtedly included in our Penal Code. This article, transcribed, states that,

"1. A crime is committed by any person who illicitly or intentionally:

a) Takes possession of a ship or exercises control over it through violence, the threat of violence or any other form of intimidation, or

b) Carries out an act of violence against a person who is on board a ship, if said act can put the safe navigation of the ship in danger; or

c) Destroys a ship or causes damage to a ship or its cargo that could put the safe navigation of the ship in danger; or

d) Places an artefact or a substance that could destroy the ship or cause damage to the ship or its cargo that put or could put the safe navigation of the ship in danger; or

e) Destroys or causes important damage in the maritime navigation facilities and services or seriously hinders their operation, if any of these acts could put the safe navigation of the ship in danger; or

f) Distributes information knowing that it is false, thus putting the safe navigation of the ship in danger; or

g) Injures or kills any person, while committing or trying to commit any of the crimes described in sections a) to f).

2. A crime is also committed by any person who:

a) Tries to commit any of the acts described in paragraph 1; or

b) Induces someone to commit any of the crimes described in paragraph 1, perpetrated by anyone, or is an accomplice in any way of the person who commits the crime; or

c) Threatens to commit, by formulating a condition or not in accordance with the stipulations of national legislation. with the intention of obliging an individual or entity to carry out or to refrain from doing it, any of the crimes described in sections b), c) and e) of paragraph 1, if the threat could put the safe navigation of the ship in question."

Another instrument is the Protocol for the repression of illicit acts against the security of landing platforms located on the continental shelf. Article 2 includes the criminal conducts which are almost identical but which are adapted to the specific problem. Thus:

"1. A crime is committed by any person who illicitly or intentionally:

a) Takes possession of a landing platform or exercises control over it through violence, the threat of violence or any other form of intimidation, or

b) Carries out an act of violence against a person who is on a landing platform, if said act can put its safety in danger; or

c) Destroys a landing platform or causes damage to it could put its safety in danger; or

d) Places an artefact or a substance that could destroy the ship or cause damage to the landing platform that put or could put its safety in danger; or

e) Injures or kills any person while committing or trying to commit any of the crimes described in sections a) to d).

2. A crime is also committed by any person who:

a) Tries to commit any of the crimes described in paragraph 1; or

b) Induces someone to commit any of the crimes described in paragraph 1, perpetrated by anyone, or is an accomplice in any way of the person who commits the crime; or

c) Threatens to commit, by formulating a condition or not in accordance with the stipulations of national legislation. with the intention of obliging an individual or entity to carry out or to refrain from doing it, any of the crimes described in sections b), c) and e) of paragraph 1, if the threat could put the safe navigation of the ship in question."

The proposal of the Government of the United States will go hand in hand with the commitment to modify those articles, among others, to typify conducts such as those that we describe:

A crime is committed by any person who elaborates, transports, commercialises or has the intention of introducing substances from the sea that are susceptible to being used as weapons of mass destruction and their systems or elements related to their fabrication.

The same goes for anyone who induces or provokes or conceals these conducts.

Spain must join in with this type of proposal from its natural allies as the nuclear, chemical or bioterrorist threat represents a real possibility today that could put weapons with a huge capacity of destruction in the hands of terrorist groups.

The sea represents a huge navigational platform on which millions of tons of licit goods are transported and wherein this type of weapons or their components could be introduced. The increase in controls and sanctions must make it possible to improve the prevention and defence systems against these threats. Controls in which the ports play a fundamental and decisive role.

Once these conducts have been typified at an international level, to make them more precise specifications must be introduced to them in Spanish national penal legislation and extradition protocols in accordance with the principles established in this rule that we are analysing.

On the other hand article 6 of the Agreement extends the scope of sovereignty and therefore the jurisdiction for this purpose to the territorial sea. Thus it explains that "each Participating State shall take the necessary measures to establish its jurisdiction with regard to the crimes described in article 3 when the crime is committed:

a) Against a ship or on board a ship which is carrying the flag of this State at the moment a crime is committed; or

b) In the territory of that State, including its territorial sea; or

c) By a national of said State."

It would not be excessive to take this protection to the neighbouring zone, as has already been done in other matters such as taxes, customs, health, protection of the underwater heritage, immigration....

All of these modifications that are being implemented, on international instruments relating to the ports and to maritime navigation, must open up a debate recommended by the IV Conference of the United Nations on the Law of the Sea so that the states can reach better and more mutually binding commitments in matters that threaten the international arena. The Convention of the United Nations on the Law of the Sea of 1982 is starting to be a legal instrument that is overwhelmed by the speed and evolution with which certain events are happening and by the gravity and importance that they have.

Therefore it seems prudent and opportune at this time to join in with the initiatives that make possible a better control of maritime navigation and safer ports.

The Ministry of Development and the Ministry of the Interior must make an effort to define a concise model of port security that is capable of assuming the demands that a modern State demands in the current context.

10. Project of general regulation of port services and policing in the Ports of General Interest, now called the "Regulation of exploitation and policing"

10.1 The sanctioning power

The administrative right to sanction is such an important power in the hands of the Administration that some treaty writers have not doubted in calling it *bastard* because, at the beginning, in the origins of democracy and the division of powers, only judges could impose sanctions. Despite this, during this century the administrative sanctioning power of the Administration has been generalised, to a great extent, as another instrument of legal organisation and coercion to deal with the fact that conducts are carried out that are considered socially positive and others that go against general interests are banned.

In our Constitution (CE), this power is given its base in article 25[1], paragraphs 1 and 3, and in article 45[2] regarding the environment. However, for a better guarantee and to the extent that its consequences affect the rights and interests of those administrated this power, which is not native, has been subjected to a revision by the judges and the courts. Thus the contentious administrative jurisdiction law appears as the reviewer of the acts of encumbrance and others, dictated by the public Administrations. It has been granted other guarantees in its exercise with certain Public Authorities which have been given sanctioning competence power. These authorities, generally speaking, exercise their function on certain matters, on certain territories and to a larger extent the greater their hierarchy is.

In the scenario of the port it has been traditional to reserve the sanction for the lighter non-compliances to the sphere of the activity and decision of the Port Authorities. These non-compliances which are translated into facts and conducts were contemplated in the Port Regulations such as that of 1976 whose validity is being questioned. Now, for better or for worse, they are housed in the anomalous situation within the Law of Ports and with the Regulation of Exploitation and Policing. Thus, the Port Authority, or its Board of Administrators, is attributed:

---

[1] 25 CE."1. No-one can be condemned or sanctioned for actions or omissions that do not constitute a crime, offence or administrative breach, in accordance with the legislation of the moment
   3. The Civil Administration cannot impose sanctions which directly or subsiduarily involve imprisonment."

[2] 45 CE."1. Everyone has the right to enjoy an adequate environment for the development of the person as well as the duty to preserve it.
   3. For those who violate the above, in the terms that the Law establishes, penal or administrative sanctions shall be established as well as the obligation to repair the damage caused."

- A limited sanctioning power granted by the Law of Ports[3] and which is reflected in a list of serious and light breaches established and typified in the Law, plus the detailed list of the old Regulation.

- The power to exercise it in a limited fashion over a certain territory which is the service area of the port.[4]

- The faculty to exercise this power in accordance with its hierarchy as the very serious breaches reside at a higher level (Ministry of Development or Council of Ministers)

During more than a decade with the Law of Ports, which has an enormous list of breaches and sanctions, it has been seen that its sanctioning regime has been quantitatively applied much more to activities related with the Merchant Navy than to those relating to ports. This is logical because the ports have commercial functions, they have decentralised services and, in short, have lost a lot of their roles to the Autonomous Communities, concession holders and private managers. On the other hand, the port activity, due to the demands of trends of the moment and of the economic environment, has been liberalised and has little intervention: even the public functions that the ports carried out have been pushed aside for commercial reasons and there is no objection to it. This is the tendency in the world. For this and for other reasons that are not from here, the sanctioning part, which is within the competences and responsibilities of the Public Entity Ports of the State, has been in the background. This is not a criticism but an experience that must be taken into account in order to be able to analyse the current situation.

Another factor that might go along the same lines is that a large part of the interests that are present in the development of the port activity are on the Port Board of Administration. Indirectly there are judge and party easements that mitigate the exercising of the sanctioning power and they make it uncomfortable given the conflicting interests.

The sanctioning power requires a Law reserve, but it is allowed in our legal legislation and even the complementary regulation through regulations[5] because of the clarity and the homogeneity it brings and besides it represents an important utility to complement the principle of legality: "the regulatory provisions of development may introduce specifications or graduations to the table of legally established breaches or sanctions which, without constituting new breaches or sanctions or altering the nature or the limits that the law contemplates, contribute to the most correct identification of the conducts or to the more precise determination of the corresponding sanctions."

---

[3] "Article 123. Competence.
1. The competence for imposing the sanctions established in this Law will correspond to:
- The Board of Administration of the Port Authority for the cases of less important breaches relating to the use of the port and the exercise of the activities provided therein.
- The Board of Administration of the Port Authority..., in the areas of their competences for the cases of serious breaches typified in this Law."

[4] The Directive Proposal requires limiting the port areas for protection..

[5] Article 129.3 of Law 30/92 on the Legal Regime of the Public Administrations and of the Common Administrative Procedure.

The Law of Ports has always needed regulatory development. An RD or two[6] should have been published: one for the activities, functions and responsibilities of the Merchant Navy and another for Ports of the State and concession holders of public domain spaces.

As this has not been the case, the development, both sectorial and fragmented of different matters, through an RD or Ministerial Order, has produced the sensation of regulatory chaos in its recipients, at least with regard to the Merchant Navy. Several articles have been developed separately. There are numerous regulations and the user is confused. A Regulation (or maybe two) of global development of the Law of Ports is needed, as that which in its day was developed for the Law of Coasts. It is a question of will. The current legal commitment[7] can be used to repeal the different laws of ports into a single one, to include recent security demands and especially those that are going to be required by the Directive[8], if it is approved in its current terms to immediately implement the regulatory development of the Law.

But as a minimum, an RD should be developed for the regime of breaches and sanctions and to complete the administrative procedure established in the Law of Ports. As there is no RD in the sanctioning area, the ample criteria of application of the Law may become somewhat different according to the Maritime Provinces, ports, problems and moments in which legal security could see itself questioned. An attempt is already being made to avoid an excess of discretionality based in the internal memos. With these memos, which only produce *ad intra* effects, there is the risk of interpreting or particularising the application of the Law which is a task reserved for the development Regulation, on which the added control of the process of accommodation of the legality that the Council of Ministers issues is projected.

In a coherent scenario – there could be others because nothing must be taken for granted but rather new points of view and working hypotheses should be brought forward – we would have, for our purposes, a development RD of the Law in port matters which would affect the precepts relating to the Spanish port organisation. Within this RD, of executive development, in a chapter apart at the end appear the breaches and sanctions with the criteria to grade the sanctions and with the nuances and formalities that the sanctioning procedure requires.

On this point, with an RD developing the Law, including a list of sanctions, breaches; of competent Authorities; of specifications and modifications, etc., we could ask whether the future Regulation of Exploitation and Policing is going to contain a list of small breaches and sanctions in the port area, as well as an agile and simplified sanctioning procedure which, in the hands of the Board of Administration, will correct small negligences, lack of discipline and deviations from the mandates of the Port Authority and of the Board of Administration, with the speed and immediacy that these formulas of regulatory power allow and which in another area, give so much to Municipal power as has been described.

This is how it has been historically in the port area, until now at least. We just need to take a look at the obsolete regulations of 1976 for proof. Besides, there is a very extensive list of facts and conducts

---

[6] When Law 27/92 was elaborated it presented the dilemma of opting for a Law of orts and another of the Merchant Navy or of trying to deal with both disciplines in one single regulation. In the end the option was for a joint treatment based on considering the ports according to the types of navigation that they serve.

[7] Law 48/2003. Sixth Final Provision. Authorisation to the Government to dictate a revised text.

[8] A summary of the Directive proposal is included later on.

and a very dense and awkward table of breaches and sanctions. What is more, it is still applied today because despite the time that has elapsed it has not been replaced by any other, although as we have already seen when considering its validity and application, there are other complexities.

As was described earlier, the less important non-compliances can be sanctioned immediately by certain authorities that are invested with regulatory power, but of course, the power that is attributed to them is less, because the procedural formality is less, although it will always be under the umbrella represented by legality and other guarantees. This power to dictate public ordinances and regulations which has been attributed to certain entities and which is exercised by the Entities of Local Administration has fallen by the wayside in other special areas of administration. It is or it was, but following the latest events, the situation could be reconsidered in light of the point of inflection represented by the threat of international terrorism for maritime transport and the port activity. Besides it would be useful to introduce some of the demands of the Directive that is to be issued into the port area.

10.2 The scope of the Regulation of Exploitation and Policing

When addressing any topic and proceeding to study and analyse it, it is recommendable to limit the terms so as to gradually advance towards the proposed targets. At the moment it seems that there is no agreement regarding what should be the contents of a Regulation of Exploitation and Policing. What is more and given the current status of the port organisation, the profound changes they have undergone in recent years, those that will come, the recent threats and the different organisational methods of the European ports, the matter could even be dealt with separately, thus disconnecting the Regulation of Exploitation from the concept of Policing:

- On the one hand we would have the Regulation of Exploitation with organisational contents that would be projected on the port activity.
- On the other hand a Regulation of Policing in which, apart form organising the port Police Service and its activities, a list of small breaches and sanctions would be contemplated to maintain the order and to sanction minor non-compliances committed by the more undisciplined and least respectful users.

Until now the Law, in its article 106, has opted for a joint treatment of the two functions but, as already explained, the Regulation of Exploitation and Policing has yet to be developed since Law 27/1992 of 24th November, on Ports of the State and the Merchant Navy was issued. It has become clear that there are doubts about what this Regulation should be, regarding both its objectives and its contents .The doubts were made clear in the successive legislative reforms of the Law of Ports of 1997 and 2003, where these aspects were changed significantly. The names were also changed. The same could be said of the successive drafts and projects of the Regulation that have circulated up to now without being published in the BOE.

If we concentrate on the part of the special police of the port public domain that is in the Regulation, the concept is not really of what is now called the Port Police Service[9] is not defined, nor who is a part

---

[9] Law 48/2003. Thirteenth Additional Provision. Port Police Service.

of them, nor who can carry out these functions and which of them are of a private nature. Now the Law says that the harbour guards and other personnel are registered in the Police Service; as the harbour guards are Agents of the Authority, their mere registration in this service, creates Agents of the Authority. To begin with we would have to ask if all the personnel working for the Port Authority is going to be invested with duties and responsibilities of Agents of the Authority. On the other hand the structure of the Police Service has not been statutorily established and if we wish to know what their functions and professional categories are, or at least understand them, we have to go to the Collective Agreement, although this is not its function as is obvious.

The regulatory power is a power in force. It performs its function and is a powerful instrument which, in itself, does not imply more than the possibility of exercising it when necessary or the redirection of certain behaviours or facts that distort a certain area of activity, in this case the port activity.

If we take a close look at the Project of October 2000 or the list of minor breaches in the Law of Ports we can observe that the Ordinances are not present, but their essence is; the form is not there but they contain the essential part of them, under formulas such as "complying with the agreements of the Board of Administration", "non-compliance with the instructions give by the Port Authority". These expressions contain the essence of the power to dictate ordinances for a better control of certain activities at specific moments and for certain matters that require rapid and flexible responses to redirect certain situations that cannot be delayed. In the opinion of the public, because of their discretional nature, Ordinances have become full of negative connotations. They are now rarely used even at a municipal level. Indeed the Regulatory power is in the faculty to give instructions whose non-compliance may be sanctioned and the demand to comply with the agreements, the Regulations and the Ordinances as instruments that perform several functions, among which are those of sanctioning certain very minor breaches.

The current situation in which there is certain confusion should not continue. Some even think they have the right, when initiating a sanctioning procedure to opt for a direct application of the Law of Ports or the old Regulation which is not in line with the security and certainty that the regulations require.

Going back to the Regulation, if in the future the option goes in line with tradition to the formula of dedicating a chapter to the sanctioning regime, we will have to consider what its content will be. Taking into account the enormous list of facts and conducts that could be determined as breaches, the Law of Ports has left a space for the Regulation and has given it legal cover with a view to its future development.

The regulatory framework to be developed is accounted for among the minor breaches of the Law of Ports, and on the other hand within the regulatory development. Maybe the whole myriad of minor breaches should be regulated and particularised in matters relating to the ports within the Regulation, if as is feared it takes years for the Law of Ports to be developed and completed with a RD. In the end the Law is the law and the field that it has left the Regulation is that which we discuss below in an approximate fashion.

In relating to minor breaches article 114 of the Law of Ports defines them as actions or omissions which do not have the consideration of serious or very serious breach due to their importance or the importance of the damage caused, and are typified in some of the following cases. Here we have looked closely at those which make a reference to the Regulation or are a consequence of other breaches or are directly related to them.

This will be, approximately, the field in which the Regulation and the Ordinances reach a potential status. If a sanctioning regime is not included in these instruments, based on these empowerments, it will be necessary to include a list of obligations and prohibitions. Otherwise, in order to sanction certain conducts that are linked to generic non-compliances with references to the Regulation and/or the Ordinances, continuous inferences and evaluations, always subjective, will be necessary to typify certain vague concepts that appear in the various open types that the Law of Ports contains and which we can look at:

The following are breaches of article 114 of Law 27/92:

"1. With reference to the use of the port and its facilities[10]:

- Non-compliance with the provisions established in the Regulation of Exploitation and Policing of the port.
- Non-compliance with the ordinance established or .instructions[11] given by the Port Authority relating to maritime operations in the port.
- Carrying out these maritime operations in the port with a danger for work, facilities, port equipment or other ships or without taking the necessary precautions.
- Non-compliance with the ordinances established or instructions give by the Port Authority referring to operations of stowing and unstowing, loading and unloading, storage, delivery and reception and any other related to the goods.
- Non-compliance with the ordinances established or instructions give by the Port Authority in the area of its competences on the ordering of traffic and means of land and sea traffic,

2. With respect to the activities subject to prior authority, concession or provided through contracts;

- Partial or total non-compliance of other obligations established in this Law and in the provisions that develop and apply it and the omission of acts that are mandatory according to them.
- Non-compliance with the regulations of exploitation and policing of the port, of the General Regulation of Piloting and other regulatory standards that regulated port activities.

4. Breaches of maritime traffic control.

- The use, in the port, of acoustic signals which are not authorised by the corresponding regulation[12].

---

[10] They are all very general types and blank precepts with the complication that they refer to a Regulation of the year 1976, when the Law is from 1992 and has been significantly reformed twice, in 1997 and 2003. What these lax references do is to give the Regulation the faculty of typifying the breaches and the Port Authority that of creating breaches in line with the instructions. This could almost be legal safety and the principle of legality.

[11] Here the power of the Port Authority has been taken too far because the simple fact that a breach is dictated gives it the category of being typified Other formulas with more guarantee could have been used.

[12] Although this breach could be within the competences of the Harbour Masters the acoustic environment today is part id the environment and therefore this breach should be sanctioned in the port. Besides, it is a breach committed inside the port. In any case it is arguable.

5. Breaches relating to the contamination of the marine environment.

- Non-compliance with the regulations or the non-observance of the prohibitions container in the port policing regulations or of other waters on keeping the waters clean or the common uses of the maritime environment.
- Non-compliance with the regulation and of the instructions dictated by the competent Authority relating to the obligations of delivering the waste generated by ships and the waste from cargos."

In this list the Law already tells us what it wants to regulate in the Regulation, apart form other matters to which it makes specific reference in other places and which appear throughout the articles of the Law of Ports and in Law 48/2003 LREPS.

10.3 ISPS Code. EU Regulation and Directive Project

This was the status of affairs before the ISPS Code came into force on 1st July 2004 and the Regulation and Community Directive which will do so shortly; the former already is and will be applied directly as the deadlines to implement the new security demands elapse and the latter shall do so through the transposition to national regulation.

The Communication of the Commission to the Council, the European Parliament, the Economic Committee and the Committee of the Regions (Brussels, 02-05-2003) already stated something that, despite being repeated, is no less true. In paragraph 3, when dealing with maritime security, it specifies that it is a challenge of efficiency, coherence and mutual recognition and at the same time explains that the aspects related to the security of maritime traffic, which means that they should not lead to a proliferation of disproportionate and exaggeratedly costly measures, dictated by simple emulation and which may be more for the gallery than for efficiency.

For this reason, it goes on, it is essential to start with a realistic analysis of the risks. Such an analysis must be subjected to periodical revisions that make it possible to approve essential security measures in the current international environment at the same time as the costs are controlled. Any protective means involves permanent measures, such as the establishment of plans, the designation of responsible authorities or the implementation of technologies, but also includes variable provisions that are only applied according to a healthy risk management when the situation justifies it. Quite often, these complementary measures are those which eat up more resources of all kinds and therefore it is convenient to justify their use. This type of focus characterises the measures adopted by the IMO.

This avoids other explanations and puts things into perspective. The simple fact that this study has focused mainly on everything related to security, taking it a bit further than where it was in the area of awareness of the those responsible in the port, should not lead to exaggerating the emphasis. Therefore in this part of the study we wish to start by making a specific reference in the direction of the reflection of this document of European work.

Returning to the matter that occupies and concerns us, among the objectives when preparing the Report of this current Project, was that of a logical link between the ISPS Code and the Port Ordinances. By Port Ordinances here we understand a wider concept than that referred to in article 106 of the Law of Ports, including the Regulation of Exploitation and Policing.

The idea was that the new security regime for international maritime transport, which came into force on 1st July 2004, having been developed by the IMO and integrated into the reformed SOLAS of 1974, would be analysed from the perspective of national legislation and of its adaptation to the newly created situation. The ISPS Code established a series of measures aimed at strengthening the maritime security of the ship and of the port facilities and at preventing and suppressing terrorist acts against the maritime transport activity.

In this sense, an examination has been made of the aspects related to the port security Authorities at a national level, the Security Forces and Corps, the Port Police, the surveillance of the security of the port facility, the different figures created by the ISPS Code and the Port Ordinances and their insertion and coherence with the Spanish port system. At the same time, there are two new instruments at a Community level which have an extraordinary interest in so far as the EU accepts the Code in its entirety but it wishes to go further and extend the field of security to new traffics and to new port spaces.

Therefore the Regulation of the European Parliament and of the Council of 31st March of 2004 relating to the improvement of the protection of ships and of port facilities was taken into account. This instrument is applied immediately and has a direct effect and according to article 3.2 extends the application of the Code to maritime traffic of passenger ships directed at national traffic and belonging to Class A[13], according to the definition of article 4 of Directive 98/18/CE of the Council, of 17th March 1998 on regulations and standards applicable to passenger ships, as well as to their companies, and in force since 1st July, 2005.

Paragraph 3 of the same article states that "Following a mandatory evaluation of the risks for security, the member States shall decide to what extent the provisions of this Regulation will be applied no later than 1st July 2007 to the different categories of ships aimed at the different national traffics f those mentioned in paragraph 2, as well as to their companies and to the port facilities to which they provide services." Many of the provisions of Part B of the Code, which in themselves are not mandatory, will be in the EU because the Regulation so provides.

The European Parliament also elaborates a Directive for the improvement of port security, taking to the port area only the security measures that the Code contemplates for the ship-port interface that is called *port facility*. It will make amore ample Port Security Plan obligatory which presumably will contemplate the different PFSP as subareas of the port.

---

[13] "Types of passenger ships. 1. Passenger ships are divided into the following categories, according to the areas in which they operate:
Class A: passenger ships that make national voyages other than those defined for classes B, C and D.
Class B: passenger ships that make national voyages in which they do not go more than 20 miles from the coast line, counted at the average height of the tide, where the passengers can take refuge in case of a shipwreck.
Class C: passenger ships that make national voyages in maritime areas where the likelihood of a typical height of the waves of 2.5m is less than 10% in a period of a year – if the ship is going to be used all the year – or a determined period of less duration, if the ship is going to be used exclusively for that period (for example, in summer) and that at no time go more than 15 miles form a shelter or more than 5 miles from the coast line, counted at the average height of the tide, where the passengers can take refuge in case of a shipwreck.
Class D: passenger ships that make national voyages in maritime areas where the likelihood of a typical height of the waves of 1.5m is less than 10% in a period of a year – if the ship is going to be used all the year – or a determined period of less duration, if the ship is going to be used exclusively for that period (for example, in summer) and that at no time go more than 6 miles form a shelter or more than 3 miles from the coast line, counted at the average height of the tide, where the passengers can take refuge in case of a shipwreck.

In short, Europe intends to include more protected traffic and larger areas of security by also creating a Committee of port security, essential for helping to the Authorities that are responsible for the ports.

All of this will bring reforms in port matters and what is more important for the purpose of this study, will oblige the Regulation and the Port Ordinances to include tasks and contents that are unknown to them at the moment.

Attending these and other considerations, the intention is to cover the following objectives in this study:

- Mark the relationships and dependences of the ISPS and the Port Ordinances with other security plans to harmonise them in the Spanish regulatory system.
- Define the role of the concession holders in a port facility.
- Designation and intervention of the Port and the Port Authority as a recognised security organisation.
- Identify the legal aspects of the ship-port facility interface.

It is possible that, given the amplitude of the contents developed, more accent has been put on security measures, on the supposition that the Spanish port maritime organisation and those who make it up, at the different levels of participation, responsibility and organisation are more familiarised and to a greater extent, as is logical, with the aspects of maritime security and of port security that with this new preventive and operative public security that is now delegated, pardon the expression, in public and private port maritime operators, in its first stage, form the understanding of security as a global concept that involves everyone.

The Ministry of the Interior intervenes when the situation or the threats and the risks are situated at levels that require responses for which only the State Security Forces and Corps are prepared. Besides it is its specific task under OL 1/92 on the Protection of Public Safety and OL 2/86, of 13th March, on Security Forces and Corps.

It was intended to make an analysis of the regulatory provisions that will make it possible to implement the precepts contained in the ISPS Code with special attention, because it is so recent and novel, on article 132 of the Law of the Economic Regime and of the Rendering of Services of the Ports of General Interest (LREPS).

An analysis was also intended of the legal foundations, the regulations and trends to be able to define the interrelation between the ISPS Code, the Port Ordinances and the other legal bodies that are required to achieve its implementation and coherence within the Spanish legal system.

Although it has already been seen, article 132 of Law 48/2003, of 26th November, on the economic regime and of the rendering of services of the ports of general interest, which will probably be affected by the Directive, deals with the emergency and security plans.

- "In the port area the Port Authority shall control compliance with the regulation that affects the admission, handling and storage of dangerous goods, as well as compliance with the obligation of coordinating activities established in article 24 of Law 31/1995 of 8th November

on the Prevention of Occupational Hazards and of the regulation that affects security systems, including those that refer to protection against antisocial and terrorist acts, notwithstanding the competences that correspond to other bodies of the public Administrations and of the responsibilities that correspond in this matter to the users and concessionaires of the port.
- In accordance with the provisions of the current legislation on the prevention and control of emergencies, each Port Authority shall elaborate an internal emergency plan for each port that it manages. Once approved in accordance with the applicable legislation it shall form part of the port ordinances.
- Following a favourable report from the Ministry of the Interior and of the autonomic entity with competences in matters relating to public safety on those aspects of their competence, each Port Authority shall elaborate a security plan for ships, passengers and goods in port areas against antisocial and terrorist acts which, once approved in accordance with the applicable legislation, shall form part of the port ordinances."

With respect to paragraph 1, the port Authority is competent and shall control "the regulation that affects the security systems, including those that refer to the protection against antisocial and terrorist acts, the competences that correspond to other bodies of the public Administrations and of the responsibilities that correspond in this matter to the users and concessionaires of the port."

Paragraph 3 once again refers to security in a much broader sense. "Following a favourable report from the Ministry of the Interior and of the autonomic entity with competences in matters relating to public safety on those aspects of their competence, each Port Authority shall elaborate a security plan for ships, passengers and goods in port areas against antisocial and terrorist acts which, once approved in accordance with the applicable legislation, shall form part of the port ordinances"

No matter how we look at them, these are public safety measures that go much further than what is understood as maritime or port security, the extension of competences made in safety matters by Law 48/2003 are very important and lead to a change in the trend in the understanding of the question of security in the Ports of General Interest, which are those considered, but it is necessary to consider that it also affects the concession holders and the autonomic port that are obliged by the demands of the ISPS Code and still more, by the demands of EU regulations.

While it is true that this function of public safety, regardless of who provides it, admits nuances in that is contemplates, indifferently, the more professionalised, specific safety of the special police that is provided by the harbour guards in state ports and private surveillance whose costs must be borne by the concession holders of the port facilities as prime and most immediate beneficiaries and perhaps, some Autonomous Communities.

The Code does not mind who provides the service, the important thing is the result. We can conclude that the argument in the sense that the public and private port maritime operators now demand a greater involvement in security and perhaps the extension of their functions to fields which were unknown to them. Whether we recognise it or not, they now start to provide public safety activities although they are in the early stages of gathering and channelling information, putting preventive measures and safety plans into practice and naming a group of people responsible for everything. This is the *globalisation* of safety, because at the beginning of the XXI Century, the threat represented by the presence of international terrorism which is very strong and capable of causing a lot of damage is global.

Security in general, without adjectives, is entering a critical phase in which profound reforms will be required, both in the Law of Security Forces and Corps and in the Law of Private Security. The former is from 1986 and the latter from 1992. Time has passed. Apart from the public or private field there is another reduced one, that of special police, which although within a certain legal and statutory uncertainty, have survived this polarisation. Within these police are the harbour guards, the Assistant Department of Customs surveillance, etc. Their field of action and their functions have been dragged along by specific facts and challenges. The adequate legal status which is to be given to them within the security laws has not been specified. Besides, security areas which were public because of their function are now in the field of private security depending on who provides the service on the one hand and who benefits from it and bears the costs on the other.

We now enter into other considerations in the field of legal reflection, without evaluating the function of the PFSO in the ports of general interest who, after all, clearly performs public functions. In which field of security are we going to place the SSO and the PFSO of a concession? What importance will their duties and responsibilities have and who shall they be accountable to? Is it not true that they perform public functions, albeit with certain nuances? What is the relationship of the SSO with the Captain of the ship, whose public status has been regulated in the Code of Commerce since the last century, including the power to impose certain sanctions on the crew and the passengers? It is true that this whole sphere of security can be performed by private security or even outside of it, such as the functions performed by the SSO, the CSO and the PFSO of port facilities that do not depend on the Public Entity Ports of the State, within the Ministry of Development. But it has to be agreed that this importance is public because of the question in hand which is non other than that of preventing and countering the threat of terrorism. The Spanish State must answer the Community of Nations and the EU regarding these demands.

We must ask whether the current organisation and the security system in the ports, regardless of who it belongs to, is in a position to perform these responsibilities in an efficient manner or whether the structure of port security must be modified in a much more profound manner. The increasing traffic of people; the departmentalisation of the port spaces; their opening to the surroundings: the greater presence of local entities which have taken their seats on the Boards of Administration, the leading role taken on by the Autonomous Communities, the transformation produced by the liberalisation of goods and traffic; the disappearance of duties in European frontiers; the arrival of leisure and catering activities in the port areas, etc. lead to profound changes that justify this approach here and now.

Going back to the main argument, after this digression, this study intends to draw conclusions to bond and to give formal coherence to the security of the Spanish port system, by guaranteeing coordination and homogeneity among the different security plans and other regulations of mandatory application. The reforms will be plentiful in the coming months.

To this end an examination has been made of the texts and provisions of the ISPS, with reference to the duties and obligations of the contracting governments. This knowledge will make it possible to declare that the initiation and maintenance of the processes and procedures required for the implementation of the applicable elements of the ISPS is a question for the national governments which are members of the IMO and signatories of the Code and of the corresponding conventions. More so in Europe, which together with the United States is the main target of the most radical Islamic threat, as we can see every day.

The Governments may delegate some tasks to a recognised security organisation, though others because of their importance cannot be delegated:

- Determination of the applicable security level.
- Approval of an evaluation of the security of the port facility and later amendments to an approved evaluation.
- Determination of the port facilities that must designate a PFSO.
- Approval of a PFSP and later amendments of an approved plan.
- Execution of the measures of control and compliance.
- Defining in which case the declaration of maritime security is necessary.

The LREPS establishes an ample and thorough control by the Port Authority, in the port areas, with relation to certain areas (dangerous goods, occupational risks, environment, etc.) notwithstanding the competences that correspond to other bodies of the public Administrations and of the responsibilities that correspond in this matter to the users and concessionaires of the port, which are not very important and do not suffer innovations from the perspective of the Code. These matters do not require reforms and urgent legislative development as in the case of security which is under threat and requires the implementation of legal answers and required operations.

10.4 The Proposal for the Community Directive

If it is published in the terms of the current proposal and is developed in an orderly and coherent manner, the Directive shall imply reforms in the Law of Ports and as a consequence the publication of a transposition rule that can help to clarify the competences, responsibilities, demands, organisation and, in short, to unravel the confusing panorama of security in Spanish ports, a concept which includes all the ports, including the concessions and the autonomous ports, many of which in the near future will be affected and to a greater extent than with the ISPS Code.

We must not waste this chance to update the organisation of the port maritime security. The transposition rule of the Directive, aside from the reforms it might provoke in the Law of Ports, must give the regulation new content; it shall specify and extend the demands of the new reinforced European port security and at the same time can be used to update the organisation of port security in our country and especially is police organisation.

The importance that the Directive will have in the port organisation for the purpose of security is going to bring about a big change in the approach to port security as we have understood it until now of course. As it will affect the Regulation of Exploitation and Policing and the Ordinances to a large extent, we transcribe a summary of the Directive which includes some points of interest. Although the entire content of each article has not been respected, we have respected the numbering of those quoted for a better understanding. Thus the contents are approximate; it will be necessary to go to the text of the Proposal for a more profound analysis and wait for its publication for the references to be correct. In any case it will not differ much from the current text.

Summary of the Proposal for the Directive of the European Parliament and of the improvement of port security.

In so far as it is consider that port security must cover both the port as a whole and the interface between the port and the *hinterland*[14]. The need for security extends to people who work in the ports or go through them as well as the infrastructure and equipment, including the methods of transport.
The amendments to the SOLAS Agreement, the ISPS Code and the Regulation will improve maritime security. The Regulation circumscribes its area of application to the area of the port that acts as an interface with the ship, that is, the terminal. The Proposal for the Directive improves the security of the areas of the ports in which the Regulation does not apply and guarantees that security measures adopted in the Regulation benefit from the increase in the security in adjacent port areas. The proposal does not create new obligations in the areas in which the Regulation is applicable.

The European Commission considers that the directive must make sure:

- To guarantee and monitor at a community level a high enough level of port protection, completing and maintaining the security measures applicable to the ship-port interface.
- Guarantee a harmonised application and equal conditions in the whole EU, preventing the appearance of differences for the commercial users of the port.
- Guaranteeing that the security measures required for the whole port can be applied as far as possible on the basis of the instruments already introduced by the Regulation to obtain maximum results with a minimum additional load for the ports.

Given the clear diversity that characterises the ports a Directive constitutes the most adequate legal instrument to introduce the necessary flexibility, while at the same time establishing the necessary common level of port security throughout the Community.

The measures that are required to improve the security of the ports would be adapted to the following principles:

- The security of the ports complements maritime security and that of the ship-port interface, strengthening it with the adoption of measures for the whole port area.
- An evaluation of the port security decides which measures are necessary and where and when to apply them.
- The levels of security distinguish between a normal, elevated or imminent threat.
- A port security plan specifies all the measures and actions aimed at port security[15].
- The port security authority is responsible for the definition and the application of the adequate measures of security through evaluation and the security Plan mentioned.
- The port security official[16] coordinates the elaboration and application of the security plan..
- The port security committee advises the responsible authority.
- Training initiatives and surveillance in favour of the application of the necessary measures are adopted.

The proposal used the same structures and organs of security (evaluations, protection officials, etc.,) as the Regulation, which provides a wide range of protection for the whole chain of maritime logistics, from the ship to the port and the port-*hinterland* interface through the ship-port interface. This

---

[14] Area of influence, dependent or closely related in economical aspects with the port.
[15] Not to be confused with the PFSP. This Plan will include all the facility plans that are included inside the defined port.
[16] This is not the PFSO.

approach makes it possible to simplify procedures and offers synergies in the area of security. The Directive specifically proposes the following:

- It obliges the member States to establish the limits of their ports[17] for the purpose of the new legal text.
- It obliges the member States to make sure they elaborate the appropriate evaluations and security plans for their ports.
- It obliges the member States to establish and communicate the levels of security that are used and any changes made to them.
- It obliges the member States to designate a port security Authority for each port or group of ports. Said public Authority will be responsible for the correct definition and execution of the port security measures.
- It obliges the designation of a port security officer for each port who shall make sure there is adequate coordination with respect to the establishment, updating and follow up of the evaluations and security plans.
- It establishes the general obligation of a consulting security Committee in which all the appropriate functions of a port are represented, including those of an operative nature and those which are the competence of the public Administration.
- It defines the minimum requisites for the evaluations and security Plans.
- It provides for the designation of contact points in the member States for the necessary communication with other member states and with the Commission.
- It provides inspection procedures to monitor the application of the port security measures.
- It establishes a procedure for adopting its provisions.

In order to protect the port and maritime sectors as far as possible, it is recommendable to introduce security measures into the ports. These actions must transcend the ship-port interface and be extended to the whole port which, on the one hand, will help to protect the port areas and, on the other, will contribute to the security measures applied in virtue of the Regulation, thanks to the higher level of security that the surrounding areas will have. These measures shall be applied to all those ports in which there is one or several port facilities subject to the provisions of the Regulation.

Notwithstanding the regulations of the member States in the area of national security and of the initiatives that may be adopted in virtue of Title VI of the Treaty of the European Union, carrying out the objective of security requires the application of useful measures in the port policies and the definition of common criteria to establish an adequate level of port security in all the ports of the Community.

The member States must use detailed evaluations as a basis to accurately define the limits of the corresponding port areas for security as well as the different measures that are necessary to guarantee the adequate protection of the ports. These measures will vary according to the level of security in place and will reflect the differences in the risk profile of the various port subareas.

---

[17] From the point of view of security this is essential even though, in fact, it means reducing the surface of the current ports without it being necessary for these limits to be equivalent to the service area or to the whole surface of public domain included in the port.

The member States shall establish port security plans that are a true reflection of the conclusions of the security evaluations.

The member States shall make sure that all of the interested parties are clearly aware of their responsibilities with regard to port security. The member States shall makes sure to monitor compliance with the security rules and establish an authority with clear competence over all the ports, approve all the evaluations and port security Plans, establish and communicate the levels of security, make sure that the measures are correctly communicated, applied and coordinated, and contribute to the efficiency of the security measures through an advisory platform in the port context.

The member States shall approve the evaluation and Plans and monitor their application in the ports. The efficiency of this monitoring activity shall be subjected to inspections supervised by the Commission.

The member States shall guarantee the presence of a contact with the Commission.

As the objectives of this action which are the balanced introduction and application of useful measures in maritime and port policies, cannot be achieved adequately by the member States and therefore, given the European dimension of this Directive, they can be achieved at a community level, the Community may adopt measures, in accordance with the principle of subsidiarity described in article 5 of the Treaty. In accordance with the principle of proportionality described in the same article, the Directive is limited to the common basic rules required to achieve the objectives of port security without going too far to achieve them.

Article 1. Purpose

The main purpose of this Directive is to introduce and apply community measures aimed at improving security in the ports against the threat of deliberate illicit acts.

At the same time this Directive will see that the security measures adopted in application of the Regulation benefit from the higher level of security in the adjacent port areas.

The measures referred to in section 1 shall consist of:

a) establishing the common basic rules relating to the port security measures
b) establishing a mechanism for applying the rules,
c) establishing appropriate mechanisms for monitoring compliance with the mentioned rules

Article 2. Area of application

This Directive regulates the security measures to which people, infrastructures and equipment, including means of transport, shall be adjusted both in the ports themselves and in the adjacent areas when these have a direct or indirect influence on port security.
The measures established in this Directive will be applied to every port located in the territory of the member State that houses one or more port facilities that is subject to the provisions of the Regulation.

The member States shall establish the corresponding limits for each port for the purpose of the Directive, taking into due account the information derived from the corresponding port security evaluation.

When the limits of a port facility, in the sense of the Regulation, cover the port, the corresponding provisions of the Regulation will override the obligations of this Directive.
Article 3. Definitions

For the purpose of this Directive the following definitions are understood;
- *port or maritime port:* area of land and water so equipped so as to permit the reception of ships, their loading and unloading and the storage, reception and delivery of goods, as well as the embarkation and disembarkation of passengers;
- *ship-port interface:* interaction that occurs when a ship is affected directly or indirectly by activities that include the movement of people or goods or the rendering of port services to the ship or from the ship.
- *port facility:* place where the ship-port interface takes place; this will include, as required, areas such as anchor areas, standby docks and accesses from the sea;
- *contact point for maritime security:* organism designated by each member State to serve as a point of contact for the Commission and other member States, as well as to facilitate and supervise the maritime security measures established in the Regulation.
- *port security authority:* the competent authority in security matters in a specific port.

Article 5. Port security authority

The member States shall designate a port security Authority for each port that is subject to the provisions of this Directive. A security Authority may be designated for more than one port.

This Authority will be responsible for the definition and application of the adequate port security measures, through the corresponding evaluations and security plans.

The member States may designate a "competent maritime security authority" as a port security Authority, as it appears in the Regulation.

Article 7. Port security plan

The member States shall make sure that, as a result of the evaluations of port security, the corresponding port security Plans are elaborated, maintained and updated. The port security Plans shall adequately address the peculiarities of the different parts of the port and shall integrate the security plans of the port facilities that are within their limits.

The port security Plans shall specify the following for each of the different levels of security referred to in article 8:

a) the procedures that must be followed,

b) the measures to be applied,

c) the actions that must be taken.

The member States shall make sure that the application of the port security Plans is coordinated with other control activities that are carried out in the port.

Article 8. Levels of security

There will be three levels of security, according to the definitions of the Regulation.
Security level 1: level in which the minimum adequate security measures must be maintained at all times,

Security level 2: level in which the additional adequate security measures must be maintained for a period of time, as a result of the increase in the risk of an event affecting security happening.

Security level 3: level in which the specific security measures must be maintained for a limited period of time when an event that affects security is likely or imminent, even though it is not possible to determine the specific target.

The member States shall establish the security levels that they use. At each of the levels, a member State may determine the application of different security measures in different parts of the port, depending on the result of the evaluation of port security.

The member States shall communicate the level of security in force at each port, as well as any changes that may be made to it. The communication of the levels of security will be made in accordance with the principle of "need to know" in accordance with the port security Plan.

Article 9. Port security officer

A port security Officer shall be designated to each port. Each port shall have a different officer. Small adjacent ports may share the same port security officer[18].

The port security Officers shall perform the function of contact point for matters relating to port security and shall have sufficient authority and knowledge at a local level to guarantee and adequately coordinate the establishment, updating and follow up of the evaluations and port security plans.

When the port security Officer is not the same person as the security officer of the port facility or facilities in virtue of the Regulation a close collaboration between them must be guaranteed.

Article 10. Port security committee

The member States shall make sure that port security Committees are created to facilitate practical advice to the ports to which this Directive is applied, unless the specific characteristics of one of them makes these committees superfluous.

---

[18] This is difficult in Spain because most of the small ports are the competence of the Autonomous Communities.

The composition of the port security Committee may vary according to the ports, but shall always reflect both the operative functions of the port and those exercised by the public Authority therein. The committee shall act in accordance with the principle of "need to know".

Article 12. Recognised port security organisation

The member States may designate recognised port security organisations for the purposes of this Directive. The recognised port security organisations must meet the conditions specified in annex IV.
Article 13. Contact point for port security

For aspects relating to port security, the member States shall name the contact point designated for maritime and port facility security in accordance with the Regulation.

Article 17. Confidentiality and distribution of information

For the application of this Directive, the Commission shall, in accordance with the provisions of the Decision of the Commission 2001/844 CE, CECA, Euratom[19] the appropriate measures to protect the information subjected to the requisite of confidentiality to which it has access or which is communicated to it by the member States.

The member States shall adopt equivalent measures in accordance with national legislations.

All personnel that carries out security inspections or who is in charge of dealing with confidential information relating to this Directive shall be subjected to the corresponding procedure of empowerment by the member State of their nationality.

Notwithstanding the public's right to access to documents contemplated in Regulation (CE) no. 1049/2001 of the European Parliament and the Council[20], these shall be secret and the inspection reports and the replies of the state Members referred to in section 4 of article 14 shall not be published.

In so far as possible and in accordance with the applicable national legislation, the member States shall deal with the information referring to other member States that is derived from the inspection reports and the replies of the member States with confidentiality.

Article 18. Sanctions

The member States shall make sure that efficient, dissuasive and proportionate sanctions are introduced for those cases of breaches of the provisions adopted in virtue of this Directive.

Thus far the summary of the Proposal for the Directive, which has been included for its extraordinary interest and for the importance that it will have in the future instruments of port ordinance and especially in the elaboration and development of the Port Ordinances herein.

---

[19] DO L 317 of 03.12.2001. p. 1.
[20] DO L 145, of 31.05.2001, p.43.

10.4.1 The hypothetical Regulation of Exploitation and Policing

We shall now take a quick look at what would be in the future law important aspects of this hypothetical Regulation of Exploitation and Policing and of the fields to be developed in matters of security. First of all it would be necessary to agree measures with the Autonomous Communities to give the same solutions, from national legislation, to the same problems, because the demands of the ISPS Code and European legislation are the same. This will mean more demands and involve more autonomic ports.

This hypothetical Regulation should be agreed by the Ministries of the Interior and Development in so far as the custody and surveillance of the ports, as stated in another part, is the competence of the Ministry of the Interior. OL 2/86, of 13th March, of Security Forces and Corps, delegate the custody and surveillance of the ports of the State to the Civil Guard with the same missions and responsibilities as in the airports. Passenger and cruise traffic has similarities in ports and airports and the Law does not distinguish between ports and airports when it comes to rendering these services. In the field of goods there will be other nuances.

If it is not so there is the risk that the measures that are implemented are more of a formality than a remedy and although measures are exteriorised to the users, we will have lost the opportunity to give the ports real security by integrating and gathering together all the possibilities of security which at the moment are totally uncoordinated, if not confused.

Without wishing to be exhaustive, we include a draft of what the Regulation should include regarding security, in a very general manner. Throughout this study we have expressed ideas and opinions and have performed analyses of what a Port Police is and what it should be at an administrative level and the extent to which it should collaborate with the Security Forces and Corps.

This security is not only port security. It is in the early stages of immediate prevention, control of accesses, gathering information, the supervision of cargos, of provisions, of containers, static protection, etc.

The demands of the new regulations must go beyond involving the Security Forces and Corps in the control of people and their personal belongings, in the analysis of risks, in the elaboration of the information available and in the investigation of the crimes and the groups related to terrorism which represent the main threat to port security.

Establishing the procedures that lead to a perfectly structured and coordinated port security so that it does not appear that we have a model of autonomous security in each port is a pending matter. The Regulation of Exploitation and Policing or the Regulation of Policing if it is decided to deal with the two matters separately, can help to structure a model for the Port Police Service in accordance with these demands which can be coordinated with the Security Forces and Corps. Before this the transposition regulation of the Community Directive will make it possible to discuss the model if the matter is to be addressed.

10.5 Security contents of the Regulation and the Ordinances

As an example and without any other intention than that of outlining some principles and references, in identifying maximums on what would be the framework to facilitate the coherence of the Port Police Service with its security functions, we indicate some articles about what could be a policing Regulation for the ports of general interest.

Legal grounds and area of application.
Article 1. Legal grounds

This Regulation of Exploitation and Policing develops and gives compliance to:

- Article 4 of OL 1/92, of 21st February, on the Protection of Public Safety.
- Article 4 of OL 2/86, of 13th March on Security Forces and Corps.
- The mandate established in articles 106, 111, 113, 114.1.2.5, 115.1.4.5, 117, 118 and the provisions of Chapter IV relating to sanctions and in Chapter V of Law 27/1992, of 24th November, on Ports of the State and the Merchant Navy, in the draft of Law 62/97, of 26th December, on Ports of the State and the Merchant Navy.
- The provisions of Law 48/2003, of 26th September, of economic regime and of the rendering of services in the ports of general interest in its articles 24, 58, 59, 64, 95, 99, 132 and in the Twelfth and Thirteenth Additional Provisions.
- Regulation (CE) of the European Parliament and of the Council, of 31st March, relating to the enhancement of the security of ships and of the port facilities.
- Part A, relating to the obligatory prescriptions of the provisions of Chapter XI-2 of the International Agreement for the Safety of Life at Sea, 1974, amended, relating to the International Code for the Security of Ships and of Port Facilities.

Article 2. Purpose

The purposes of this RD are the following:

- The organisation of the Port Police Service.
- The general and special policing of the service area of the port.
- The surveillance and control of the services provided by people and entities other than the Port Authority.
- Establish measures of cooperation and specifically, regulate together with the Ministry of the Interior, those circumstances in which the Ministry of Development might request the collaboration of the Ministry of the Interior of its maritime services when so required by needs of general interest in the civil marine area, or of the safety of people or objects or of maritime transport.
- Develop the sanctioning regime established in Law 27/92 on Ports of the State and of the Merchant Navy in order to accommodate it to the demands:
    a. Of the ISPS Code: "the SSP shall include provisions on the updating of the systems of identification so that abuses are subjected to a disciplinary sanction" and when it states that "the PFSP shall include provisions for the systems of identification to be updated and for the abuses to be subjected to a disciplinary sanction."
    b. Of the community Regulation, "the member States shall guarantee that efficient, proportionate and dissuasive sanctions are introduced for not observing this Regulation."

c. Of the Directive, which in article 18 states that "the member states shall make sure that efficient, proportionate and dissuasive sanctions are introduced for those cases in which there is a breach of the provisions adopted in virtue of this Directive."

- Regulate the use of platform port facilities by ships, passengers and goods, which will be governed by this RD and by the corresponding Port Ordinances.

- Collaboration with the Ministry of the Interior and, when appropriate, with the corresponding bodies of the Autonomous Communities for the safety of people and objects and for maintaining public safety.

- Limiting the transit and manoeuvre areas into which the area of commercial uses is divided.

- Develop the surveillance, security and policing services in the common areas, notwithstanding the competences that correspond to other Administrations.

- Implement the general services that are manager by the Port Authority. These Services will be provided, in accordance with the technical regulations and criteria established in this RD and in the port Ordinances, by Port Authority personnel, notwithstanding the fact that they can be delegated to third parties in certain cases when security is not put at risk or does not imply an exercise of authority.

- Provide basic services that shall guarantee, among other objectives, the security of the interests of the Port Authority and of public safety.

- The use of the port public domain shall be governed by the stipulations of the Law, in this RD and in the corresponding port ordinances, which shall establish the areas open to general use and if the case may be, free. Anything that is not stipulated in the above provisions will be subject to the law of coasts.

- Ordering and performing operations and services provided by the Port Authority.

- Sanctioning, in the port area, of non-compliances with the General Regulation of Piloting and other regulations that regulate port activities.

Article 3. Area of application[21]

1. According to the proposal for the Directive, "the member States shall use detailed evaluations to accurately define the limits of the corresponding port areas for security, as well as the different measures that are necessary for guaranteeing the adequate protection of the ports. These measures will vary according to the level of security in place and shall reflect the differences in the risk profile of the different port subareas."
2. For each port the member States shall establish the limits corresponding to the purpose of this Directive, taking due account of the information derived from the corresponding evaluation of

---

[21] As the service area of the ports has been defined fir the purpose of taxes and uses, it will be necessary to define the surface of the port for the purposes of security. For the Project for the Directive it is almost an obsession. We only cite a few paragraphs. As the Directive will need legislative development in the national area, it will be the moment and the opportunity to specify the different spaces that are subjected to security controls. It is the moment to exclude the sports harbours and fishing docks from the area of security referred to in the ISPS Code, the Regulation and the Directive. In recent years, some Port Authorities have placed these activities in the centre of the port which would break the port into pieces and break the principle of unity for the purposes of security.

port security. When the limits of a port facility, in the sense of the Regulation, cover the port, the corresponding provisions of the Regulation will override the obligations of this Directive. The Directive obliges the member States to establish the limits of the ports subject to it. The member States shall elaborate a security policy for the areas and make sure that they establish and update the corresponding evaluations and security Plans. The introduction and application of any national port security policy shall be monitored by a central national Authority. In order to conveniently homogenise their application, the directive includes priority aspects in its annexes relating to the evaluation and the port security plans.

The Regulation Project made a reference to the service area to which the repealed article 15 of Law 27/92 referred and is not exactly the same as the Directive. Therefore we state its content.

3. Article 2. Community Directive. Area of application

- This Directive regulates the security measures to which people, infrastructures and equipment, including means of transport, shall be adjusted both in the ports themselves and in the adjacent areas when these have a direct or indirect influence on port security.

- The measures established in this Directive will be applied to every port located in the territory of the member State that houses one or more port facilities subject to the provisions of the Regulation.

- For each port the member States shall establish the limits corresponding to the purpose of this Directive, taking into due consideration the information derived from the corresponding port security evaluation.

- When the limits of a port facility, in the sense of the Regulation, cover the port, the corresponding provisions of the Regulation will override the obligations of this Directive.

It is obvious that it is not the limits of the public domain specified for a defined service area, basically for commercial purposes with which it will not be possible to coincide. The criterion now is the security with which the limits will be determined in the EU.

With respect to the authorities and their competences:

Article 4. Competent authorities and bodies

- It corresponds to the Government, through the Ministries of Development and of the Interior to implement the measures required to achieve the standards of security defined in the ISPS Code, the Regulation, the Directive and the Law of Ports applicable to the Ports of General Interest and the demands of its compliance for the concession holders. When security level 3 is declared in the port facility in question, the Ministry of the Interior, in so far as it determines the levels of security and is responsible for the security policy, which is the exclusive competence of the State, shall take over the management and control to neutralise the incident that determined such a security level and shall give the appropriate instructions to those responsible in the port for public safety matters. The competences and functions that are established in the Law of Ports of the State and of the Merchant Navy relating to the functions of special policing of the port maritime public domain correspond to the Port Authorities and their bodies.

- The competences and functions that are established in the Law of Ports of the State and of the Merchant Navy, in RD 1246/1995, of 14th July, and in the rest of the applicable legislation correspond to the Harbour Masters.

- The competences of the Port Authority and of the Harbour Masters are understood without prejudice or detriment to those which correspond to the Autonomous Community, to the towns in whose municipality the service area of the port is located and to other organisms or public entities that develop their activity within the area in accordance with its own legislation.

Article 5. Surveillance and policing of the port
- The functions of special police, described in article 4.1 of the OL on the Protection of Public Safety, with respect to article 1.2 of the same Law, and in article 4 of OL 2/86 on the Security Forces and Corps, regarding the collaborations required for those who carry out public safety functions, attributed to the Port Authority by the Law of Ports of the State and of the Merchant Navy, correspond to the Board of Administration of the Port Authority[22].

- These functions will be exercised, in the manner determined by the Regulation of Exploitation and Policing, by the harbour guards and other personnel of the Port Authority, duly qualified and registered with the Police Service, for the purpose of which they will have the consideration of agents of authority of the Port Administration in exercising the powers of port police included in the Law of Ports of the State and of the Merchant Navy, notwithstanding the obligation to collaborate whenever necessary with the Security Forces and Corps.

- The security services referred to in this RD will always be performed in uniform and the security task will not be compatible with any other. For this purpose, the harbour guard Service can be divided into different sections so as to be able to complete tasks which are not strictly security related and which therefore can be performed without a uniform.

- The remaining surveillance functions may also be performed by private security personnel, in accordance with the stipulations of Law 23/92 on Private Security, provided it does not involve the exercise of authority or the performance of public functions. Inside the port, with the approval of the Port Authority, they may also provide private security services, for the custody and protection of certain private assets, tools, materials and cargos deposited temporarily in the docks by their proprietors. The same goes for the custody of buildings provided that this takes place inside the area. In any case they will have a special obligation to collaborate with the Police Service[23].

- The policing faculties attributed to the Port Authorities include the following functions, among others:

---

[22] These two Organic Laws on security contain, with the exception of the recent modification introduced by Law 48/2003, the only references to public security other than the Security Forces and Corps. This must be the starting point for the development of all legislation that justifies the existence and the performance of the functions of Port Police in security matters, apart from their functions as Administrative Police of the Port Maritime Public Domain.

[23] This is what it is now called in Law 48/2003.

- Control, inspection and coordination of the demands derived from the ISPS Code and the Regulation and Development of the Directive, inside the different port facilities and the rest of the port public domain surfaces.
- Control, inspection and coordination of the provisions contained in the Port Security Plan and in the different PFSP within their area of responsibility.
- Control, inspection and coordination of the port services and those of aiding navigation, provided directly by the Port Authority or through indirect management.
- Control, inspection and coordination of the operations and activities that require their authorisation and concession.
- Surveillance of the compliance of the clauses and conditions imposed in the act of awarding the concessions and authorisations.
- Control and inspection of the works, facilities and equipment located in the port area in the area of their competences.
- Control and inspection of the goods and containers located in the port area in the area of their competences.
- Control in the port area of compliance with the regulations for dangerous goods and health and safety, as well as for security systems and fire fighting, notwithstanding the competences that correspond to other bodies of the Administration.
- Control of access of people to buildings, works, port facilities and restricted or limited access areas within the service area of the port or which are restricted for security reasons.
- Make sure that the regulations of this RD and the Port Ordinances are complied with.

- The harbour guards and other personnel to whom the Port Authority entrusts surveillance functions within the service area of the port shall give the Security Forces and Corps the support they require to attain the security objectives established in article 1 of the OL on the Protection of Public Safety.

- At the same time and in order to attain these objectives, the Port Authority may require the support of the Security Forces and Corps in accordance with article 4 of the OL on the Protection of Public Safety.

- Notwithstanding the orders and instructions that could be given by the President of the Port Authority, the immediate and direct management of all the surveillance and policing services in the service area of the port, will be exercised by the Manager of the Port Authority. The Port Authorities may regulate the regime of organisation and operation of these services.

- In accordance with the stipulations of the Law of Ports of the State and the Merchant Navy and within the limits established in current legislation[24], the harbour guards and other

---

[24] In reference to the inexistence of legal authorisation for entering and registering a car or a ship, jurisprudential doctrine is very reiterated that indicates that the cars and ships, as a mere possession and means of transport, lack the special protection given to the intimacy of the residence by article 18.2 of the Spanish Constitution – except for exceptional cases in which boats or caravans for example are used as mobile homes – which means that their inspection or registration is subjected to the rigorous requisites established in articles 545 and following of the Law of Criminal Procedures and may carry out police investigations, in the tasks of prevention and investigation of criminal acts, without the need for legal authorisation, but always under the principles of proportionality and justification.

personnel of the Port Authority may access the different facilities, ships or platforms located inside the service area of the port, in order to carry out the inspection, surveillance and control tasks attributed to the Port Authorities by the Law.

- The personnel of any surveillance and security service that may be established by the port users, either occasionally or permanently, must have the prior authorisation of the Port Authority and, besides complying with the specific tasks given them, shall make sure that this Regulation is complied with and give their cooperation to the harbour guards and other agents of authority.

- The harbour guards that will perform the security and surveillance functions in the port facilities, shall do so in uniform, and when they do it in their condition of agents of authority, apart from their functions of administrative police, shall:

- Carry out identity controls at the access to or inside certain buildings, though at no time may they retain personal documentation, except for carrying out the necessary checks or requesting checks of the Security Forces and Corps of the State through the PFSO.

- Refuse access to those who do not prove their identity or justify the need for access.

- Prevent criminal acts or breaches from being committed in relation to the purpose of their protection for which they will organise their services to monitor the area of the port that is limited for the purposes of security including the surface of the water under their responsibility.

- Immediately hand over delinquents to the members of the Security Forces and Corps in relation with the purpose of their protection, as well as the instruments, effects and proof of the criminal acts and may not proceed to interrogate them.

- Give support or collaborate with the Security Forces and Corps in the investigation and persecution of these criminal acts, in discovering and arresting the delinquents or in carrying out the acts of inspections or control corresponding to them.

- Prepare a report on any breach or incident that they observe.

Article 6. Functions of the Port Police Service.

As a consequence the absence of judicial authorisation or of the interested party in the police investigations of a criminal act, which justifyingly and proportionally include the inspection of a motor vehicle, does not imply a violation of constitutional rights.
An STS argument says: "It is logical that on a mailing ship, if you sail at night or the weather turns bad, you go to a place protected from it to shelter or sleep, which does not mean that it constitute a place in which you habitually exercise the minimum living habits.
The absence of furniture or instruments to cover these vital functions at the moment of the intervention and the accidental or provisional nature of their use, which is imposed by the circumstances of the moment, does not make a means of locomotion (in this case at sea) the dwelling or home of a person. It could be considered as such in a flexible interpretation of the question during the voyage. Not once it is over."
For this reason in the case of doubt it will be necessary to use the Security Forces and Corps when faced with these unjustified refusals or sanction the obstructions to this control requirement.

The security services shall be carried out through static surveillance, access control and guards, including patrols on foot, in motor vehicles and in boats.

- Gather information on the threats to maritime security and report them to their superiors, or if the emergency so requires, to the Security Forces and Corps.
- Keep communications available to them operative and remain alert at all times.
- Prevent the unauthorised access to ships and port facilities and to the restricted areas under their responsibility.
- Prevent the introduction of unauthorised weapons, incendiary devices or explosives into ships and port facilities.
- Raise the alarm when there is a threat to security.
- Comply with the demands of the port and port facility security plans.
- Participate in the required training and in the drills and practices to be familiarised with the security procedures.
- Within the port facility they shall act according to the security level, with the rigour that the situation requires while minimising the inconveniences to passengers, ships, personnel and visitors to ship, goods and services all of which they will treat with care and deference.
- At security level 1, within the missions they have, they shall carry out the security measures required by the port facility performing the activities indicated in order to take the necessary measures required against the events that affect security. They must be aware of:

    - Guaranteeing the execution of their tasks related with the security of the port facility.
    - Controlling access to the port facility.
    - .Monitoring the port facility and the anchoring berths and docking areas.
    - Monitoring the restricted areas so that only authorised people have access.
    - Supervising the handling of cargo and the handling of the provisions of the ship.
    - Guaranteeing the immediate availability of the means of communication on security.

At security level 2, and in so far as they are responsible for it, they shall apply the additional security measures specified in the PFSP.

At security level 3, if so delegated, they shall apply other specific security measures as specified in the PFSP for the activities indicated and shall follow all the security instructions that they receive from their superiors in the port facility and in the port area. They shall collaborate with the Security Forces and Corps in charge of controlling the incident that provoked such a high security level.

This service shall be aware of and be available to adopt:

- Measures to prevent weapons, dangerous substances and devices to be used against people, ships or ports from being taken on board a ship or being taken into a port facility.
- Measures to prevent unauthorised access to the port facility, to docked ships and to restricted areas.
- Procedures to address threats or failures in the security measures.
- Procedures to respond to any instruction on security given by the Government at security level 3.

- Procedures for evacuation in the case of a threat to security or a failure of the security measures.
- Tasks of port facility personnel assigned with security responsibilities and the rest of port authority personnel relating to security.
- Procedures for the interface with activities relating to ship security.
- Procedures for the periodical revision of the plan and its updating.
- Procedures to report the events that affect maritime security.
- Identification of the PFSP and around the clock contact data.
- Measures to protect the information contained in the plan.
- Measures to guarantee the efficient security of the cargo and of the equipment for handling the cargo in the port facility.
- Procedures for verifying the PFSP.
- Procedures for responding in the case of the activation of the security alert system on a ship in the port facility.

A port facility security officer, registered with the Port Police Service, will be designated for each port facility. The same person may be designated security Officer for more than one port facility.

Without being limited to the following the duties and responsibilities of the PFSO shall be:

- Carry out an initial evaluation of the port facility, considering the security evaluation of the port facility.
- Guarantee the elaboration and maintenance of the PFSP.
- Implement the PFSP and carry out drills with it.
- Make periodical inspections on the port facility to make sure that the security measures are adequate.
- Recommend and include, as appropriate, modifications in the PFSP in order to correct deficiencies and update the Plan.
- Increase the awareness of security and surveillance of the port facility personnel.
- Make sure that adequate training has been given to the personnel responsible for port facility security.
- Report to the authorities any event that implies a threat to port security and keep a record of the events.
- Coordinate the implementation of the PFSP with the SSO and the CSO.
- Coordinate with the necessary security services.
- Guarantee that the rules relating to the personnel responsible for the security of the port facility are complied with.
- Guarantee the adequate performance, testing, calibration and maintenance of the security equipment, if it exists.
- Help the SSO to confirm the identity of the people who wish to go on board when so requested.

The PFSO and the personnel of the port facility Police Service shall have knowledge about and have received training on the guidelines given in part B of the ISPS Code.

The personnel of the port facility that carry out specific security tasks, especially the harbour guards, must know their functions and responsibilities as included in the PFSP and have the capacity to carry out the tasks that are assigned to them.

In order to guarantee the efficient implementation of the Port and port facility Security Plan, they shall perform drills at adequate intervals.

The PFSO shall guarantee the efficient coordination and implementation of the PFSP through his participation in the drills at adequate intervals, taking into account the guidelines given in part B of the ISPS Code.

Apart form these obligations, which are hardly described, they shall perform all the functions that this Service has been doing to date.

It will be interesting to work with the hypothesis that the Regulation contemplates for the security of the whole port and of the new and novel demands to be implemented in the Proposal for the Directive, which has already been discussed and to which we must refer to complement the elaboration of the Regulation of Exploitation and Policing.

11. Conclusions

Throughout this study, among other aspects, we have tried to analyse the most recent legislation regarding port and maritime security. This has led to discovering the reality of the organisation of both public and private security in Spain. The following were considered.

- In the context of maritime transport that we analysed, security has a new predominantly dynamic, flexible and preventive concept. It must be activated, always in accordance with the principle of proportionality, at different levels according to the entity of the threats faced. In the current circumstances, in accordance with the world situation, it must be globally understood and managed. The preventive dimension involves everyone and especially those who may be affected either directly or indirectly. Costs must be shared in this measure.

- We must conclude that public safety, maritime security, port security and private security are merely partial aspects of a security without adjectives. Though acting in their own area, these different subjects must be put on common ground and coordinated through joint bodies that are capable of elaborating and analysing the information available so that, in a crisis situation that could put the maritime transport network in danger, they can react quickly and efficiently or otherwise minimise the consequences.

- For this study the threat is specified in the means of maritime transport in so far as it could well be a susceptible target for large scale terrorist attacks. Spain, which on the one hand has a complex port maritime organisation and a security organisation on the other, must unite the state, autonomic and private port interests to present a common front in response to the emerging demands of world security in this sector of activity which is essential and strategic for the economy.

- Spain is at the crossroads of the world maritime transport routes and of civilisations – the rich north and the poor south, Europe and Africa. At this historical moment, it receives a large contingent of regular and irregular immigration which can partly serve as camouflage and infrastructure for radical Islamic groups. Therefore, Spain must be especially aware of and concerned about these evidences.

- With respect to the IMO. The fanaticism shown by the most radical and indiscriminate Islamic terrorism, which does not hold back in its methods or procedures to cause as much harm to people and damage to things as possible, has sparked off legislative reactions around the world which has led to the IMO organising a series of protocols for preventive and operative actions which are specified in Part A of the ISPS Code and in its inclusion in SOLAS, which means that they are mandatory for the countries that enter the agreement. SOLAS which is intended to govern all over the world is, like any universal agreement, a commitment of minimums among many parties that seek a generalised consensus. Thus the intention of SOLAS is essentially, in a very specific space such as the terminal and for the limited time that the ship remains in port, to activate specific security measures specified in certain plans to counter any attack. At the same time it makes certain people, the Security Officers, responsible of coordinating these security measures and making sure that they are completed.

- With respect to the EU. The European Union has seen the need to increase this agreement of minimums in its common space as the threats have become a greater risk. As it felt hypothetically and especially threatened it published a Regulation[1] which extends the demands of the Code to other types of traffic and imposes a calendar which will gradually come into force by 2007. On the other hand a Community Directive[2] will spark off the activation of new demands in matters of port security at the same time as creating new organs and procedures to achieve these objectives. The Directive, which must be transferred to national legislation within six months of its publication, will oblige the Spanish State to adopt specific measures, extend the security measures to all the port beyond the security of the port facilities that the Code refers to. The Directive will demand the evaluation of port security deciding which measures are necessary and where and when to apply them. It will require a port security Plan that specifies all the measures and actions aimed at protecting the port. It will require the designation of the port security Authority and the port security Officer to coordinate the elaboration and application of the security Plan. It will also create a port security Committee to advise the responsible Authority.

- Related with national legislation. It is obvious that all of these international regulations are going to condition national legislation in the near future. It will have to adapt to the new security demands and make an effort to give operational and organisational responses. It is the moment to contemplate port security together, beyond the responsibilities of the Public Entity Ports of the State, while very important and potentially threatened traffic is under the control of and being managed by private companies. Examples are containers, tankers or chemical or gas products. Other ports, such as those in the hands of Autonomous Communities, will also be affected and equally bound, which means that there will have to be a prior agreement with the port officials of the coastal Autonomous Communities. All of those involved must be aware of the entity of the changes and be in a position to meet the new demands in the expected fashion.

---

[1] Regulation (CE) Nº 725/2004 of the European Parliament and Council, of 31st March, 2004 relating to the improvement in the security of ships and port facilities.

[2] Proposal for a Directive of the European Parliament and Council for the improvement of port security.

The most recent regulation, aware of the sensitivity of the world to the terrorist threats, has tried to create the conditions that make it possible to introduce these new International rules into the Spanish legal network as can be seen in Law 47/2003, of 26th November of economic regime and the rendering of services in the ports of general interest. In article 132.3 it states that "Following a favourable report form the Ministry of the Interior and of the autonomic entity with competences in matters relating to public safety on those aspects of their competence, each Port Authority shall elaborate a security plan for ships, passengers and goods in port areas against antisocial and terrorist acts which, once approved in accordance with the applicable legislation, shall form part of the port ordinances."

This is not exactly what has been put into practice as not only have the Port Authorities had to elaborate Plans but other port operators, both autonomous and private, have been obliged to do the same. The ships affected have also had to do it and it was not the Port Authorities who approved these plans but the General Directorate of the Merchant Navy. These failures are justified in the understanding that Law 48/2003, which is prior to the Code, introduced these precepts when the content of the Code had still not been defined and less still the EU Regulation and the Proposal for the Directive.

A document, to be used on a daily basis, adapted to the reality of the ports of general interest, such as the Regulation of Exploitation and Policing, will necessarily have to be affected by all of these changes relating to the management of port and maritime security. When this document and the Port Ordinances, both the general ones and those of free configuration in each Autonomous Community, have been elaborated they must be capable of understanding, organising and responding to the new security needs. Specifically this will be in the development, very shortly, of the Community Directive which will require the creation of new spaces, of new bodies and of an efficient port security structure subjected to continuous evaluations. The weak point in all of this matter, as we have seen throughout this study, is that the port facilities that are not state operated but rather by autonomous or private operators seem to have been left to one side in the process.

Together with the above, the study has shown that:

- Port security, in general terms, is for the moment structured here in Spain. When interpreted as public safety, in so far as it gives a response to terrorist attacks, or at least to preventing them, it can be observed that while the Civil Guard and the harbour guards as representatives of public safety are present in the ports of general interest, although with different levels of involvement, this is not the case in autonomic ports. There is a well organised private security in the port facilities that operate under concession but this will have to be strengthened and adapted to the new demands and responses to the threats. The Ministries of Development and of the Interior must redefine and specify the mission and functions of public safety in the ports of general interest and establish measures for the rest of the port facilities, private or autonomous and determine what their level of involvement and control is going to be.

- We have the paradoxical circumstance that there is a point of inflection and a more than clear contradiction between the policy of opening the ports and the new security demands. This contradiction is only going to be resolved when the large ports are excluded from the cities. In the medium term only passenger traffic and cruise ships, for obvious reasons, should remain on the facades of the cities that surround them.

- The need for preventive security to reach the anchor points and the side of the ship that faces the sea is a weak point. In the most dangerous hypothesis, an attack from the sea against a ship docked at port or anchored in an estuary is comparatively much easier and at first sight would seem to have greater consequences than an attack from land. In this task the harbour guards and private security have a new field to get involved one, once they have been trained.

In its development, the text has tried to maintain an attitude of positive criticism, stating those deficiencies which are important in the organisational area and which come from time ago and are due to the inertias of a past in which the design of security and the scenario in which the threat of terrorism appeared were basically very different. Therefore the following benefits should be derived:

- A calm and critical reflection on the new demands and on the national legislation that develop this security organisation. Legislation that must consider and define which part of security and to what extent it can be considered preventive and operative and therefore private or which can be privatised and where and when the step has to be taken to make it public and subject it to the leading role of the Ministry of the Interior and the Security Forces and Corps.

- On the other hand there are new people responsible for security, both public and private and where they fit in the organisation of State security must be defined. Thus the SSO, the PFSO or the CSO will be integrated in the Law of Private Security as if they were Security Managers or they will remain in the limbo of legal uncertainty. The same could be said of the new figures that the Directive is going to create, such as the Port Security Authority and Port Security Officer and what their interdependence will be. Because no matter how we look at it we are talking about security, about public safety and port and maritime security must serve them. We cannot get lost in arguments. The basic question here is the concern to prevent terrorism.

- In short, the immediate future brings the possibility and the opportunity, although forced upon us by the horrific recent events, to review maritime and port security from the point of view of organisation and the distribution of competences. The Ministries of Development and of the Interior must be capable of finding common ground and solutions to modernise security in Spanish ports. Disconnecting the competences of the Security Forces and Corps from those of the harbour guards and defining just how far private security must be legally involved are unavoidable requirements. It is no good relying on external demands to find formal solutions. The question must be addressed and these solutions are not going to come form the IMO or the EU.

Bibliography

Publications

MARÍ, R. *Crisis situations on passenger ships*. Barcelona: Edicions UPC. I.S.B.N 847653 6852. 1998

MARÍ, R., Librán A. *Public safety on passenger ships*. Barcelona. Edicions UPC. I.S.B.N. 84-8301-692-3. 2003

MARÍ, R. *IPEN Journal (Pan-American Institute of Naval Engineering)* "The ISPS and the challenge for naval construction." n° 28th September 2003. ISSN: 1011-5951. 2003

MARÍ, R. *International Congress on Maritime Technological innovations and research.* "Influence of the Maritime Environment on the casuistry of organised crime". 2nd. University of Cadiz. Publications Service of the UCA, recorded on CD. 2000

MARÍ, R. *The ISPS-1 Code. Operability in the ship-port interface.* Barcelona; Edicions UPC. I.S.B.N. 978-84-8301-895-8

Research work

Identification and analysis of the influence of the maritime environment on the casuistry of organized crime. European Commission. Task Force for Cooperation on Justice and Home Affairs. Police and Customs. October 1998 / April 2000. Main researcher: Ricard Marí Sagarra. UPC

Methodology and programme framework for the development of port facility security plans (PFSP). Public entity Ports of the State. November 2003 / March 2004. Main researcher: Ricard Marí Sagarra. UPC

www.ingramcontent.com/pod-product-compliance
Lightning Source LLC
Chambersburg PA
CBHW081215230426
43666CB00015B/2736